Vietnam War
Biographies

Volume 1: A–K

11/01

Vietnam War
Biographies

**Kevin Hillstrom
and Laurie Collier
Hillstrom**
Diane Sawinski, Editor

AN IMPRINT OF THE GALE GROUP

DETROIT · SAN FRANCISCO · LONDON
BOSTON · WOODBRIDGE, CT

Vietnam War: Biographies

Kevin Hillstrom and Laurie Collier Hillstrom

Staff

Diane Sawinski and Allison McNeill, *U•X•L Senior Editors*
Carol DeKane Nagel, *U•X•L Managing Editor*
Thomas L. Romig, *U•X•L Publisher*

Sarah Tomasek, *Permissions Specialist*

Randy Bassett, *Image Database Supervisor*
Robert Duncan, *Imaging Specialist*
Pamela A. Reed, *Image Coordinator*
Dean Dauphinais, *Senior Image Editor*

Michelle DiMercurio, *Senior Art Director*

Mary Beth Trimper, *Manager, Composition and Electronic Prepress*
Evi Seoud, *Assistant Manager, Composition Purchasing and Electronic Prepress*

Rita Wimberley, *Senior Buyer*
Dorothy Maki, *Manufacturing Manager*

LM Design, *Typesetting*

Front cover photographs: Abbie Hoffman (reproduced by permission of New York Times Co./Archive Photos); Lyndon Johnson with troops (reproduced by permission of Corbis Corporation); Back cover photograph: Ngo Dinh Nhu (reproduced by permission of AP/Wide World Photos).

Library of Congress Cataloging-in-Publication Data

Hillstrom, Kevin, 1963-
  Vietnam War: biographies/Kevin Hillstrom and Laurie Collier Hillstrom; Diane Sawinski, editor.
    p. cm.
  Includes bibliographical references and index.
  ISBN 0-7876-4884-1 (set) - ISBN 0-7876-4885-X (vol. 1) - ISBN 0-7876-4886-8 (vol. 2)
    1. Vietnamese Conflict, 1961-1975-Biography-Juvenile literature. 2. United States-Biography-Juvenile literature. 3. Vietnam-Biography-Juvenile literature. [1. Vietnamese Conflict, 1961-1975-Biography. 2. United States-Biography.] I. Hillstrom, Laurie Collier, 1965- II. Sawinski, Diane M. III. Title.

DS557.5 .H55 2001
959.704'3'0922-dc21
[B]   00-056378

Contents

Reader's Guide

V*ietnam War: Biographies* presents biographies of sixty men and women who participated in or were affected by the Vietnam War. These two volumes profile a diverse mix of personalities from both the United States and Vietnam, including politicians, military leaders, antiwar activists, journalists, authors, nurses, veterans, and civilians who got caught in the middle of the conflict.

Detailed biographies of major Vietnam War figures (such as Ho Chi Minh, Lyndon B. Johnson, Robert McNamara, Ngo Dinh Diem, and Richard M. Nixon) are included. But *Vietnam War: Biographies* also provides biographical information on lesser-known but nonetheless important and fascinating men and women of that era. Examples include Daniel Berrigan, a Catholic priest who went to prison for burning military draft files as a form of protest against the war; Jeremiah Denton, an American prisoner-of-war who blinked the word "torture" in Morse code during a televised interview with his North Vietnamese captors; Tim Page, a daring British combat photographer who produced some of the best known images of the war before being seriously wounded; Phan Thi Kim

Phuc, a nine-year-old Vietnamese girl who was photographed running naked down a country road after suffering terrible burns from a U.S.-ordered napalm attack in her village; and Jan Scruggs, an American veteran who led the drive to create the Vietnam Veterans Memorial in Washington, D.C.

Vietnam War: Biographies also features sidebars containing interesting facts, excerpts from memoirs, diaries, and speeches, and short biographies of people who are in some way connected with the leading figures of the era. Within each full-length biography, cross-references direct readers to other individuals profiled in the two-volume set. More than seventy black and white photographs enhance the text. In addition, each volume contains a timeline that lists significant dates and events of the Vietnam War era, a glossary, further readings, and a cumulative subject index.

Vietnam War Reference Library

Vietnam War: Biographies is only one component of the three-part U•X•L Vietnam War Reference Library. The other two titles in this set are:

- *Vietnam War: Almanac:* This work presents a comprehensive overview of the Vietnam War. The volume's sixteen chapters cover all aspects of the conflict, from the reasons behind American involvement, to the antiwar protests that rocked the nation, to the fall of Saigon to Communist forces in 1975. The chapters are arranged chronologically and explore such topics as Vietnam's struggles under French colonial rule, the introduction of U.S. combat troops in 1965, the Tet Offensive, and the lasting impact of the war on both the United States and Vietnam. Interspersed are four chapters that cover the growth of the American antiwar movement, the experiences of U.S. soldiers in Vietnam, Vietnam veterans in American society, and the effect of the war on Vietnam's land and people. The Almanac also contains "Words to Know" and "People to Know" sections, a timeline, research and activity ideas and a subject index.

- *Vietnam War: Primary Sources:* This title presents thirteen full or excerpted speeches and written works from the Vietnam War era. The volume includes excerpts from civil rights leader Martin Luther King, Jr.'s 1967 antiwar speech at Riverside Church in New York City; President Richard Nixon's 1969 "Silent Majority" speech; Le Ly Hayslip's memoir *When Heaven and Earth Changed Places,* about growing up in a war-torn Vietnamese village and becoming involved with the Viet Cong; and Admiral James Stockdale's memoir about his years in a Vietnamese prisoner-of-war camp, *In Love and War.* Each entry includes an introduction, things to remember while reading the excerpt, information on what happened after the work was published or the event took place, and other interesting facts. Photographs, source information, and an index supplement the work.

- A cumulative index of all three titles in the U•X•L Vietnam War Reference Library is also available.

Acknowledgments

The authors extend thanks to U•X•L Senior Editor Diane Sawinski and U•X•L Publisher Tom Romig at the Gale Group for their assistance throughout the production of this series.

Comments and Suggestions

We welcome your comments on *Vietnam War: Biographies* and suggestions for other topics in history to consider. Please write: Editors, *Vietnam War: Biographies,* U•X•L, 27500 Drake Rd., Farmington Hills, Michigan 48331-3535; call toll-free 800-877-4253; fax to 248-414-5043; or send e-mail via http://www.galegroup.com.

Vietnam War Timeline

1862   Under the Treaty of Saigon, Vietnam gives control of three eastern provinces to France.

1863   France makes Cambodia a French colony.

1883   Under the Treaty of Hue, France expands its control over all of Vietnam.

1887   France turns its holdings in Southeast Asia into one colony, called Indochina.

1893   France makes Laos a French colony.

1930   Ho Chi Minh creates the Indochinese Communist Party to oppose French colonial rule.

1940   Japan occupies Indochina during World War II.

1890
The Battle of Wounded
Knee ends the last
major Indian resistance
to white settlement
in America

1861–65
U.S. Civil
War

1929
Onset of the
Great
Depression

1939–45
World
War II

1860   1900   1940

1941 The Communist-led Vietnamese nationalist organization known as the Viet Minh is established.

March 1945 Emperor Bao Dai proclaims Vietnam an independent nation under Japan's protection.

April 1945 U.S. president Franklin Roosevelt dies; Harry S. Truman takes office.

August 1945 Japan surrenders to end World War II.

August 1945 Bao Dai is removed from power in the August Revolution.

September 1945 Ho Chi Minh establishes the Democratic Republic of Vietnam and declares himself president.

September 1945 U.S. Army Major A. Peter Dewey becomes the first American soldier to die in Vietnam.

March 1946 France declares Vietnam an independent state within the French Union.

November 1946 The First Indochina War begins with a Viet Minh attack on French forces in Hanoi.

1949 France creates the independent State of Vietnam under Bao Dai.

January 1950 Communist countries China, Yugoslavia, and the Soviet Union formally recognize the Democratic Republic of Vietnam under Ho Chi Minh.

February 1950 Democratic countries Great Britain and the United States formally recognize the State of Vietnam under Bao Dai.

May 1950 The United States begins providing military and economic aid to French forces in Vietnam.

June 1950 Truman sends U.S. troops into Korea to begin the Korean War.

Ho Chi Minh.

1944
Anne Frank and family are captured by the Nazis after two years in hiding and taken to the concentration camp at Auschwitz

1946
The Cold War between the United States and the Soviet Union begins

1949
People's Republic of China proclaimed by Mao Tse-tung

1950
Korean War begins

1942

1946

1950

1952 Dwight Eisenhower becomes president of the United States.

1954 An estimated one million Vietnamese flee North Vietnam for South Vietnam. Many credit Edward Lansdale, a secret agent for the U.S. Central Intelligence Agency (CIA), as a key reason for this mass exodus.

March 1954 The Viet Minh set up a siege of the French outpost at Dien Bien Phu.

May 1954 Viet Minh forces defeat the French in the Battle of Dien Bien Phu.

June 1954 Bao Dai selects Ngo Dinh Diem as prime minister of the State of Vietnam.

July 1954 The Geneva Accords divide Vietnam into two sections: North Vietnam, led by Communists under Ho Chi Minh; and South Vietnam, led by a U.S.-supported government under Ngo Dinh Diem.

July 1954 Laos and Cambodia are granted full independence from France.

October 1954 French troops are withdrawn from Vietnam.

July 1955 Ngo Dinh Diem refuses to proceed with national elections required by the Geneva Accords.

September 1955 Cambodia gains independence from France; Norodom Sihanouk becomes prime minister.

October 1955 Diem takes control of the South Vietnamese government from Bao Dai and establishes the Republic of Vietnam.

1957 Communist rebels begin fighting for control of South Vietnam.

1959 Construction begins on the Ho Chi Minh Trail, a major supply and communications route for Communist forces.

1953	1954	1956	1959
James Watson and Francis Crick decipher the structure of DNA	Egypt and Britain conclude a pact on the Suez Canal, ending 72 years of British military occupation	Soviet troops suppress a revolution in Hungary	Ruth and Eliot Handler, owners of Mattel, unveil the Barbie Doll

1953   **1956**   **1959** ▶

Robert McNamara.
Reproduced by permission of AP/Wide World Photos.

Lyndon B. Johnson.
Reproduced by permission of AP/Wide World Photos.

1960 Le Duan is elevated to secretary general of the Communist Party, making him one of the most powerful men in North Vietnam during the Vietnam War.

November 1960 Rebels try to overthrow the Diem government.

November 1960 John F. Kennedy becomes president of the United States.

November 1960 The National Liberation Front is established in North Vietnam to overthrow Diem and reunite the two parts of Vietnam.

1961 Kennedy offers military assistance to Diem and sends the first U.S. advisors to South Vietnam.

January 1963 The Battle of Ap Bac brings American public attention to Vietnam.

April 1963 Buddhists begin demonstrating against the Diem government.

June 1963 The suicide of a Buddhist monk draws international attention to the situation in Vietnam.

September 1963 President Kennedy sends military advisor Maxwell Taylor and Secretary of Defense Robert McNamara to Vietnam to conduct a study of the escalating situation between South Vietnam and the Viet Cong.

November 1963 Ngo Dinh Diem and other members of his government are assassinated; the Military Revolutionary Council takes control of South Vietnam.

November 1963 President Kennedy is assassinated; Lyndon Johnson takes office.

July 1964 Senator Barry Goldwater loses to Lyndon Johnson in one of the most lopsided presidential elections in American history.

August 1964 North Vietnamese patrol boats reportedly attack American warships in the Gulf of Tonkin.

1960
Theodore Maiman builds the first working laser

1961
CIA-backed invasion of Cuba at the Bay of Pigs

1962
Television satellite Telstar put into orbit by U.S.A.

1960   1961   1962

August 1964 The U.S. Congress passes the Gulf of Tonkin Resolution, which allows Johnson to use any means necessary to prevent North Vietnamese aggression.

November 1964 Johnson is reelected as president of the United States.

1965 Nguyen Thi Dinh is named deputy commander of the Communist-led National Liberation Front (NLF) armed forces, which is the highest combat position held by a woman during the Vietnam War.

February 1965 Viet Cong guerillas attack a U.S. base at Pleiku; the U.S. military retaliates with air attacks.

March 1965 The American bombing campaign known as Operation Rolling Thunder begins over North Vietnam.

March 1965 The first U.S. combat troops are sent to Vietnam.

March 1965 Faculty of the University of Michigan organize a teach-in to protest the war.

June 1965 Nguyen Cao Ky becomes premier of South Vietnam.

August 1965 Henry Cabot Lodge is appointed as American ambassador to South Vietnam.

November 1965 Antiwar demonstrations become widespread in the United States.

1966 U.S. national security advisor McGeorge Bundy resigns from office due to doubts about U.S. policy toward Vietnam.

1966 American prisoner-of-war Jeremiah Denton blinks "torture" in Morse code during a televised interview with his North Vietnamese captors.

January 1966 Senator J. William Fulbright arranges for the Senate Foreign Relations Committee to hold public hearings on American military involvement in Viet-

1963
Freedom March held in Washington, D.C.

1964
The Civil Rights Act, which forbids employers and other businesses from discriminating against minorities, is signed into law

1965
Former British prime minister Winston Churchill dies

1963   1964   1965

Martin Luther King, Jr.
Reproduced by permission of National Archives and Records.

Robert F. Kennedy.
Library of Congress.

nam. The hearings are widely credited with increasing public skepticism about the Johnson administration's handling of the Vietnam War.

February 1967 French journalist Bernard Fall is killed by a land mine while covering the war in Vietnam.

April 1967 Civil rights leader Martin Luther King, Jr., speaks out against the Vietnam War.

September 1967 Nguyen Van Thieu becomes president of South Vietnam.

October 1967 The March on the Pentagon draws 50,000 anti-war protesters to Washington, D.C.

October 1967 Navy pilot John McCain's fighter plane is shot down over Hanoi. He becomes a prisoner-of-war (POW) for more than five years in North Vietnam.

January 1968 The Siege of Khe Sanh begins.

January 1968 North Vietnamese forces, headed up by Vo Nguyen Giap, launch the Tet Offensive.

January 1968 The Battle for Hue begins.

February 1968 Clark Clifford replaces Robert McNamara as U.S. secretary of defense.

March 1968 U.S. troops kill hundreds of Vietnamese civilians in the My Lai Massacre.

March 1968 Johnson announces he will not seek reelection.

April 1968 Civil rights leader Martin Luther King, Jr., is assassinated.

May 1968 The United States and North Vietnam begin peace negotiations in Paris.

May 1968 Catholic priest Daniel Berrigan burns military draft files in Catonsville, Maryland, to protest the Vietnam War.

1966
Cultural Revolution
begins in China

1966

1967
Dr. Christiaan Barnard
performs the first
human heart transplant

1967

1967
Rolling Stone
magazine begins
publication

1968
Ralph Lauren
introduces his Polo
line of clothing

1968

June 1968 U.S. senator and Democratic presidential candidate Robert F. Kennedy is assassinated.

June 1968 William Westmoreland is relieved of his command over U.S. troops in Vietnam.

August 1968 Antiwar protestors disrupt the Democratic National Convention in Chicago. Chicago police, under the leadership of Chicago mayor Richard J. Daley, are criticized for their use of violence to quiet angry protestors.

October 1968 Johnson announces an end to the bombing of North Vietnam.

November 1968 Richard M. Nixon is elected president of the United States.

January 1969 Former U.S. attorney general Ramsey Clark leaves office and becomes an outspoken member of the antiwar movement.

February 1969 Secret bombing of Cambodia begins.

April 1969 U.S. troop levels in Vietnam peak at 543,400.

June 1969 Nixon puts his "Vietnamization" policy into effect, reducing U.S. troop levels by 25,000.

September 1969 North Vietnamese leader Ho Chi Minh dies.

September 1969 The "Chicago Seven" trial begins, in which David Dellinger, Abbie Hoffman, Tom Hayden, and other prominent antiwar activists are charged with conspiracy for disrupting the Democratic National Convention.

April 1970 Lon Nol seizes power from Norodom Sihanouk in Cambodia.

April 1970 Nixon authorizes American troops to invade Cambodia.

William Westmoreland.
Reproduced by permission of Archive Photos.

Abbie Hoffman.
Library of Congress.

July 1969 U.S. astronaut Neil Armstrong becomes the first man to walk on the moon	**August 1969** Woodstock Music Fair attracts three hundred thousand people	**1970** Television and radio cigarette ads are banned in the U.S.	**1971** Greenpeace founded in Vancouver, Canada
1969		1970	1971

Bobby Seale.
*Reproduced by permission of
AP/Wide World Photos.*

May 1970 The National Guard kills four student protestors during an antiwar demonstration at Kent State University in Ohio.

June 1970 U.S. troops withdraw from Cambodia.

October 1970 Antiwar groups hold the first Moratorium Day protests.

November 1970 Nixon makes his "Silent Majority" speech.

November 1970 The My Lai Massacre is revealed to the American people.

November 1970 Lt. William Calley is put on trial for his role in the My Lai Massacre.

December 1970 The U.S. Congress repeals the Tonkin Gulf Resolution.

February 1971 Daniel Ellsberg leaks the top-secret Pentagon Papers to reporter Neil Sheehan.

June 1971 The *New York Times* begins publishing the Pentagon Papers.

1972 Actress Jane Fonda makes a controversial visit to North Vietnam.

1972 American journalist Frances FitzGerald publishes *Fire in the Lake,* which looks at the war from a Vietnamese perspective.

1972 American journalist David Halberstam publishes *The Best and the Brightest,* about the U.S. officials who developed the government's policy toward Vietnam.

March 1972 North Vietnamese troops, under the leadership of Vo Nguyen Giap, begin the Easter Offensive.

June 1972 Republican agents associated with Nixon break into the Democratic presidential campaign headquarters at the Watergate Hotel in Washington, D.C.

Vo Nguyen Giap.
*Reproduced by permission of
Archive Photos.*

1971
The Twenty-sixth Amendment, which lowers U.S. voting age from 21 to 18, is ratified

1972
President Nixon makes historic visit to China

1973
Artist Pablo Picasso dies

1971   1972   1973

August 1972 The last U.S. combat troops withdraw from Vietnam.

November 1972 Nixon is reelected as president after defeating Democratic nominee George McGovern.

December 1972 U.S. warplanes begin the Christmas bombing campaign.

January 1973 The United States and North Vietnam sign the Paris Peace Accords.

February 1973 North Vietnam releases American prisoners of war (POWs).

June 1973 The U.S. Congress passes the Case-Church Amendment, prohibiting further American military involvement in Southeast Asia.

October 1973 Spiro T. Agnew resigns as vice president of the United States.

October 1973 North Vietnamese negotiator Le Duc Tho and U.S. secretary of state Henry Kissinger are awarded the Nobel Peace Prize.

November 1973 The U.S. Congress passes the War Powers Act over Nixon's veto, reducing the president's authority to commit U.S. military forces.

August 1974 Threatened with impeachment over the Watergate scandal, Nixon resigns from office; Gerald R. Ford becomes president of the United States.

September 1974 President Ford pardons Richard Nixon.

March 1975 North Vietnamese forces capture Hue, Da Nang, and other South Vietnamese cities.

March 1975 President Nguyen Van Thieu orders South Vietnamese forces to withdraw from the central provinces, causing the "Convoy of Tears."

1974
Anthropologists discover "Lucy,"
a hominid skeleton more than
three million years old

1975
Bill Gates organizes
Microsoft Corp.

1976
Viking I and *Viking II*
space probes land
on Mars

1974   1975   1976

Joan Baez.
Reproduced by permission of Jack Vartoogian.

April 1975 The U.S. embassy in Saigon is evacuated by military helicopters.

April 1975 North Vietnamese forces capture the South Vietnamese capital of Saigon to win the Vietnam War.

April 1975 Communist Khmer Rouge rebels capture the capital of Phnom Penh and take control of Cambodia.

May 1975 Khmer Rouge forces capture the U.S. merchant ship *Mayaguez.*

August 1975 The Communist-led Pathet Lao take control of Laos, removing prime minister Souvanna Phouma from rule.

1976 Vietnam veteran Ron Kovic publishes his memoir *Born on the Fourth of July.*

July 1976 Vietnam is reunited as one country under Communist rule, called the Socialist Republic of Vietnam. Pham Van Dong becomes premier of the newly formed country.

November 1976 Jimmy Carter is elected president of the United States.

1977 Carter pardons most Vietnam War draft evaders.

1977 Journalist Michael Herr publishes *Dispatches,* based on his experiences reporting on the war in Vietnam.

1978 Thousands of refugees known as "boat people" flee from Vietnam, creating an international crisis.

1978 Vietnam invades Cambodia and takes control of the government away from the violent Khmer Rouge.

1978 Veteran Bobby Muller cofounds the support organization Vietnam Veterans of America.

1979 China reacts to the Vietnamese invasion of Cambodia by invading northern Vietnam.

1977
Steven Jobs and Steve Wozniak found the Apple Computer Co.

1978
U.S. Senate ratifies Panama Canal Agreement

1979
Political action group "Moral Majority" is founded by Jerry Falwell

1980
Former Beatle John Lennon is shot and killed

1977	1978	1979	1980

| 1979 | Vietnam veteran Jan Scruggs cofounds the Vietnam Veterans Memorial Fund (VVMF). |

1979   Vietnam veteran Jan Scruggs cofounds the Vietnam Veterans Memorial Fund (VVMF).

1979   Joan Baez forms a group called Humanitas to raise money for food and medical supplies for the many refugees from Vietnam, Cambodia, and Laos in refugee camps in northern Thailand.

Lynda Van Devanter.
Reproduced by permission of AP/Wide World Photos.

1980   Ronald Reagan is elected president of the United States.

1980   U.S. Army nurse Lynda Van Devanter founds the Vietnam Veterans of America Women's Project to assist female veterans.

1982   The Vietnam Veterans Memorial, designed by Maya Lin, is dedicated in Washington, D.C.

1983   Photojournalist Tim Page publishes *Tim Page's Nam,* a collection of his best known images of the war.

1984   American Vietnam veterans reach an out-of-court settlement with chemical companies over health problems related to their wartime exposure to the poisonous herbicide Agent Orange.

1984   Diane Carlson Evans founds the Vietnam Women's Memorial Project to raise funds for a memorial for female veterans.

1986   Nguyen Van Linh becomes head of the Communist Party in Vietnam and introduces the *Doi Moi* economic reforms.

1986   *Platoon,* the award-winning film about a young American soldier in Vietnam, is released. It is directed by Vietnam veteran Oliver Stone.

1988   George Bush becomes president of the United States.

1988   Reporter Neil Sheehan publishes *A Bright Shining Lie: John Paul Vann and America in Vietnam.*

Diane Carlson Evans.
Reproduced by permission of AP/Wide World Photos.

1981	1984	1986	1988
Acquired Immune Deficiency virus (AIDS) is identified	Olympic Games at Los Angeles, California, are boycotted by Soviet bloc countries	U.S. space shuttle *Challenger* explodes seconds after takeoff, killing seven astronauts including teacher Christa McAuliffe	Colin Powell becomes first black 4-star general in U.S. Army

1982   1984   1986   1988

Le Ly Hayslip.
Reproduced by permission of AP/Wide World Photos.

Nguyen Thi Binh.
Reproduced by permission of Corbis Corporation.

1989 Vietnam withdraws its troops from Cambodia.

1989 Le Ly Hayslip publishes *When Heaven and Earth Changed Places,* her memoir about growing up in South Vietnam during the Vietnam War.

1990 Tim O'Brien publishes *The Things They Carried,* which is regarded as the single greatest work of literature ever written about the American experience in Vietnam.

1992 Bill Clinton is elected president of the United States.

1993 The United Nations sponsors free elections in Cambodia; Norodom Sihanouk regains his position as king.

1993 The Vietnam Women's Memorial is dedicated in Washington, D.C.

1993 Nguyen Thi Binh, the second-ranking negotiator for the North Vietnamese side in the Paris peace talks, is elected vice president of Vietnam.

1994 President Clinton ends the economic embargo against trade with Vietnam.

1995 The United States restores full diplomatic relations with Vietnam.

1995 Former secretary of defense Robert McNamara publishes *In Retrospect,* in which he reveals his personal doubts about U.S. actions in Vietnam.

1998 Pol Pot, former leader of the Cambodian Communists known as the Khmer Rouge, dies under mysterious circumstances.

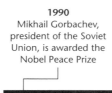

1990
Mikhail Gorbachev, president of the Soviet Union, is awarded the Nobel Peace Prize

1993
North American Free Trade Agreement (NAFTA) is signed

1997
U.S. diplomat Madeline Albright becomes the first woman secretary of state

1998
President Bill Clinton is impeached by the House of Representatives

| 1990 | 1993 | 1996 | 1999 |

Words to Know

A

ARVN: The South Vietnamese army, officially known as the Army of the Republic of South Vietnam. The ARVN fought on the same side as U.S. troops during the Vietnam War.

B

Buddhism: A religion based on the teaching of Gautama Buddha, in which followers seek moral purity and spiritual enlightenment.

C

Cambodia: Southeast Asian nation located on the western border of South Vietnam. During the Vietnam War, Cambodia experienced its own civil war between its pro-U.S. government forces and Communist rebels known as the Khmer Rouge.

Cold War: A period of intense rivalry between the United States and the Soviet Union as both nations competed to spread their political philosophies and influence around the world after the end of World War II. The climate of distrust and hostility between the two nations and their allies dominated international politics until the 1980s.

Colonialism: A practice in which one country assumes political control over another country. Most colonial powers established colonies in foreign lands in order to take possession of valuable natural resources and increase their own power. They often showed little concern for the rights and well-being of the native people.

Communism: A political system in which the government controls all resources and means of producing wealth. By eliminating private property, this system is designed to create an equal society with no social classes. However, Communist governments in practice often limit personal freedom and individual rights.

Coup d'etat: A sudden, decisive attempt to overthrow an existing government.

D

Dien Bien Phu: A French fort in northwestern Vietnam that was the site of a major battle in the Indochina War in 1954.

Domino Theory: A political theory that held that the fall of one country's government to communism usually triggered similar collapses in neighboring countries, as if the nations were dominoes falling in sequence.

E

Escalation: A policy of increasing the size, scope, and intensity of military activity.

G

Great Society: A set of social programs proposed by President Lyndon Johnson designed to end segregation and reduce poverty in the United States.

Guerrilla: A member of a native military force operating in small units in occupied territory to harass the enemy, often with surprise attacks.

H

Hanoi: The capital city of Communist North Vietnam. Also an unofficial shorthand way of referring to the North Vietnamese government.

I

Indochina: The name sometimes given to the peninsula between India and China in Southeast Asia. The term narrowly refers to Cambodia, Laos, and Vietnam, which were united under the name French Indochina during the colonial period, 1893-1954.

Indochina War: Later known as the First Indochina War (the Vietnam War became the Second Indochina War), this conflict took place between France and Communist-led Viet Minh forces in Vietnam, 1946-54.

K

Khmer Rouge: Communist-led rebel forces that fought for control of Cambodia during the Vietnam War years. The Khmer Rouge overthrew the U.S.-backed government of Lon Nol in 1975.

L

Laos: A Southeast Asian nation located on the western border of North Vietnam. During the Vietnam War, Laos experienced its own civil war between U.S.-backed forces and Communist rebels known as the Pathet Lao.

M

MIAs: Soldiers classified as "missing in action," meaning that their status is unknown to military leaders or that their bodies have not been recovered.

Military Revolutionary Council: A group of South Vietnamese military officers that overthrew President Ngo Dinh Diem and took control of South Vietnam's government in 1963.

N

Nationalism: A feeling of intense loyalty and devotion to a country or homeland. Some people argued that nationalism, rather than communism, was the main factor that caused the Viet Minh to fight the French for control of Vietnam.

North Vietnam: The Geneva Accords of 1954, which ended the First Indochina War, divided the nation of Vietnam into two sections. The northern section, which was led by a Communist government under Ho Chi Minh, was officially known as the Democratic Republic of Vietnam but was usually called North Vietnam.

NVA: The North Vietnamese Army, which assisted the Viet Cong guerilla fighters in trying to conquer South Vietnam. These forces opposed the United States in the Vietnam War.

O

Offensive: A sudden, aggressive attack by one side during a war.

P

Paris Peace Accords: A peace agreement, signed on January 25, 1973, between the United States and North Vietnam that ended direct American involvement in the Vietnam War.

Pentagon Papers: A set of secret U.S. Department of Defense documents that explained American military policy toward Vietnam from 1945 to 1968. They created a controversy when they were leaked to the national media in 1971.

Post-Traumatic Stress Syndrome (PTSS): A set of psychological problems that are caused by exposure to a dangerous or disturbing situation, such as combat. People who suffer from PTSS may have symptoms like depression, flashbacks, nightmares, and angry outbursts.

S

Saigon: The capital city of U.S.-supported South Vietnam. Also an unofficial shorthand way of referring to the South Vietnamese government.

Silent Majority: A term used by President Richard Nixon to describe the large number of American people he believed quietly supported his Vietnam War policies. In contrast, Nixon referred to the antiwar movement in the United States as a vocal minority.

Socialist Republic of Vietnam (SRV): The country created in 1976, after North Vietnam won the Vietnam War and reunited with South Vietnam.

South Vietnam: Created under the Geneva Accords of 1954, the southern section of Vietnam was known as the Republic of South Vietnam. It was led by a U.S.-supported government.

T

Tonkin Gulf Resolution: Passed by Congress after U.S. Navy ships supposedly came under attack in the Gulf of Tonkin, this resolution gave President Lyndon Johnson the authority to wage war against North Vietnam.

V

Veteran: A former member of the armed forces.

Veterans Administration: A U.S. government agency responsible for providing medical care, insurance, pensions, and other benefits to American veterans of Vietnam and other wars.

Viet Cong: Vietnamese Communist guerilla fighters who worked with the North Vietnamese Army to conquer South Vietnam.

Viet Minh: Communist-led nationalist group that worked to gain Vietnam's independence from French colonial rule.

Vietnamization: A policy proposed by President Richard Nixon that involved returning responsibility for the war to the South Vietnamese. It was intended to allow the United States to reduce its military involvement without allowing the country to fall to communism.

W

Watergate: A political scandal that forced U.S. President Richard Nixon to resign from office in 1974. In June 1972, Republican agents associated with Nixon's reelection campaign broke into the Democratic campaign headquarters in the Watergate Hotel in Washington, D.C., to gather secret information. Nixon and several members of his administration attempted to cover up the burglary.

Vietnam War
Biographies

Spiro T. Agnew

Born November 9, 1918
Baltimore, Maryland
Died September 18, 1996
Berlin, Maryland

Vice President of the United States, 1969–1973

During President Richard Nixon's (see entry) first term in the White House (1969–1973), Vice President Spiro Agnew emerged as an outspoken defender of the president and his administration. He regularly criticized the American news media for providing slanted coverage of Vietnam and other issues. In addition, he became known for his critical remarks about antiwar groups and people who held liberal political beliefs. In 1973, though, investigations revealed that Agnew had accepted bribes and engaged in other illegal activities during his years as governor of Maryland. The scandal eventually forced Agnew to resign from the vice presidency in disgrace.

"We can . . . afford to separate [antiwar protestors] from our society with no more regret than we should feel over discarding rotten apples from a barrel."

Early political career

Spiro Theodore Agnew was born on November 9, 1918, in Baltimore, Maryland. The son of a Greek immigrant, Agnew attended Johns Hopkins University and the University of Baltimore Law School. In 1942 he married Elinn Judefind, with whom he eventually had four children. That same year he left school to enlist in the U.S. military and fight in World War II

Spiro T. Agnew.
Courtesy of the Library of Congress.

(1939–1945). He served during the war as a captain in an armored division, earning a Bronze Star medal.

After the war ended in 1945, Agnew returned home to Baltimore. He resumed his education, earning a law degree from Baltimore Law School in 1947. He established a successful law practice in the city's suburbs, but as the years passed he expressed increasing interest in seeking a new career in politics. By the late 1950s Agnew had established himself as one of the state's promising young Republican leaders. In 1962 he upset his Democratic opponent to win election as Baltimore County Executive.

Four years later, Agnew won the Republican nomination for governor of Maryland. He then defeated the state's Democratic governor in a big upset. Agnew's victory was due in large part to strong support from Baltimore's black community, which opposed his Democratic opponent's support for segregation (keeping members of different races separated in society).

Governor of Maryland

When Agnew became governor of Maryland in early 1967, most residents of the state viewed him as a moderate Republican. They believed that he did not hold radical or extreme views on the Vietnam War, civil rights, and other issues that were dividing many American communities. In April 1968, however, riots broke out in Baltimore's black neighborhoods following the assassination of civil rights leader Martin Luther King, Jr. (see entry). The riots infuriated Agnew. He harshly criticized the city's black community leaders for permitting—or in some cases, encouraging—the violence to take place. Agnew's reaction angered some segments of Maryland's black community. But it pleased Republican conservatives across the nation who were appalled by the riots.

In 1968 Republican presidential nominee Richard M. Nixon selected Agnew as his vice presidential running mate after his first two choices (Robert Finch and Gerald Ford) declined his offer. Nixon and his advisors correctly predicted that the selection of Agnew would meet with approval from various groups within the Republican Party. The party's moderate wing did not actively oppose his selection, and conservatives expressed outright enthusiasm for Agnew.

As the presidential campaign progressed, Agnew proved to be an effective campaigner. He paid special attention to the Vietnam War, which was a source of great concern to the American people. By 1968 American troops had been fighting and dying in Vietnam for more than three years, with little indication that the war would end any time soon. As a result, public support for the war effort was decreasing across the country.

On the campaign trail during the summer of 1968, Agnew claimed that Nixon had a secret plan to end the war in Vietnam. By contrast, Agnew charged that Democratic presidential nominee Hubert Humphrey was incapable of winning the war in Vietnam. Humphrey had great difficulty overcoming these charges. After all, he had spent the past four years as vice president under President Lyndon Johnson (see entry), whose Vietnam policies had made him increasingly unpopular.

Defender of the Nixon administration

In the fall of 1968 Nixon and Agnew defeated the Democratic candidates of Hubert Humphrey and Edmund Muskie to win the presidency and vice presidency of the United States. When Nixon and Agnew took office in early 1969, the president gave his vice president very little to do. Nixon and his advisors worried that Agnew did not possess the diplomatic or strategic instincts to be an effective member of the Nixon team, so they did not include him in some key policy discussions.

In the meantime, Nixon began withdrawing American troops from Vietnam. He was reluctant to leave Vietnam without gaining some sort of military or political victory, however, so he periodically increased other kinds of U.S. military operations in the region. These decisions generated great controversy across America, so Nixon launched a special public relations campaign to increase support for the administration's Vietnam policies. Agnew soon emerged as a leading figure in this campaign.

Beginning in late 1969 Agnew traveled around the country delivering speeches in which he defended the Nixon White House and blasted the administration's opponents. Agnew targeted antiwar activists and journalists for particularly tough treatment. He labeled antiwar protestors as "an effete [feminine and weak] corps of impudent [disrespectful] snobs who characterize themselves as intellectuals." At other times, he referred to members of the antiwar movement as "Communists" and "vultures" who transformed "honest concern" about the war into "something sick and rancid [decayed and offensive]." At one point, Agnew stated that the United States would be better off without the people who made up the antiwar movement. "We can . . . afford to separate them from our society with no more regret than we should feel over discarding rotten apples from a barrel," he said. These attacks made him deeply hated within the antiwar movement. But they transformed Agnew into an immensely popular figure among conservative Americans who supported U.S. involvement in Vietnam.

Agnew also became well known in late 1969 and 1970 for his attacks on America's news media. He claimed that U.S. journalists purposely provided negative coverage of the war because they opposed it. He charged that the media was "a small and unelected elite" that did not represent the views of ordinary Americans. These speeches further added to Agnew's popularity among conservatives.

Agnew's political career crashes

Agnew's willingness to attack groups that Nixon disliked made him a valuable asset to the White House. Nixon appreciated Agnew's campaigning because he knew that the vice president's speeches aroused greater support for his policies among conservatives. In fact, Agnew became so effective that Nixon at one point instructed White House Chief of Staff H. R. Haldeman to "keep building and using him" against the administration's political enemies. Still, Nixon's confidence in Agnew's abilities remained low. In fact, Nixon considered dumping his vice president in favor of someone else on a number of occasions, though he never went through with it.

Agnew continued to act as the Nixon administration's primary spokesperson on war-related issues throughout 1970 and 1971. He also regularly campaigned on behalf of Republican candidates during the congressional elections of 1970. Throughout this period, Agnew remained an outspoken critic of antiwar protestors, journalists, and others who questioned administration policies.

In 1972 Nixon and Agnew were reelected to second terms, easily defeating Democratic presidential nominee George McGovern (see entry) and vice-presidential running mate Sargent Shriver. Since Nixon was forbidden by law from running for a third term as president, Agnew began making plans to succeed him in 1976, when the next presidential election would be held. But in the spring of 1973 Agnew learned that he was under investigation for accepting bribes during his years as governor of Maryland. The investigations centered on evidence that real estate developers had secretly paid Agnew thousands of dollars in exchange for valuable business contracts from the state.

Agnew called the charges "damned lies" and tried to rally public opinion to his side. But the American people gave most of their attention to the growing Watergate scandal. This scandal concerned the efforts of Nixon and several of his top aides to cover up a 1972 burglary of the Democratic campaign headquarters at Washington, D.C.'s Watergate hotel. Investigations into the burglary and cover-up eventually forced Nixon to resign from office in August 1974.

Agnew, meanwhile, was forced to resign after the Maryland bribery investigation turned up overwhelming evidence of illegal activity by the vice president. On October 10, 1973, Agnew appeared in court and pleaded no contest to a charge of income tax evasion. He received a $10,000 fine and three years of probation. Later that day, he submitted his resignation.

After leaving office, Agnew became an international business consultant. He continued to proclaim his innocence throughout the remainder of his life, despite the strong evidence against him. In his 1980 autobiography, *Go Quietly . . . Or Else,* he even claimed that he resigned because he worried that White House Chief of Staff Alexander Haig might try to have him murdered if he stayed. Historians, though, dismiss this claim as ridiculous. In 1983 Agnew was forced to pay $268,000 to the state of Maryland as reimbursement and penalty for his illegal activities as governor.

Agnew died on September 18, 1996, of a previously undiagnosed case of acute leukemia, a fatal disease that attacks blood cells.

Sources

Agnew, Spiro. *Go Quietly . . . or Else.* New York: William Morrow, 1980.

Cohen, Richard M., and Jules Witcover. *A Heartbeat Away: The Investigation and Resignation of Vice President Spiro T. Agnew.* New York: Viking Press, 1977.

Lukas, Anthony J. *Nightmare: The Underside of the Nixon Years.* New York: Viking Press, 1976.

Safire, William. *Before the Fall: An Inside View of the Pre-Watergate White House.* New York: Doubleday, 1975.

Small, Melvin. *Johnson, Nixon, and the Doves.* New Brunswick, NJ: Rutgers University Press, 1988.

White, Theodore H. *The Making of the President, 1972.* New York: Atheneum, 1973.

Joan Baez

Born January 9, 1941
Staten Island, New York

American folk singer, songwriter, and activist

T hroughout her career Joan Baez has used her talent and fame as a folk singer to bring attention to social causes, including ending world hunger and gaining civil rights for African Americans. During the Vietnam War, she focused her energy on protesting U.S. involvement in the conflict. By the late 1960s Baez was a well-known and highly influential anti-war activist. Her music and her visible presence at demonstrations encouraged many young Americans to speak out against the war. "Her songs . . . helped mobilize young people to take an interest in the world around them for the first time," Jeffrey Heller wrote in *Joan Baez: Singer with a Cause.*

Develops social conscience as a child

Joan Chandos Baez was born on January 9, 1941, in Staten Island, New York. She was the second of three daughters born to Alberto Vinicio Baez, who had moved to the United States from Mexico as a boy, and Joan Bridge Baez. Throughout her childhood, her family always pronounced their last name "BICE." But years later, as Joan gained attention as a folk singer, the media mispronounced her name as "BY-ezz." She

"I do think of myself as a symbol of following through on your beliefs, using your talents to do so."

Joan Baez.
Photograph by Jack Vartoogian.
Reproduced by permission.

did not bother to correct the error, and that is how she is known today.

Joan's father held a doctoral degree in physics. He could have earned a lot of money designing bombs and other weapons for the U.S. government. But he believed that war was wrong, so he took a lower-paying job as a college professor instead. "We would never have all the fine and useless things little girls want when they are growing up," Baez said of her father's career decision in her memoir *A Voice to Sing With*. "Instead we would have a father with a clear conscience. Decency would be his legacy to us."

In 1951 Alberto Baez took a job with the United Nations Educational, Scientific, and Cultural Organization (UNESCO). The job involved building a physics lab in Baghdad, Iraq. Joan and her family spent a year in Baghdad, where they saw terrible poverty and hunger for the first time. In her memoir Baez recalled seeing "people rooting for food in our family garbage pails, and legless children dragging themselves along the streets on cardboard . . . begging for money." Her year in Iraq helped her develop great sympathy for poor and hungry people around the world.

When the Baez family returned to the United States, they settled in California. Joan began expressing her social and political views in school, and they did not always make her popular with fellow students. At this time, the United States and the Soviet Union were involved in an intense rivalry known as the Cold War. Both nations competed to increase their military strength and to spread their political influence around the world. Many Americans became caught up in the Cold War and strongly supported the government's efforts to wipe out communism.

But Baez felt that the United States would never achieve world peace by trying to build more destructive weapons than the Soviet Union. In high school she staged a personal protest against the country's military buildup. One day, her teacher informed the class that the school was conducting an air-raid drill. The school would pretend that the United States was coming under attack from Soviet missiles. The students were supposed to leave school calmly and return home. But Baez knew from her father that if a real attack occurred, the students would never have enough time to make it home from school. So in protest she refused to leave the classroom. The next day, she was featured in an article in the local newspaper.

Also during her high school years, Baez attended a student conference sponsored by the Society of Friends religious group. Also known as the Quakers, this group has traditionally opposed war. The featured speaker at the conference was civil rights leader Martin Luther King, Jr. (see entry). Baez strongly agreed with King's ideas about achieving social change through nonviolent protest.

Becomes a well-known folk singer

As a girl, Baez took piano lessons and enjoyed listening to classical music with her family. But it was not until high school that she began concentrating on music. After failing to make her school's glee club, she practiced singing during her spare time. She also learned to play a miniature guitar called a ukelele (pronounced u-ka-LAY-lee). Before long, she was entertaining fellow students in the courtyard at school, doing impressions of popular singers, and appearing in school talent shows.

In 1958 Baez and her family moved back east to Boston, Massachusetts. Baez started college at Boston University, but she dropped out after a year. She found that she would rather spend her time singing and playing the guitar in Boston coffee houses. Baez grew her hair long, wore colorful Mexican blouses, and often appeared barefoot on stage. She sang traditional folk songs of Europe and the United States, as well as original songs about problems in American society. She quickly developed a large following of fans in Boston. In 1959 she was invited to appear at the first annual Newport Folk Festival in Rhode Island. The following year, she recorded her first album, *Joan Baez*. It soon became the third most popular album in the United States.

As the popularity of folk music spread across the country, Baez became a symbol of the folk movement and the growing hippie culture. She even appeared on the cover of *Time* magazine. "In the book of my destiny the first page had been turned," she recalled. "This book could no longer be exchanged for any other."

Phil Ochs (1940–1976)

One of the best-known singers and writers of antiwar protest songs during the Vietnam War was Phil Ochs. Ochs was born on December 19, 1940, in El Paso, Texas. Growing up in New York and Ohio, he learned to play the clarinet and showed a great deal of musical talent. He first began writing songs as a student at Ohio State University. He also became interested in journalism during his college days and published a radical student newspaper. He left the university a few credits short of graduation when his political views prevented him from becoming editor of the official school newspaper.

In the early 1960s Ochs decided to focus on music rather than journalism. He based his decision on the advice of union organizer and songwriter Joe Hill, who said that "a pamphlet, no matter how good, is never read more than once, but a song is learned by heart and repeated over and over." Ochs took up the guitar and began playing at folk clubs in New York City, alongside such rising stars as Joan Baez and Bob Dylan. In 1963 he appeared at the prestigious Newport Folk Festival in Rhode Island.

Ochs released his first album, *All the News That's Fit to Sing*, in 1964. A review in *Rolling Stone* magazine called it "a manifesto of social urgency." But it was his second album, *I Ain't Marchin' Anymore*, that brought him to national attention. The title track became a theme song of the antiwar movement. For the next few years, Ochs was a fixture at antiwar rallies, folk festivals, and benefit concerts around the United States. Each time he performed, he encouraged his audience to protest against the Vietnam War and support the civil rights movement.

While her popularity as a musician grew, Baez remained committed to the cause of social change. For example, she continued to support Martin Luther King, Jr., in his fight to gain equal rights and opportunities for African Americans. At this time, parts of the United States had laws that segregated (separated) people by race. White people and "colored" people were required to use separate restrooms, drinking fountains, schools, theaters, and restaurants. These laws, called Jim Crow laws, discriminated against blacks and placed them in an inferior position in society.

During a concert tour of southern states in 1962, Baez refused to perform anywhere that did not allow black people. She

Phil Ochs. *Reproduced by permission of AP/Wide World Photos.*

government watched him closely and even banned him from appearing on television for several years. He also received several death threats. But Ochs viewed himself as a patriotic person. He claimed that his songs were intended to pressure America to live up to the principles on which it was founded.

During the late 1960s Ochs grew increasingly disillusioned with American society. As he became less hopeful about the possibility of seeing positive changes, he also lost confidence in his singing and song writing abilities. He began drinking heavily and slipped into depression. Ochs released his last studio album, *Greatest Hits,* in 1970. He committed suicide on April 9, 1976, in Far Rockaway, New York. A number of well-known musicians organized a tribute concert three months after his death at Madison Square Garden in New York City.

Not everyone appreciated the messages of protest contained in Ochs' songs. Some people felt that his views were radical and un-American. The U.S.

also appeared at several African American churches and sang "We Shall Overcome," which became a theme song of the civil rights movement. In 1963 Baez sang at the rally in Washington, D.C., where King gave his famous "I Have a Dream" speech.

Joins the antiwar movement

Throughout the early 1960s, the United States became more and more involved in the conflict in Vietnam. The Vietnam War pitted the Communist nation of North Vietnam and its secret allies, the South Vietnamese Communists known as the Viet Cong, against the U.S.-supported nation of South Vietnam.

North Vietnam wanted to overthrow the South Vietnamese government and reunite the two countries under one Communist government. But U.S. government officials felt that a Communist government in Vietnam would increase the power of the Soviet Union and threaten the security of the United States. In the late 1950s and early 1960s the U.S. government sent money, weapons, and military advisors to help South Vietnam defend itself. In 1965 President Lyndon Johnson (see entry) sent American combat troops to join the fight on the side of South Vietnam.

But deepening U.S. involvement in the war failed to defeat the Communists. Instead, the war turned into a bloody stalemate. The American public became bitterly divided about how to proceed in Vietnam, and antiwar demonstrations took place across the country. Like many other Americans, Baez felt that the U.S. government's actions were wrong. She did not think that the United States should interfere with the reunification of Vietnam. Instead, she believed that the Vietnamese people should be allowed to decide their own future. As U.S. involvement increased to all-out war against North Vietnam, Baez joined the antiwar movement.

As one form of protest, Baez refused to pay 60 percent of her federal taxes. She chose this number because she estimated that 60 percent of the money the government received in taxes was used for military purposes. Baez knew that failing to pay taxes could result in severe financial penalties and even time in prison, but she wanted to make a statement. She did not want the U.S. government to use her money to pay for what she believed was an immoral war in Vietnam. The Internal Revenue Service (the government agency that collects taxes) eventually claimed her house, car, and concert earnings as a penalty for her unpaid taxes. Still, Baez continued her protest for ten years.

Baez also appeared on many television talk shows to share her views on U.S. involvement in Vietnam. She believed that she had a responsibility to use her celebrity to make a difference. "I must be ready not to die for something, but to live for it, which is really much harder," she explained in a letter to her parents in 1965. "I have a choice of things to do with my life. I think it is time to charge in head first. I want to start a peace movement." Toward that end, she founded the Institute for the Study of Nonviolence in California.

In 1967 Baez released one of her best-known albums,

Joan. It included a mixture of traditional folk songs, antiwar songs, and versions of modern pop songs by artists like Paul Simon and the Beatles. Later that year, she was arrested at an antiwar demonstration that encouraged young men to refuse to be drafted into the U.S. military. While she was in jail, Baez met fellow antiwar activist David Harris. The two were married in March 1968. Just over a year later, Harris was sentenced to a term in prison for draft evasion.

In the summer of 1969 Baez performed at Woodstock—a weekend-long concert and party in upstate New York that attracted 250,000 fans. Her son, Gabriel, was born shortly afterwards. But her marriage broke up when her husband got out of prison. "We split up, when we did, because I couldn't breathe," she recalled, "and because I belonged alone, which is how I have been since then, with occasional interruptions."

Travels to Southeast Asia to witness the effects of the war

In 1972 Baez and several other American antiwar activists were invited to visit Hanoi, the capital of Communist North Vietnam. She agreed to go to Hanoi because she wanted to see how the North Vietnamese people were coping during the war. She made the trip even though some people criticized her decision and called her a traitor or a Communist. During her time in Hanoi, Baez was caught in a series of American bombing raids. She recorded many sounds of her experience, including planes flying overhead, air-raid sirens, bombs exploding, Vietnamese voices, songs, and even a church service. When she returned to the United States, she incorporated these sounds into an album of poetry and songs called *Where Are You Now, My Son.*

The U.S. government withdrew the last American troops from Vietnam in 1973. Two years later, North Vietnam captured the South Vietnamese capital of Saigon to win the war. After the war ended, many American musicians turned their focus away from songs of social protest and began focusing on their inner thoughts and feelings. As a result, Baez's folk songs seemed to fall behind the times. In 1975 she recorded a more upbeat album on the advice of her record company. This album, *Diamonds and Rust,* included covers of songs by Jackson Browne, Stevie Wonder, and the Allman Brothers.

Through the late 1970s Baez continued performing in concerts around the world to spread her message of peace and human rights. She also became active in the humanitarian organization Amnesty International and helped organize chapters in California. In 1979 Baez grew concerned about conditions in Vietnam and Southeast Asia. Vietnam's Communist government had put many of its political opponents in prison or sent them away to "reeducation" camps. In fact, conditions in Vietnam had become so bad that thousands of Vietnamese people fled the country as refugees. Baez wrote an open letter to the Vietnamese government, asking for an end to the repression (the denial of basic rights).

Later that year, Baez organized a trip to Southeast Asia. With a group of American reporters and photographers, she visited refugee camps in northern Thailand. She met with many refugees from Vietnam, Cambodia, and Laos and heard stories about how they had been imprisoned and tortured by their countries' new Communist governments. Upon returning home, Baez formed a group called Humanitas to raise money for food and medical supplies for the refugees.

In the 1980s folk music came back into style, and Baez regained some of her popularity as a singer and performer. In 1985 she was selected to open Live Aid, a huge benefit concert event that attracted 90,000 spectators and a worldwide television audience. Live Aid eventually raised $70 million to fight world hunger. Baez continued to perform in the 1990s. Many people still consider her a symbol of how an individual can create social change. "I do think of myself as a symbol," she noted in her memoir, "of following through on your beliefs, using your talents to do so."

Sources

Baez, Joan. *And a Voice to Sing With*. New York: Summit Books, 1978.

Baez, Joan. *Daybreak*. New York: Dial Press, 1968.

Heller, Jeffrey. *Joan Baez: Singer with a Cause*. Chicago: Children's Press, 1991.

Loder, Kurt. "Joan Baez: The Rolling Stone Interview." *Rolling Stone,* April 14, 1983.

Robbins, Mary Susannah, ed. *Against the Vietnam War: Writings by Activists*. Syracuse, NY: Syracuse University Press, 1999.

Sager, Mike. "Joan Baez." *Rolling Stone,* November 15, 1987.

Daniel Berrigan

Born May 9, 1921
Virginia, Minnesota

American antiwar activist and Catholic priest

Daniel Berrigan is a Roman Catholic priest whose vocal opposition to U.S. involvement in Vietnam made him one of America's most visible and controversial antiwar activists. He participated in numerous peace demonstrations during the Vietnam War, and in 1966 he helped found Clergy and Laity Concerned About Vietnam (CALCAV), one of the most respected groups within the antiwar movement. Berrigan's fame peaked in 1968, when he and eight other Roman Catholic antiwar protestors (including his youngest brother, Philip Berrigan, who was also a priest) burned military draft files in Catonsville, Maryland. This action, which ultimately resulted in the imprisonment of both Berrigan brothers, was one of the most famous acts of protest of the entire Vietnam War era.

Early interest in the priesthood

Daniel Berrigan was born on May 9, 1921, in Virginia, Minnesota, to Thomas Berrigan, a union activist, and Frieda (Fromhart) Berrigan. One of six sons (he and his brother Philip were the two youngest), Berrigan became interested in religion and helping people at an early age. "From the age of six, Daniel

Philip and Daniel Berrigan.
Reproduced by permission of Corbis Corporation.

was obsessed by the suffering in the world," his mother recalled in Francine du Plessix Gray's book *Divine Disobedience*. "[He was] the most sensitive and studious . . . and the most devout [religious] of the six children."

During high school Berrigan decided that he wanted to enter the priesthood of the Roman Catholic Church. As a senior he chose to join the Society of Jesus, or Jesuits, a religious order of men within the Roman Catholic Church. He began his training for the priesthood in 1939, immediately after graduating from high school. He spent the next thirteen years studying theology, philosophy, foreign languages, and other subjects at Jesuit schools around the world.

Berrigan was ordained (appointed by church authorities) into the Jesuit priesthood on June 19, 1952. He spent the following year on a spiritual retreat in France. Berrigan was strongly influenced during this period by his daily involvement with French Roman Catholic priests who were dedicated to addressing social problems such as poverty, hunger, and prejudice. These members of the Catholic clergy believed that they had a responsibility to apply their religious beliefs to real-world issues. By the time Berrigan returned to the United States in 1954, he had become a firm believer in this philosophy of religious activism.

Writer, educator, and activist

In the mid-1950s Berrigan taught French and theology at a Jesuit-operated school in Brooklyn, New York. During this time, the energetic priest organized a variety of projects to help poor families in surrounding neighborhoods and directed the activities of several other local Catholic groups. But Berrigan still found time to pursue his lifelong interest in poetry and literature, often crafting poems late into the evening. In 1957 he published his first collection of poetry, titled *Time without Number*. Reviewers praised the collection, both for its rich language and for its joyful exploration of religious faith and other themes. The volume won several awards, including the prestigious Lamont Poetry Award from the American Academy of Poets.

Berrigan continued to write poetry throughout the late 1950s and early 1960s, when he served as professor of New Testament studies at Le Moyne College in Syracuse, New York.

Berrigan first arrived at the Jesuit-run school in 1957, and within months he emerged as the most admired instructor on the faculty. In fact, Berrigan's religious teachings and emphasis on social activism inspired many of the school's students to volunteer in antipoverty programs or join the civil rights movement that was taking shape in the American South.

Over time, however, other members of the Le Moyne College faculty expressed concern about Berrigan's influence over some students and his unconventional teaching style. He became an increasingly controversial figure at the school, and in 1963 the Jesuit leadership told him to take a year-long sabbatical (study leave) in Europe. Berrigan spent the following year roaming throughout Europe, Russia, and Africa, where he witnessed troubling instances of religious persecution, racial prejudice, and other social ills. These experiences deepened his commitment to faith-based activism.

Opposes the Vietnam War

Berrigan returned to the United States in 1964, a time when America was on the verge of escalating its involvement in the Vietnam War. Over the previous ten years, the U.S. government had sent military and financial aid to the young country of South Vietnam to help it establish a strong economy and a democratic government. But by the early 1960s America had become gravely concerned that South Vietnam was going to be conquered by the Communist nation of North Vietnam and its Viet Cong allies in the South. Most U.S. analysts believed that if the South were taken over by the Communists, other nations would become more vulnerable to Communist aggression as a result. For this reason, many American officials came to believe that the United States should commit military forces to the region in order to keep South Vietnam out of the hands of the Communists.

Berrigan, however, strongly disagreed with this viewpoint. "I returned to the United States in the autumn of 1964 convinced . . . of one simple thing," he wrote in *No Bars to Manhood* (1970). "We [the United States] were spoiling for a fight; we were determined not to yield before a poor and despised people, whose 'underdeveloped, non-white status' made them 'prime expendable targets.' . . . I began . . . as loudly as I could, to say 'no' to the war."

Philip Berrigan (1923–)

During the course of the Vietnam conflict, Roman Catholic priest Philip Berrigan engaged in numerous radical protests against U.S. involvement in the war. In his early years as a priest, Philip actively participated in the civil rights movement. He also became a firm pacifist (one who refuses to consider war or violence as a way of settling disagreements).

As the Vietnam War developed, Philip and his older brother Daniel—also a Catholic priest—became the center of controversy both inside and outside the Catholic Church because of their antiwar activities. In 1966 Philip conducted a series of demonstrations around the United States, including rallies outside the homes of Secretary of State Dean Rusk (see entry), Secretary of Defense Robert McNamara (see entry), and top U.S. military leaders.

In 1967 Berrigan's anguish over the war became so great that he decided to risk lengthy imprisonment in order to register his opposition. In October 1967 he and a few other activists broke into the offices of the Baltimore military draft board and poured blood on hundreds of personnel files. "To stop this war I would give my life tomorrow," he declared afterward. "I believe in revolution, and I hope to continue a nonviolent contribution to it. In my view, we are not going to save this country and mankind without it."

Berrigan was arrested for his participation in the Baltimore incident. As he awaited sentencing, however, he joined forces with his brother Daniel to strike another blow against America's military draft machine. On May 17, 1968, the Berrigan brothers and seven other protestors—collectively known as the Catonsville Nine—set fire to hundreds of personnel files from a draft board office in Catonsville, Maryland. The Berrigan brothers were convicted of conspiracy and destruction of government property. Rather than submit to prison, they tried to escape the authorities and carry on their antiwar activities, but both men were captured within a matter of months.

Philip Berrigan was released from prison on December 20, 1972, after serving thirty-two months. In 1973 he left the priesthood and announced that he had actually been married to a nun, Elizabeth McAlister, for the previous four years. Since then, Berrigan has continued to work on behalf of a wide range of peace and social justice groups.

In 1965 U.S. President Lyndon Johnson (see entry) committed American combat troops to fight on the side of South Vietnam. But despite America's awesome military might, the Viet Cong guerrillas and their North Vietnamese allies remained strong. The war soon settled into a bloody and confusing "war of attrition" (a strategy of grinding down the enemy until it cannot or will not fight any longer). As the conflict dragged on with no end in sight, many Americans joined organized protests against the war.

Berrigan soon emerged as one of the American antiwar movement's leaders. In early 1965, he and his brother Philip helped found the Catholic Peace Fellowship, the nation's first-ever Catholic antiwar organization. A short time later, the Berrigan brothers publicly declared their opposition to the Vietnam War in a "Declaration of Conscience." The Fellowship also took out a number of ads in national magazines, in which they described the Vietnam War as an immoral violation of God's laws. And in October 1965 Daniel Berrigan joined with Lutheran Reverend Richard John Neuhaus and Jewish Rabbi Abraham Heschel to create a new peace organization called Clergy Concerned About Vietnam.

A month later, Roman Catholic Cardinal Francis Spellman—who supported U.S. involvement in Vietnam—assigned Berrigan to a post in South America. Most observers interpreted this reassignment as an effort by church leaders to neutralize Berrigan's antiwar activities. But Cardinal Spellman and other Roman Catholic officials underestimated the impact of their decision. Antiwar Catholics strongly protested Berrigan's removal and demanded his return. Anger over Berrigan's treatment became so strong that church officials ended Berrigan's exile in March 1966 and brought him back to the United States. But Berrigan remained an extremely controversial figure within the Catholic Church—and the country—for the remainder of the war.

Outspoken leader of CALCAV

In May 1966 Clergy Concerned About Vietnam changed its name to Clergy and Laity Concerned about Vietnam (CALCAV), in order to encourage laypersons (non-clergy members) to join the organization. The group soon became one of the most prominent of America's mainstream national antiwar organizations. It emphasized a message of peaceful protest based on genuine moral outrage about U.S. involvement in the Vietnam War. In addition, it maintained a level of independence from the larger antiwar movement, which sometimes used radical activities and harsh language. CAL-CAV's moderate, peace-oriented stance appealed to many Americans who opposed the war but disliked the militant stances of other antiwar groups.

In addition to his CALCAV-related activities, Berrigan participated in a wide range of other antiwar rallies and events. In October 1967, for example, he took part in a massive anti-war demonstration in Washington, D.C. Berrigan was one of hundreds of protestors who were arrested on the last day of the protest outside the Pentagon, the headquarters of the U.S. military. In addition, Berrigan's writings reflected his strong outrage over the Vietnam conflict. He used both books of poetry such as *No One Walks Waters* (1966) and nonfiction works such as *They Call Us Dead Men: Reflections on Life and Conscience* (1966) to express his anger and anguish over the war.

In 1967 Berrigan moved to Cornell University in Ithaca, New York, to take a leadership position with the United Religious Work Program. In February 1968 he traveled to North Vietnam with fellow activist Howard Zinn. During their visit, the two men examined the impact of U.S. air attacks on the nation's population centers and helped gain the release of three captured U.S. pilots. Later that year, Berrigan published an account of his trip to North Vietnam, called *Night Flight to Hanoi*.

The Catonsville Nine

In the late 1960s Daniel and Philip Berrigan became so frustrated about the continuing war in Vietnam that they turned to more radical methods of protest. On May 17, 1968, the Berrigan brothers and seven other Roman Catholic activists entered a local draft board office in Catonsville, Maryland. They seized hundreds of government files containing information on potential military draftees and carried them outside to the parking lot. The protestors then set the records on fire with homemade napalm, a flammable chemical widely used in Vietnam in bombing attacks. The Berrigans then led the group in prayer until authorities arrived to arrest them.

"We are Catholic Christians who take our faith seriously," the protestors declared in a public statement. "We destroyed these draft records because they exploit our young men and represent misplaced power concentrated in the ruling class of America . . . . We confront the Catholic church, other Christian bodies [organizations], and the synagogues of America with their silence and cowardice in the face of our country's crimes."

In October 1968 the Berrigan brothers and the other activists, collectively known as the "Catonsville Nine," went on trial for conspiracy (an agreement to join with others to perform an illegal act) and destroying government property. During the trial, Daniel Berrigan explained that he burned the draft files because he felt that he needed to fight against the war with more than words. "I burned some paper because I was trying to say that the burning of children was unhuman and unbearable, and . . . a cry is the only response," he said.

The Catonsville Nine were found guilty by a jury, and sentences of varying lengths were handed down to the nine protestors. Daniel Berrigan received a three-year prison sentence for his role in the Catonsville protest. He launched a legal appeal to have his sentence overturned, but it was turned down. He was ordered to surrender to federal authorities and begin serving his jail sentence on April 10, 1970. But rather than submit to jail, Berrigan decided to go "underground" (lead a secret existence) with his brother, who had also been sentenced to prison. The two men hoped to elude authorities and continue their fight against the war.

Federal law enforcement organizations immediately launched a massive manhunt to capture the fugitive priests. Philip Berrigan was apprehended on April 21, eleven days after he went underground. But Daniel Berrigan eluded capture for four months before FBI agents finally caught him in Rhode Island. He served eighteen months in a federal prison in Connecticut before gaining an early release. During his time in prison, Berrigan wrote an award-winning play about the case called *The Trial of the Catonsville Nine* (1971).

Social activist for many causes

When Berrigan was released from prison on February 24, 1972, he quickly resumed his outspoken criticism of the war in Vietnam. U.S. forces withdrew from the conflict in 1973, and two years later, North Vietnam finally defeated South Vietnam to end the war and unite the country under Communist rule. With the war finally over, Berrigan turned his attention to other social causes, such as racial equality and improving the lives of poor and politically powerless people.

Through the 1980s and 1990s Berrigan became well-known for his counseling efforts on behalf of people suffering from cancer and AIDS. Over the years, he has also expressed strong opposition to the death penalty in America and fiercely criticized U.S. military policies toward other nations. Finally, Berrigan is known as a leading critic of nuclear weapons production in the U.S. and abroad. In fact, he has been repeatedly jailed for his protest activities against nuclear arms production. His most recent imprisonment took place in 1997, when he and five other antinuclear activists were convicted of damaging a U.S. missile cruiser during a protest.

Berrigan has also published nearly three dozen books of poetry, nonfiction essays, and religious studies over the course of his career. In 1987 he published an autobiography, *To Dwell in Peace*. Not surprisingly, critics characterized Berrigan's autobiography as a blunt and unapologetic account of his actions and statements during and after the Vietnam War. "Those readers who despised Berrigan at the peak of the Vietnam War will find him no more worthy of admiration as he reflects on the events in his life [in *To Dwell in Peace*]," wrote *Chicago Tribune* reviewer Charles Madigan. "And those who admired him, who perhaps recognized in him something of an ancient Christian ideal, will find that the fire still burns in Berrigan."

Sources

Berrigan, Daniel. *Lights on in the House of the Dead: A Prison Diary.* New York: Doubleday, 1974.

Berrigan, Daniel. *Night Flight to Hanoi.* New York: Macmillan, 1968.

Berrigan, Daniel. *No Bars to Manhood.* New York: Doubleday, 1970.

Berrigan, Daniel. *The Trial of the Catonsville Nine* (play). Beacon Press, 1970.

Berrigan, Daniel. *They Call Us Dead Men: Reflections on Life and Conscience.* New York: Macmillan, 1966.

Berrigan, Daniel. *To Dwell in Peace: An Autobiography.* New York: Harper, 1987.

Dear, John, ed. *Apostle of Peace: Essays in Honor of Daniel Berrigan.* Maryknoll, New York: Orbis, 1996.

DeBenedetti, Charles, and Charles Chatfield. *An American Ordeal: The Antiwar Movement of the Vietnam Era.* New York: Syracuse University Press, 1990.

Gray, Francine du Plessix. *Divine Disobedience: Profiles in Catholic Radicalism.* New York: Knopf, 1970.

Hall, Mitchell K. *Because of Their Faith: CALCAV and Religious Opposition to the Vietnam War.* 1990.

O'Grady, Jim, and Murray Polner. *Disarmed and Dangerous: The Radical Lives and Times of Daniel and Philip Berrigan.* New York: Basic Books, 1997.

Robbins, Mary Susannah, ed. *Against the Vietnam War: Writings by Activists.* Syracuse, NY: Syracuse University Press, 1999.

McGeorge Bundy

Born March 30, 1919
Boston, Massachusetts
Died September 16, 1996
Boston, Massachusetts

U.S. national security advisor, 1961–1966

> "I am much affected by my belief that the sentiment in the country on the war has shifted very heavily . . . . What has happened is that a great many people . . . have begun to think that Vietnam really is a bottomless pit."

McGeorge Bundy.
Courtesy of the Library of Congress.

McGeorge Bundy played a major role in shaping U.S. military policies toward Vietnam during the early and mid-1960s. During his years as national security advisor, Bundy urged both President John F. Kennedy (see entry) and President Lyndon B. Johnson (see entry) to expand America's military role in the war. By 1965, however, Bundy's confidence in an eventual U.S. victory was badly shaken. His doubts about continued American involvement in the Vietnam War became so great that he resigned from the Johnson administration in early 1966.

Early reputation for brilliance

McGeorge Bundy was born March 30, 1919, in Boston, Massachusetts. He was one of three sons of Harvey H. Bundy, an attorney and government official, and Katharine (Putnam) Bundy. Bundy's parents enrolled their sons in Massachusetts' finest schools, where all three boys excelled in their studies. After graduating from Groton School in 1936, McGeorge applied for admission into Yale University, one of the most prestigious universities in the United States. Yale gladly accepted Bundy after he posted the school's first-ever perfect score on its entrance exam.

During his years of study at Yale, Bundy distinguished himself as a brilliant and energetic student. He won numerous academic honors at the school, where he majored in mathematics. But he became even better known around the school for his active involvement in journalism and his interest in both local and national politics. After graduating from Yale in 1940, Bundy was invited to teach U.S. foreign policy at Harvard University. The young scholar soon became one of the most popular instructors at Harvard.

In 1942 Bundy managed to gain acceptance into the U.S. Army despite suffering from extremely poor eyesight. He entered the military as a private but received extensive training as an intelligence officer. He served in the army for the next four years as World War II raged across Europe and the Pacific Rim. During this time he helped devise strategy for a variety of military operations, including major invasions of France and Italy. He left the army in 1946 as a captain.

In the late 1940s and early 1950s, Bundy's image as a brilliant and ambitious young man continued to flourish. He remained a member of the Harvard faculty while simultaneously working his way into powerful political circles. In 1948 and 1949, for example, he served as a political analyst for the U.S. Council of Foreign Relations, and in 1952 he edited a collection of Secretary of State Dean Acheson's public papers. In 1950 he married Mary Buckminster Lothrop, with whom he eventually had four sons.

In 1953 Bundy was named dean of Harvard's Graduate School of Arts and Sciences. This was an amazing honor for someone of Bundy's age—he was only 34 years old at the time—and reflected his growing national reputation as a brilliant administrator and decisive leader. He spent the next several years attending to his duties at Harvard and building strong relationships with a number of prominent American politicians, including John F. Kennedy.

The best and the brightest

In November 1960 Kennedy was elected president of the United States. As Kennedy prepared to take office in January 1961, he asked dozens of bright young men from the nation's most highly regarded universities, companies, and foundations to accept important government posts in his administration. He reserved a special spot in his administration for Bundy, making him his national security advisor. Bundy and the other men selected by Kennedy eventually came to be known as "the Best and the Brightest," a new generation of capable leaders who would guide America into the future.

In earlier presidential administrations, the position of national security advisor had not always been that important. But Kennedy gave Bundy a great deal of authority and relied on him for advice on military policies and other national security issues. For example, Bundy was responsible for overseeing the National Security Council (NSC) and developing the Kennedy administration's overall military and foreign policy strategies. Before long, Bundy was widely known as one of Kennedy's closest and most trusted advisors on a wide range of issues.

In the early 1960s Bundy helped Kennedy reach decisions on many different areas of public policy. But he is best remembered for encouraging the president to increase America's military commitment to the troubled nation of South Vietnam.

South Vietnam had been created only a few years earlier, when Vietnamese forces ended decades of French colonial rule. The 1954 Geneva peace agreement that ended the French-Vietnamese conflict created two countries within Vietnam. North Vietnam was headed by a Communist government under revolutionary leader Ho Chi Minh (see entry). South Vietnam, meanwhile, was led by a U.S.-supported government under President Ngo Dinh Diem (see entry).

The Geneva agreement provided for nationwide free elections to be held in 1956 so that the two parts of Vietnam could be united under one government. But U.S. and South Vietnamese officials refused to hold the elections because they feared that the results would give the Communists control over the entire country. When the South refused to hold elections, North Vietnam and its allies in the South—known as the Viet Cong—launched a guerrilla war against Diem's government. The United States responded by sending money, weapons, and advisors to aid in South Vietnam's defense. By the early 1960s, however, Bundy and some other American analysts became concerned that South Vietnam might collapse and trigger a wave of Communist aggression around the globe.

A "hawk" on Vietnam

Bundy firmly believed that South Vietnam could be saved if the United States took a more active role in the conflict. After all, America possessed technology and military power that were far superior to those of North Vietnam. In addition, Bundy interpreted the civil war in Vietnam as a test of American resolve. He felt that the United States needed to show the world that Communist aggression would not be allowed to go unpunished. These feelings, which were shared by many other Kennedy administration "hawks" (supporters of American military involvement in Vietnam), shaped U.S. military policy toward Vietnam for the next several years.

In November 1963 Kennedy was assassinated, and Vice President Lyndon B. Johnson was sworn in as president. But Johnson retained Bundy and most other Kennedy officials for his own administration. During his first year as Johnson's national security advisor, Bundy continued to advocate an expansion of the U.S. military role in Vietnam. He and other administration hawks remained certain that as America unleashed more and more of its military power on the Viet Cong and their allies in the North, the Communists would give up the fight.

In 1965, however, Bundy's confidence in an eventual American victory began to crumble. In February of that year he made a personal tour of Vietnam that deeply troubled him. Despite massive amounts of American military and economic aid, the nation seemed to him to be tottering on the brink of a Communist takeover. The "energy and persistence [of the Viet Cong] are astonishing," he warned Johnson in a secret cable message. Bundy also stated that during his travels, he detected a "widespread belief that we [the United States] do not have the will and force and patience and determination to take the necessary action and stay the course." He concluded his message by urging the president to approve "continuous" bombing attacks on North Vietnam and other new military measures.

Over the next several months, the United States dramatically escalated its involvement in the Vietnam War. Johnson approved a major bombing campaign against North Vietnam called Operation Rolling Thunder. He also sent U.S. combat troops to fight in the conflict. But when these actions failed to stop the Communist threat, Bundy became convinced that an American victory in Vietnam was years away.

In early 1966 Bundy's doubts about the war led him to submit his resignation and leave the government. But he never publicly expressed his fears that American involvement in Vietnam was a terrible mistake. Instead, he continued to advise Johnson on an informal basis after assuming the presidency of the Ford Foundation, an organization that supports a wide range of educational, antipoverty, and nation-building programs around the world.

After Bundy's departure, the war continued to drag on with no end in sight. Public opposition exploded across the country, and Johnson's presidency came under intense criticism for its actions in Vietnam. This criticism became even stronger in early 1968, after North Vietnam launched the Tet Offensive—a massive attack against American and South Vietnamese positions throughout South Vietnam.

In March 1968 Johnson asked Bundy and other close advisors—known collectively as the "Wise Men"—to meet with him about the war. Johnson hoped that the men could help him devise a strategy to win the war. But to Johnson's great dismay, Bundy and the others urged him to withdraw American troops from Vietnam and begin peace negotiations with the Communists. "I am much affected by my belief that the sentiment in the country on the war has shifted very heavily since the Tet offensive," Bundy told Johnson. "This is not because our people are quitters . . . . What has happened is that a great many people— even very determined and loyal people—have begun to think that Vietnam really is a bottomless pit." A short time later, Johnson announced a halt to the Rolling Thunder bombing campaign and called on North Vietnam to begin peace talks.

Bundy's post-Vietnam career

Bundy remained at the Ford Foundation until 1979, when he joined the faculty of New York University as a professor of history. He taught at the school from 1979 to 1989, during which time he became a notable critic of nuclear arms proliferation around the world. He also wrote two critically acclaimed studies of this issue—*Danger and Survival: Choices about the Bomb in the First Fifty Years* (1988) and *Reducing Nuclear Danger: The Road Away from the Brink* (1993).

In 1990 Bundy accepted the chairmanship of the Carnegie Corporation's Committee on Reducing Nuclear Danger. He continued his association with the Carnegie Corporation until 1996, when he died of a heart attack in his hometown of Boston.

Sources

Berman, Larry. *Lyndon Johnson's War.* New York: W. W. Norton, 1989.

Bird, Kai. *The Color of Truth: McGeorge Bundy and William Bundy, Brothers in Arms: A Biography.* New York: Simon and Schuster, 1998.

Halberstam, David. *The Best and the Brightest.* New York: Random House, 1972.

Heath, Jim F. *Decade of Disillusionment: The Kennedy-Johnson Years.* Bloomington: Indiana University Press, 1975.

Herring, George C. *LBJ and Vietnam: A Different Kind of War.* Austin: University of Texas Press, 1994.

Isaacson, Walter. "The Best and the Brightest: McGeorge Bundy, 1919–1996." *Time,* September 30, 1996.

Just, Ward. "A Man of the Establishment." *Newsweek,* September 30, 1996.

William Calley

Born in 1943

American soldier who led the My Lai Massacre

William Calley is one of the Vietnam War's most infamous figures. In 1968 he led American troops in an attack that led to the slaughter of hundreds of defenseless Vietnamese peasants in My Lai, a small farming village. In many people's minds, this massacre stands as the single most horrible event of the entire war.

Joins the army after early struggles

William Laws Calley, Jr., grew up in a comfortable neighborhood in Miami Shores, Florida, where his father worked as a machinery salesman. Calley—who acquired the nickname "Rusty" as a child—was a poor student who had occasional discipline problems in school. He attended high school at Florida Military Academy, from which he graduated in 1962. He enrolled in Palm Beach Junior College in Florida but dropped out after a few months. Calley then spent the next few years moving from job to job.

In the meantime, American involvement in the Vietnam War was escalating rapidly. In the late 1950s the U.S. government sent generous military and financial aid packages to the young country of South Vietnam to help it establish a strong economy and a democratic government. But by the early 1960s America had become gravely concerned that South Vietnam was on the verge of falling to the Communist nation of North Vietnam and its Viet Cong allies in the South. U.S. analysts claimed that if the South were overrun by the Communists, other nations would become more vulnerable to a Communist takeover. This fear convinced U.S. President Lyndon Johnson (see entry) to send American combat troops to fight on the side of South Vietnam in 1965.

In 1966 Calley voluntarily left civilian life to enlist in the U.S. Army. He supported American intervention in Vietnam and hoped to make a career for himself in the military. After undergoing basic training at Fort Benning, Georgia, he successfully completed officer school. "When he became a lieutenant, it was the most important thing in the world to him," recalled one of Calley's friends in a 1989 *People Weekly* article. "He wanted to do the best possible job . . . . He was going to fight Communism. He believed in the war. Absolutely."

Calley goes to Vietnam

After completing his training, Second Lieutenant Calley was transferred to Vietnam, where he joined C Company (also known as Charley Company), a combat infantry unit within the U.S. Army's 20th Infantry Division. He was assigned to command one of three platoons within C Company. Calley's performance as an officer during his first months in Vietnam received mixed reviews. Some soldiers who served with Calley believed that he conducted himself well. But others thought that he was incompetent. They charged that he did not possess the intelligence or military knowledge to effectively lead troops in battle.

Calley served in Vietnam at a time when the conflict was rapidly turning into a grim war of "attrition" (a military strategy of grinding down the enemy until it is unable or unwilling to fight any longer). The United States and its South Vietnamese allies held a tremendous advantage over their Communist foes in terms of military firepower. But North Vietnamese and Viet Cong forces used guerrilla tactics, their superior knowledge of Vietnam's terrain, and their ability to blend in with Vietnamese civilians to cancel out this advantage. As a result, the war turned into a stalemate, with neither side able to gain a meaningful advantage.

As the war continued and American frustration increased, the U.S. military adopted increasingly ruthless measures to defeat the Communists. For example, they approved the use of so-called "free-fire zones" in Vietnam. Areas received this designation when military authorities decided that they were probably inhabited only by enemy soldiers. American soldiers were free to attack any Vietnamese they saw in a free-fire zone. But in many cases, areas were given "free-fire zone" status despite the continued presence of civilians. As a result, Vietnamese civilians who lived in or passed through free-fire zones came under attack from U.S. forces.

Another controversial element of the U.S. war effort was its reliance on "body counts." The U.S. military kept track of enemy casualties (killed and wounded) as a way of gauging its progress in the conflict. But as opposition to the war increased in America, U.S. troops were encouraged to take the view that all dead Vietnamese—even women and children—should be counted as Viet Cong guerrillas. Officials hoped that the inflated body count statistics would reassure both Congress and the American public that it was marching to victory in Vietnam. But the use of "body count" statistics came under harsh criticism. Critics argued that the military's decision to use such information as a measurement of progress proved that the war was immoral. Many observers also claimed that the emphasis on body counts eroded the morale and spirit of American troops and actually encouraged them to take the lives of innocent civilians.

The My Lai massacre

In early 1968 Calley and the other members of C Company went on an extended mission into the South Vietnamese countryside, where they suffered several casualties from enemy land mines and booby traps. By mid-March, when the soldiers neared a village called Son My, they were feeling frustrated and vengeful. On the morning of March 16, 1968, the soldiers entered My Lai, a small hamlet that was part of Son My village. They entered My Lai because intelligence reports indicated that Viet Cong guerrillas were using it as a base of operations. When the U.S. troops looked around, they found no evidence of a Viet Cong presence. But rather than leave the village, the soldiers—led by Calley—turned their rifles on the unarmed villagers.

Over the next several hours, the American soldiers went on a murderous rampage. They killed hundreds of helpless women, children, and elderly people (the estimated number of civilians killed in the massacre is as high as 500) as well as most of the hamlet's livestock. Calley played a leading role in supervising and carrying out the massacre. He encouraged his men to shoot the unresisting villagers and personally gunned down a number of the victims.

Most of the terrified villagers were rounded up in ditches, then mowed down by Calley and other machine-gun wielding soldiers. Others were shot as they tried to escape or protect their families. In addition, a number of women and children were raped before they were shot. Finally, the soldiers set fire to most of the homes before departing. By the time Calley and the other soldiers of Company C left My Lai, the village had been transformed into a bloody, smoking ruin.

In the days and weeks after the slaughter, Calley's superior officers tried to cover up the incident. Both Captain Ernest L. Medina and Major General Samuel Koster submitted false and misleading reports about the massacre. In fact, reports on the My Lai incident stated that Calley and his men killed sixty-nine Viet Cong, not hundreds of unarmed civilians. In April 1969, however, Vietnam veteran Ronald Ridenhour called for an investigation into My Lai after hearing disturbing rumors about what happened. Ridenhour's letters led to a new U.S. Army investigation headed by Lieutenant General William R. Peers.

Debate over the My Lai massacre

Over the next several months, investigators determined that major atrocities (extremely cruel or brutal acts) had been committed at My Lai. They began quietly issuing criminal charges against Calley and other soldiers from Company C. But the massacre did not come to public attention until November 1969, when the *New York Times* published a full report on the incident.

Hugh C. Thompson: A Hero in My Lai

One of the few American soldiers who behaved honorably during the My Lai massacre was helicopter pilot Hugh C. Thompson. He and his two-man crew (Lawrence Colburn and Glenn Andreotta) spotted dozens of dead bodies while flying over the hamlet during a reconnaissance (information gathering) mission. They quickly radioed for help, then watched in disbelief as an American soldier executed a young Vietnamese girl. Horrified by what he witnessed, Thompson quickly landed his helicopter in the village. Once he landed, the pilot urged some of Calley's troops to help him rescue the remaining villagers. But when he was told that "the only help the villagers would get was a hand grenade," Thompson realized that Calley and his platoon intended to wipe out the entire village.

Thompson knew that he could not stop the slaughter by himself. But he immediately flew his helicopter between a group of terrified villagers and a line of advancing soldiers. "These people [the villagers] were looking at me for help, and there was no way I could turn my back on them," Thompson recalled in the *National Catholic Reporter* (March 20, 1998). The pilot then ordered his crew to aim their M-60 machine gun at the murderous U.S. troops.

News of the atrocities shocked the American people, who by 1969 had come to view the war as a nightmarish event that threatened to tear the country apart. Many Americans expressed shame and anger about the massacre, and antiwar leaders claimed that the incident showed that U.S. involvement in Vietnam was evil and immoral. Thousands of U.S. soldiers joined in the criticism, condemning the bloodthirsty behavior of Calley and his troops.

But millions of Americans who supported the war or disliked the antiwar movement refused to believe that the incident had even taken place. Many others excused the conduct of the soldiers. They either blamed the violence on the basic nature of warfare or insisted that the slain villagers had really been Viet Cong. These voices expressed particularly strong support for Calley, whose leading role at My Lai made him the focus for much of the public debate over the massacre. In fact, Calley assumed hero status among some Americans. These supporters bought "Free Calley" bumper stickers for their cars,

He instructed them to open fire if the soldiers tried to interfere with the rescue.

The threat worked. Calley and his soldiers backed off as Thompson loaded the Vietnamese civilians onto his helicopter and two other helicopter gunships that responded to his radio call. After airlifting the villagers to safety, Thompson returned to the hamlet and rescued a two-year-old boy who was clinging to his dead mother in a ditch.

Thompson submitted a report on the massacre, and he urged the army to investigate. But U.S. officials did not launch a full investigation until the following year, when Vietnam veteran Ron Ridenhour's letters finally sparked an inquiry. Thompson remained in the military for another thirteen years, then worked as a helicopter pilot for the oil industry. He now works in Louisiana as a counselor for military veterans.

Thompson's actions at My Lai have also been recognized by the U.S. Army. In 1974 Thompson received the Distinguished Flying Cross in recognition of his heroism at My Lai. In 1998 he was given the prestigious Soldier's Medal for bravery at a ceremony at the Vietnam Veterans Memorial in Washington, D.C.

wrote pro-Calley letters to their congressional representatives, and sang along to the "Battle Hymn of Lieutenant Calley," a pro-Calley country song that sold 200,000 copies in the first three days after its release.

Calley also received a surprising level of support from people who opposed U.S. involvement in Vietnam. Antiwar Americans were disgusted and horrified by his actions, but they viewed him as a "pawn" (a powerless person being used by others) who was being unfairly targeted for his actions in a war that was itself immoral. In fact, many antiwar leaders charged that the true criminals were the U.S. political and military leaders who used "free-fire zones," "body counts," and other ruthless policies in conducting the war. Even Ron Ridenhour, the soldier who helped expose the massacre to the American public, charged that Calley was basically just following orders. "Calley may have been more zealous [fanatical or devoted to a goal] than others, but he was doing what was expected," Ridenhour said in *People*. "This was not the aberration [abnormal behavior] of one wild officer. My Lai was an act of policy. Calley had his guilt, but he was just one small actor in a very large play, and he did not write the script."

Calley goes on trial

In 1970 Calley and twelve other soldiers from Company C went on trial for war crimes associated with the My Lai massacre. Calley alone was charged with 102 counts of murder. An additional twelve soldiers—including General Koster— were charged with offenses relating to the cover-up of the attack.

On March 29, 1971, Calley was sentenced to life in prison for the murder of twenty-two Vietnamese civilians. But he was the only participant at My Lai who was convicted. All the other soldiers brought to trial were acquitted (found not guilty) of the charges. These "not guilty" verdicts outraged both antiwar activists and millions of ordinary Americans.

Supporters of Calley, meanwhile, mobilized to protest his sentence. In the days immediately following Calley's conviction, President Richard Nixon (see entry) reportedly received 15,000 letters from around the country demanding the soldier's immediate release. In August Calley's sentence was reduced to ten years by Secretary of the Army Howard Calloway. On November 9, 1974, President Nixon ordered Calley released from prison with a dishonorable discharge from the army. After gaining his freedom, Calley settled in Columbus, Georgia, where he became a jeweler. In 1976 he married Penny Vick, with whom he had one child.

Calley has led a quiet existence out of the public eye for the past three decades. But the My Lai massacre continues to cast a dark shadow over the American people and the nation's military. "My Lai punctured the pristine myth of American 'goodness' in war," wrote Myra MacPherson in *Long Time Passing: Vietnam and the Haunted Generation*. "GIs were not handing out bubble gum, they were slaughtering babies . . . . My Lai . . . became the massacre that will be forever synonymous with the Vietnam War."

Sources

Bilton, Michael, and Kevin Sim. *Four Hours in My Lai.* New York: Viking, 1992.

Calley, William L., as told to John Sack. *Lieutenant Calley: His Own Story.* New York: Viking Press, 1971.

Hersh, Seymour M. *My Lai 4: A Report on the Massacre and Its Aftermath.* New York: Random House, 1970.

Hewitt, Bill. "William Calley." *People Weekly,* November 20, 1989.

Knoll, Erwin, and Judith Nies McFadden. *War Crimes and the American Conscience.* New York: Holt, Rinehart and Winston, 1970.

MacPherson, Myra. *Long Time Passing: Vietnam and the Haunted Generation.* Garden City, NY: Doubleday, 1984.

Sack, John. *Body Count: Lt. Calley's Story as Told to John Sack.* London: Hutchinson, 1971.

Ramsey Clark

Born December 18, 1927
Dallas, Texas

U.S. attorney general, 1967–1969;
political activist

Ramsey Clark served as U.S. attorney general—the highest-ranking law enforcement officer in the federal government—from 1967 to 1969, when antiwar protests reached their peak in America. During his time as head of the U.S. Justice Department, he oversaw the prosecution of several prominent antiwar figures who were charged with interfering with the nation's military draft. But he also displayed considerable independence from President Lyndon Johnson (see entry) and his administration. For example, Clark's position gave him authority to break up public gatherings that threatened to create civil disorder. But he resisted the Johnson administration when it pressured him to use that authority to break up antiwar rallies. He believed that such gatherings were protected by the U.S. Constitution. In 1969 Clark left public office and joined the antiwar movement.

Son of a Supreme Court justice

Ramsey Clark learned about American politics and government at an early age. His father was Tom Campbell Clark (1899–1977), who served his country as both a U.S.

Attorney General (from 1945 to 1949) and a U.S. Supreme Court justice (from 1949 to 1967). Ramsey Clark's career eventually carried him into the world of American law and politics as well. Raised in Texas, he joined the U.S. Marines in 1945. After leaving the military one year later, he went on to college. In 1949 he graduated from the University of Texas with a bachelor's degree. That same year, he married Georgia Welch, with whom he eventually had two children. He then continued his education, securing both a master's degree and a law degree from the University of Chicago.

Clark worked from 1951 to 1961 in a Dallas law firm. In 1961 he accepted a post as an assistant attorney general with the U.S. Justice Department. Four years later, he was promoted to deputy assistant attorney general. And in 1967 President Lyndon Johnson—a longtime friend of the Clark family—selected him to succeed Nicholas Katzenbach as U.S. Attorney General. At that time, his father, Tom Clark, retired from the Supreme Court because his son, as the Johnson administration's leading law officer, would be arguing many cases in front of the Supreme Court. Tom Clark knew that if he remained on the Supreme Court, he would be faced with a serious "conflict of interest"—a circumstance in which his public obligation to make impartial (fair) rulings might clash with his personal interest in seeing his son succeed.

Clashes with Johnson and Hoover

Clark assumed his new duties at a time when Johnson was under furious attack for his Vietnam War policies. The Vietnam War was a conflict that pitted the U.S.-supported nation of South Vietnam against the Communist nation of North Vietnam and its Viet Cong allies in the South. American involvement in the conflict began in the late 1950s, when the United States sent money, weapons, and advisors to South Vietnam to help it fend off the Viet Cong. In 1965 President Lyndon Johnson sent American combat troops to fight on the side of South Vietnam. But deepening U.S. military commitments failed to defeat the Communists. Instead, the war in Vietnam settled into a bloody stalemate, and the American public became bitterly divided about continued U.S. involvement in the conflict.

In the late 1960s the American antiwar movement increasingly turned to big public rallies and demonstrations as

Dr. Benjamin Spock speaks out at a "Peace in Vietnam" meeting in 1968.
Reproduced by permission of AP/Wide World Photos.

a way of registering its anger with Johnson's Vietnam policies. These protests angered and embarrassed the president. As a result, Johnson repeatedly urged Clark to use his law enforcement powers to halt the gatherings. But the attorney general himself harbored significant doubts about the wisdom of American involvement in Vietnam. In addition, he argued that peaceful protests against the government were protected by the U.S. Constitution. For these reasons, Clark resisted Johnson's calls to break up the demonstrations. Instead, he concentrated his energies on other law enforcement issues. For example, he waged an effective campaign against organized crime activity in the United States.

As the months passed, Clark's relationship with the president continued to deteriorate. In fact, Johnson pursued alternative strategies to combat the antiwar movement that did not involve Clark. For example, he made special arrangements with Federal Bureau of Investigation (FBI) Director J. Edgar Hoover—who was technically under Clark's authority—to use wiretapping and other spying techniques against antiwar leaders. But Clark fought against these surveillance activities as well, arguing that they violated the constitutional rights of the protestors. Clark's steady defense of constitutional principles during this period has since received high praise from scholars and historians.

In 1968 Clark did supervise criminal prosecutions of a number of antiwar leaders. These activists, including William Sloan Coffin and Dr. Benjamin Spock, were charged with conspiring to encourage draft evasion among young American men eligible for military service. The defendants were eventually found guilty of the conspiracy charges, but their passionate testimony against the war drew a great deal of attention. In addition, the guilty verdicts were never enforced. Instead, Clark's Justice Department dropped all charges against the defendants after their convictions were overturned on appeal.

During the 1968 presidential campaign, Clark became a special target of Republican presidential nominee Richard M. Nixon (see entry). Eager to portray Johnson's Democratic Party as "soft" on crime, Nixon charged that the previous year's massive antiwar demonstrations showed that Clark had done a poor job of preserving "law and order" in America. Meanwhile, the attorney general's relationship with Johnson became so bad that when the president left office, he refused to invite Clark to the farewell luncheon he held with top administration officials. In November 1968 Nixon defeated Democratic nominee Hubert H. Humphrey to win the presidency. Clark's service as U.S. attorney general ended in early 1969, after Nixon's inauguration (official swearing into office).

Clark joins the antiwar movement

After leaving office, Clark quickly emerged as an outspoken member of the antiwar movement. He publicly declared his opposition to continued U.S. military involvement in Vietnam and used his legal expertise to represent Catholic priest Philip Berrigan (see entry on Daniel Berrigan), Vietnam Veterans Against the War (VVAW), and other elements of the antiwar movement. In 1972 he traveled to North Vietnam to review the impact of American bombing campaigns on the country. During his visit, he went on the *Voice of Vietnam,* North Vietnam's propaganda radio station, to condemn the U.S. bombing raids on the North. Clark claimed that U.S. air attacks had bombed the country "back to the seventeenth century" and purposely targeted civilian areas. American military and civilian officials strongly denied his charges.

In 1973 the United States finally withdrew from Vietnam after signing a peace agreement with North Vietnamese leaders. Two years later, North Vietnamese troops overran South Vietnam and reunited the war-torn country under one Communist government. In the meantime, Clark campaigned in New York in both 1974 and 1976 as a Democratic candidate for the U.S. Senate. But he failed to gain the Democratic nomination on either occasion. These defeats marked Clark's last attempts to resume his earlier career within the U.S. government.

Controversial career as political activist

Since the late 1970s Clark has worked as a lawyer and political activist, building a reputation as a harsh and persistent critic of U.S. government policies. He claims that the United States routinely bullies and mistreats poor, minority, and politically powerless peoples, both within its own borders and around the world. In fact, he has repeatedly charged that the "greatest human rights violator in the world is my own government." But Clark has also criticized the activities of other governments over the years. For example, in the 1980s and 1990s he represented Native American groups in both Canada and Mexico when they became involved in disputes with the governments of those two nations.

Clark's visibility as a political activist reached its height during the early 1990s. At that time he denounced the Persian Gulf War, in which U.S.-led forces drove Iraq out of Kuwait after Iraq had invaded its oil-rich neighbor. Clark expressed outrage over America's military strikes against Iraq, charging that U.S. air raids killed many Iraqi civilians. Since the war ended, Clark has remained a strong critic of U.S.-sponsored economic sanctions against Iraq. He claims that these sanctions, which have remained in place for nearly a decade, are hurting millions of innocent men, women, and children. Clark explained his feelings about the situation in Iraq in 1998, when he published *Challenge to Genocide: Let Iraq Live.*

Some officials, scholars, and peace activists express support for Clark's views on U.S. policies toward Iraq and other countries. But other observers differ strongly with him on these issues. For example, many people believe that U.S. military intervention in the Persian Gulf was necessary to protect political stability and oil supplies throughout the Middle East. In addition, critics note that while Clark has repeatedly criticized the United States for committing human rights violations, he has remained silent about the well-documented human rights abuses committed by Iraqi President Saddam Hussein's regime.

Clark has also been heavily criticized for other positions that he has taken during the past two decades. During the 1980s, for example, Clark became closely linked to Lyndon LaRouche, the anti-Semitic (anti-Jewish) leader of an extreme right-wing political movement. Around the same time, he began a long association with the Workers World Party, a radical political group that has repeatedly expressed support for dictatorships around the world (in 1989, for example, the party defended the Chinese government after it killed hundreds of participants in a pro-democracy demonstration in Beijing's Tiananmen Square). Clark remained affiliated with this organization into the late 1990s.

Clark has also continued to advise and defend unpopular political figures around the world. His clients during the past two decades have ranged from the men who allegedly murdered Grenada Prime Minister Maurice Bishop in 1983 to a Rwandan pastor accused of masterminding a brutal massacre of the country's Tutsi minority group during Rwanda's civil war of the mid-1990s.

Clark's most notorious clients of the 1990s, however, were Serbian leaders Slobodan Milosevic and Radovan Karadzic. Both of these men were charged with war crimes for their activities in Yugoslavia in the early 1990s, when the country dissolved into civil war. They are accused of issuing ruthless orders and developing brutal policies that resulted in the death or dislocation of millions of people from non-Serb ethnic groups in the region. But Clark has repeatedly charged that the Serb leaders are being unfairly victimized by the United States. In fact, he bitterly criticized the United States and NATO (the North Atlantic Treaty Organization, of which the United States is a powerful member) for launching a bombing campaign against Serb positions in Yugoslavia in 1995. Many observers believe, however, that NATO air raids helped convinced the Serb leaders to end the bloodshed and reach a peace accord.

Clark remains respected among some liberal groups for his long record of advocacy on behalf of economically and politically disadvantaged people. In recent years, however, his expressions of public support for Milosevic, Hussein, and other political rulers of questionable repute have had a profoundly negative impact on the way he is viewed in the United States and in many other nations. Critics charge that he is a man whose dislike for the U.S. government has become so great that he is willing to ally himself with the world's most despised leaders, provided that they are in conflict with America's political and military leadership.

Sources

Clark, Ramsey. *The Fire This Time: U.S. War Crimes in the Gulf.* New York: Thunder's Mouth Press, 1992.

Elliff, John T. *Crime, Dissent, and the Attorney General: The Justice Department in the 1960s.* 1971.

Judis, John B. "The Strange Case of Ramsey Clark." *New Republic,* April 22, 1991.

Margolick, David. "The Long and Lonely Journey of Ramsey Clark." *New York Times,* June 14, 1991.

Williams, Ian. "Ramsey Clark, the War Criminal's Best Friend." *Salon* (Internet magazine), June 21, 1999. [Online] Available http://www.salon.com/news/feature/1999/06/21/clark/index.html (accessed August 1, 2000).

Zaroulis, Nancy, and Gerald Sullivan. *Who Spoke Up? American Protest against the War in Vietnam, 1963–1975.* Garden City, NY: Doubleday, 1984.

Richard J. Daley

Born May 15, 1902
Chicago, Illinois
Died December 20, 1976
Chicago, Illinois

Mayor of Chicago, 1953–1976

R ichard J. Daley became one of the most powerful Democratic Party figures in America during his twenty-three years as mayor of Chicago. Known for his administrative abilities and sharp political instincts, he played a vital role in the city's economic growth during the 1950s and 1960s, when many other major cities in the northern United States underwent serious financial declines. But Daley's national reputation suffered permanent damage when Chicago hosted the 1968 Democratic Convention. During that event, Chicago law enforcement units engaged in a shocking "police riot" against antiwar demonstrators. Televised coverage of these clashes convinced many Americans that Democratic Party leaders could not effectively guide the nation in Vietnam or at home.

Early career in politics

Richard J. Daley was born in Chicago in 1902 to Michael Daley, a factory worker who was active in the Democratic Party, and Lillian (Dunne) Daley. As a youth, Richard acquired a solid familiarity with local politics and an early allegiance to the Democratic Party. He attended parochial

"As long as I am mayor of this city, there's going to be law and order in Chicago."

Richard J. Daley.
Courtesy of the Library of Congress.

45

(Catholic) school before earning his high school diploma from De La Salle Institute in 1918.

Daley worked as a clerk and a Democratic Party official around the neighborhood for the next several years. But he also continued his studies, eventually earning a law degree from Chicago's De Paul University. In 1933 he passed law exams that enabled him to work as an attorney in Illinois, and three years later he formed a law firm with William J. Lynch and Peter Fazio. As time passed, however, Daley turned many of his business duties over to his partners so that he could devote his time and energy to city politics.

Daley's importance as a Democratic Party official increased steadily during the late 1930s and 1940s, when he took a series of positions of increasing prestige within the city and state governments. During that same period, he began to raise a family with Eleanor Guilfoyle, whom he married on June 23, 1936. They eventually had seven children.

By 1948 Daley had risen to the post of revenue director for the state of Illinois, and two years later he took over as Cook County clerk. These important administrative positions provided Daley with important experience in the complex political and financial worlds that governed Chicago and the rest of Cook County. In 1953 Daley was elected to the chairmanship of the Cook County Democratic Party Central Committee. This victory made Daley even more powerful in Chicago, for it gave him control over the Democratic political machine that directed affairs throughout the city.

Mayor of Chicago

In 1955 Daley completed his rise to the top of Chicago's political world by winning the city's mayoral election. In addition, he continued to serve as the chairman of the Cook County Central Committee even after taking the mayoral reins. Daley exercised great power and influence over the city in these dual roles.

As mayor, Daley forged effective relationships with industry leaders, labor unions, and federal agencies. As these alliances took shape, the mayor oversaw new business growth and massive construction projects throughout the city. These projects included the world's largest airport and tallest office building, a world-class convention center, a city campus for the University of Illinois, and major improvements in metropolitan highway and subway systems. In addition, Daley introduced popular new programs that improved public services and neighborhoods in various sectors of the city.

As chairman of the central committee, meanwhile, Daley built the Cook County Democrats into a very powerful organization. By 1960 Democrats occupied every important government post in Chicago, as well as most of the city's elective offices. In addition, Daley used the Cook County political machine to further strengthen his own position within the city. In fact, Chicago voters reelected him as mayor in five consecutive elections, in 1959, 1963, 1967, 1971, and 1975.

Daley's administration was not without critics. Some observers charged that the city's political and economic existence was unduly influenced by organized crime. Others charged that the Daley administration unfairly appointed friends, relatives, and political allies to positions within city government or the mayor's political organization. And as time passed, growing numbers of blacks and other minorities living in Chicago claimed that Daley's administration ignored problems in their neighborhoods and practiced its own brand of racism. But Daley remained hugely popular among the city's business leaders, union members, and white working-class families.

Not surprisingly, Daley's ability to control Chicago politics attracted national attention. In fact, his Chicago-based political machine made him arguably the most powerful mayor in the country. He helped shape the policies and politics of the national Democratic Party and played an important role in Democratic nominee John F. Kennedy's (see entry) narrow victory over Republican nominee Richard M. Nixon (see entry) in the 1960 presidential election. Daley's political machine sparked a heavy Democratic turnout in Chicago that enabled Kennedy to defeat Nixon in Illinois. Even more importantly, news of the Illinois vote reportedly discouraged Nixon supporters from voting in several Western states that Kennedy barely won.

Daley and the Vietnam War

In 1968 Daley prepared to host the Democratic National Convention in Chicago. Daley looked forward to the convention because he knew that the event would provide a boost for Chicago's businesses, emphasize his prominent position in the Democratic Party, and shine a spotlight on the city he led. But as the August convention date approached, America's growing divisions over the Vietnam War threatened to cast a shadow over the event.

The Vietnam War was a conflict that pitted the U.S.-supported nation of South Vietnam against the Communist nation of North Vietnam and its Viet Cong allies in the South. The Viet Cong were guerrilla fighters who wanted to overthrow the South Vietnamese government and unite the two countries under one Communist government. In the late 1950s and early 1960s the United States sent money, weapons, and advisors to South Vietnam to help it fend off the Viet Cong. In 1965 the United States began using thousands of American combat troops and extensive air bombing missions to crush the Communists. But deepening U.S. involvement in the war failed to defeat the Viet Cong or the North Vietnamese. Instead, the war settled into a bloody stalemate that claimed the lives of thousands of young American troops. As disillusionment over the war increased, the American public became bitterly divided over how to proceed in Vietnam.

For his part, Daley reportedly harbored private doubts about American involvement in the conflict. But he publicly supported the Vietnam policies of President Lyndon B. Johnson (see entry), a fellow Democrat and important political ally. The mayor also criticized the antiwar movement, which he viewed as a group of disrespectful troublemakers. But despite Daley's public expressions of support for the war, none of his four draft-age and eligible sons served on active military duty during the conflict. Instead, they all joined military reserve units to avoid going to Vietnam. One son even used his father's political connections to leapfrog over a waiting list of several thousand applicants and gain special admittance into the reserve.

In the weeks prior to the Chicago convention, Daley expressed great concern that antiwar demonstrators might try to interfere with the convention proceedings. He vowed that he would not tolerate any nonsense on the streets of Chicago during the convention. Antiwar activists took this warning seriously. After all, Daley had reacted strongly to disturbances in the past. In April 1968, for example, riots broke out in some of Chicago's black neighborhoods after the assassination of civil rights leader Martin Luther King, Jr. (see entry). Daley responded to the riots by ordering city police to "shoot to kill" arsonists. Later that same month, Chicago police brutally beat dozens of people who participated in a peaceful antiwar march.

Daley's warnings convinced many antiwar demonstrators to stay away from Chicago. But about 5,000 still showed up, including leaders of some of the country's angriest and most militant antiwar groups. Daley, meanwhile, arranged for a massive security presence around the convention center and the rest of downtown Chicago. As David Levy noted in *The Debate over Vietnam,* the mayor turned the city into an "armed fortress" in preparation for the convention.

The 1968 Democratic National Convention

The 1968 Democratic National Convention opened on August 26. Daley welcomed the party officials and delegates to the event. He also assured them that "as long as I am mayor of this city, there's going to be law and order in Chicago." But clashes between antiwar protestors and police erupted almost immediately and worsened over the course of the four-day convention.

As the violence of the confrontations increased with each passing day, some observers blamed the protestors for the unrest. After all, some members of the antiwar crowd engaged in angry and defiant behavior. They used drugs in public, waved North Vietnam flags, chanted obscene slogans, and engaged in petty vandalism during their time in Chicago. "They monopolized media attention," wrote David Levy in *The Debate over Vietnam,* "provoking terror and hatred among those Americans who still believed in order, and they were able to quite overwhelm the more respectable, reasoned, and dignified opponents of the war."

But as the convention continued, citizens of Chicago and American television viewers nationwide expressed even greater alarm about the behavior of the Chicago police. In many instances, the police acted like an angry mob. They stalked the city's streets with billy clubs, tear gas, and police dogs, brutally attacking peaceful demonstrators, journalists, and innocent onlookers alike. "By [the second day of the convention] it was irrelevant to the police whether the person they clubbed was young or old, male or female, a protestor or a hapless neighborhood resident who happened to be on his way home from work," wrote Mike Royko in *Boss: Richard J. Daley of Chicago.* "Clergymen trying to calm the situation were beaten . . . . Scores of people were beaten badly enough to require hospital treatment, including twenty newsmen. After [the first day's] jolting experience, reporters had mistakenly taken to wearing even bigger press credentials, which only served to attract the police like hungry sharks . . . .To a nation and a world, [Daley's] Chicago was beginning to look like a madhouse, and the famous TV commentators were being blunt about it. By [the last day of the convention], there was more interest in Daley and his policemen than in the expected nomination of [Hubert] Humphrey," the Democrats' candidate for the U.S. presidency.

Many Democratic officials who gathered for the convention were outraged by the behavior of the Chicago police. They angrily demanded a halt to the police violence, which eventually forced an estimated 1,000 people to seek medical assistance. But Daley and his staff dismissed their complaints and furiously defended the performance of the Chicago police. As the convention continued, public shouting matches erupted between the two camps. In the meantime, the convention floor also became the setting for a bitter debate over the party's Vietnam War policies. The delegates eventually voted to support a continuation of Johnson's war policies. But the chaotic debate, which was televised to a national audience, revealed that the party was deeply divided over the issue.

By the time the convention finally ended, nearly everyone agreed that the event had been a nightmarish disaster for both Humphrey and the Democratic Party. Televised images of rampaging police and furious party officials lingered long after the convention closed. The events in Chicago convinced many voters that the Democratic Party was too troubled and confused to lead the U.S. to victory in Vietnam or heal American communities that had become divided over the war, civil rights, and other issues. In fact, many scholars believe that the ugliness of the Chicago convention was an important factor in Humphrey's loss to Republican nominee Richard M. Nixon in the November 1968 presidential election.

Daley continues as mayor

The convention seriously tarnished Daley's national reputation and reduced his influence among national leaders of the Democratic Party. But he remained the most powerful politician in Chicago, winning reelection in both 1971 and 1975. He died on December 20, 1976. Thirteen years later, his oldest son, Richard M. Daley, was elected mayor of Chicago. In 1997 he won election to a third consecutive term as mayor of the city.

Sources

Farber, David. *Chicago '68*. Chicago: University of Chicago Press, 1988.

Kahn, Melvin. *The Winning Ticket: Daley, the Chicago Machine, and Illinois Politics*. New York: Praeger, 1984.

Kennedy, Eugene. *Himself: The Life and Times of Mayor Richard J. Daley*. New York: Viking, 1978.

Royko, Mike. *Boss: Richard J. Daley of Chicago*. New York: New American Library, 1970.

David Dellinger

Born August 22, 1915
Wakefield, Massachusetts

American peace activist; Chairman of the National Mobilization Committee to End the War in Vietnam (MOBE)

"I think I shall sleep better and happier . . . in whatever jails I am in for however many years than if I had compromised, if I had pretended the problems were less real than they are . . . ."

David Dellinger.
Courtesy of the Library of Congress.

David Dellinger is a traditional pacifist who opposes war on moral grounds. The son of a prominent Boston family, Dellinger graduated from Yale University and then spent the next few years in prison for resisting the military draft during World War II (1939–1945). He went on to become a leader in the protest movement against the Vietnam War. As chairman of the National Mobilization Committee to End the War in Vietnam (MOBE), Dellinger helped organize a number of large demonstrations against the war, including the one that took place during the 1968 Democratic National Convention in Chicago. The demonstration turned into a violent confrontation between protestors and Chicago police. Afterward, Dellinger and seven other activists—who became known as the Chicago Eight—were put on trial for causing the riot.

Yale man opposes World War II

David Dellinger was born into a wealthy and prominent family in Wakefield, Massachusetts, on August 22, 1915. Both his father, Raymond Pennington Dellinger, and mother, Marie Fiske Dellinger, traced their ancestors back to families that arrived in the United States before the American Revolution. As a boy, Dellinger spent most of his time playing sports and chasing girls. But he also made friends with children from poor, ethnic neighborhoods and began to question class and racial discrimination.

Upon graduating from high school, Dellinger went along with his family's expectations and enrolled at Yale University. While there, he supported a group of janitors and other university employees who went on strike in an effort to obtain higher wages. After earning a bachelor's degree in economics in 1936, Dellinger received a scholarship to attend Oxford University in England for a year. He then studied religion at Yale Divinity School and Union Theological Seminary. When he graduated in 1940, he became associate minister at a church in Newark, New Jersey. A short time later, he married Elizabeth Peterson, with whom he eventually had five children.

During his religious training, Dellinger gave a great deal of thought to his personal values and his direction in life. He decided to dedicate himself to pacifism—actively opposing war and working for peace. By the time Dellinger completed his education, nations around the world were being drawn into World War II (1939–45). In this conflict the United States, Great Britain, and the Soviet Union fought to prevent Germany and its allies from taking control of Europe. Many Americans felt that fighting the Germans was a worthy cause, and large numbers of young men volunteered to serve their country.

But Dellinger believed that war was morally wrong. "I couldn't believe that armed struggle, with the bloodshed and hatred it would generate, was the way to build a better world," he wrote in his autobiography, *From Yale to Jail*. As a minister, Dellinger could have avoided military service by filing for a deferment (an official delay in military induction). But he refused to file a deferment request. Instead, Dellinger's pacifist philosophy led him to believe that he should resist the military draft as a way of voicing his opposition to the war.

In 1940 Dellinger was sentenced to a year in prison for illegally avoiding the draft. In 1943 he received another three years in prison for organizing a demonstration against large-scale bombing attacks on German cities. During his time in prison, Dellinger continued to fight against what he viewed as unjust policies. For example, he was put in solitary confinement for refusing to sit in the white section of the racially segregated prison dining hall.

Dellinger soon discovered that he found standing up for his beliefs to be very satisfying. "I had gone from freedom to jail, from regular jail to solitary confinement, from solitary confinement to a damp, black dungeon they called punitive isolation—and I never felt so free before," he wrote in *From Yale to Jail*. "For the first time in my life I had nothing. And for the first time in my life I had everything."

Protests against the Vietnam War

By the time Dellinger was released from prison, World War II had ended. Over the next twenty years, he concentrated his efforts on fighting discrimination and poverty in American society. In the 1950s he started a printing cooperative with a group of other peace activists. He also founded a journal called *Liberation* that was intended to inspire readers to think critically about issues and take action according to their beliefs. In addition, he published books and articles encouraging people to join social protest movements.

In the early 1960s the United States became more and more involved in a conflict in Vietnam. The Vietnam War pitted the Communist nation of North Vietnam and its secret allies, the South Vietnamese Communists known as the Viet Cong, against the U.S.-supported nation of South Vietnam. North Vietnam wanted to overthrow the South Vietnamese government and reunite the two countries under one Communist government. But U.S. government officials felt that a Communist government in Vietnam would increase the power of the Soviet Union and threaten the security of the United States.

In the late 1950s and early 1960s the U.S. government sent money, weapons, and military advisors to help South Vietnam defend itself. In 1965 President Lyndon Johnson (see entry) sent American combat troops to join the fight on the side of South Vietnam. But deepening U.S. involvement in the war failed to defeat the Communists. Instead, the war turned into a bloody stalemate. The American public became bitterly divided about how to proceed in Vietnam, and antiwar demonstrations took place across the country.

Like many other Americans, Dellinger felt that the U.S. government's actions were wrong. As the U.S. involvement increased to all-out war against North Vietnam, he emerged as a leader in the growing antiwar movement. In contrast to other prominent antiwar activists—who tended to be young hippies or college students—Dellinger was in his fifties and often wore business suits. Still, he spoke on numerous college campuses, calling for an immediate withdrawal of American forces from Vietnam. He urged people to protest against the war using various methods of nonviolent resistance, such as marches and sit-ins.

In 1965 Dellinger joined a group of antiwar activists in visiting North Vietnam. While there, he met North Vietnamese President Ho Chi Minh (see entry). During this visit, Dellinger became convinced that the majority of the Vietnamese people wanted U.S. troops to leave Vietnam and allow them to settle their own disputes. He also accepted the word of Ho and other Communist leaders that American prisoners of war (POWs) were being treated well.

Afterward, many people criticized Dellinger for spending time with America's enemy and for believing what Ho Chi Minh had to say. In fact, some people called him a traitor. But he felt it was important to establish ties between North Vietnamese leaders and the American antiwar movement in order to reach a peaceful settlement to the conflict. With this goal in mind, Dellinger visited North Vietnam several more times over the next few years.

Member of the Chicago Eight

By 1967 Dellinger had become the chairman of the National Mobilization Committee to End the War in Vietnam (MOBE). This antiwar group organized rallies and demonstrations against the war throughout the United States. One of the best-known events sponsored by MOBE was the 1967 March on the Pentagon, which attracted 100,000 protesters to Washington, D.C.

At this event Dellinger spoke with several other well-known antiwar activists—such as Tom Hayden (see entry) and Rennie Davis of Students for a Democratic Society (SDS)—about staging a major protest in Chicago the following summer. They wanted the antiwar demonstration to take place during the Democratic National Convention, when the Democratic Party would formally choose its candidate for the presidency. They knew that this event would attract a great deal of attention from political leaders and the media, so it would be an ideal opportunity to get their message across.

When the Democrats met in the summer of 1968, thousands of protesters showed up outside the convention hall. Dellinger repeatedly asked the members of the various antiwar groups not to resort to violence. But as the protests went on, some of the demonstrators began throwing rocks and bottles. Chicago Mayor Richard J. Daley (see entry) sent his police force to control the protestors, and the situation quickly turned into a riot. Scenes of fights between antiwar activists and police officers dominated television newscasts and overshadowed the convention. As the convention continued, many reporters, demonstrators, and other observers charged that the police used excessive force against the protestors. In the end, more than one thousand protestors and two hundred police officers were injured in the fighting.

A year later, Dellinger and seven other organizers of the demonstrations—known in the media as the Chicago Eight— were put on trial for conspiracy to cause a riot. But the antiwar activists refused to cooperate with the justice system. Instead, they used their appearance in court as an opportunity to present their political views. The six-month trial turned into a media circus. Dellinger and the other activists disrupted the proceedings with frequent outbursts. They even draped a Viet Cong flag over the table where they sat.

At the end of the trial, Dellinger was found guilty of causing a riot and contempt of court. Facing another prison sentence, he made a defiant final statement before the court: "I think I shall sleep better and happier with a greater sense of fulfillment in whatever jails I am in for however many years than if I had compromised, if I had pretended the problems were less real than they are, or if I had sat here passively in the courthouse while justice was being throttled and the truth was being denied." A year later, a higher court overturned Dellinger's conviction following an appeal.

Continues working for peace

With the publicity of the Chicago Eight trial, Dellinger became even more prominent in the antiwar movement. In

1969 he helped organize the Moratorium Day demonstrations, in which thousands of people participated in antiwar events in cities across the nation. Dellinger remained active in MOBE, which was eventually renamed the People's Coalition for Peace and Justice, until the war ended in a North Vietnamese victory in 1975.

Dellinger remained a committed pacifist after the Vietnam War ended, turning his attention to ending war in other parts of the world. In the 1980s, for example, he led demonstrations against U.S. military involvement in Central America. In 1993 Dellinger published a book about his life as an activist, *From Yale to Jail: The Life Story of a Moral Dissenter*. In a review for *The Progressive,* Samuel H. Day, Jr., called the book "a key to understanding what's wrong with American democracy and a model for those who would pursue solutions."

Sources

Day, Samuel H., Jr. Review of *From Yale to Jail*. *The Progressive,* September 1993.

Dellinger, David. *From Yale to Jail: The Life Story of a Moral Dissenter*. New York: Pantheon, 1993.

Farber, David, ed. *The Sixties: From Memory to History*. Chapel Hill, NC: University of North Carolina Press, 1994.

Robbins, Mary Susannah, ed. *Against the Vietnam War: Writings by Activists*. New York: Syracuse University Press, 1999.

Jeremiah Denton

Born July 15, 1924
Mobile, Alabama

U.S. Navy pilot and prisoner of war during the Vietnam War

Jeremiah Denton was one of the best-known American soldiers to be captured by North Vietnam during the Vietnam War. He was shot down over North Vietnam in 1965 while leading a squadron of navy jets on a bombing run. After his capture, he spent the next seven years and eight months as a prisoner of war (POW), enduring years of torture, isolation, and near starvation at the hands of the North Vietnamese. After his release in 1973, Denton wrote *When Hell Was in Session,* a gripping account of his years in captivity. Seven years later, he was elected to represent his native Alabama in the U.S. Senate.

Chooses a military life

Jeremiah A. Denton, Jr., was born on July 15, 1924, in Mobile, Alabama. He was the son of Jeremiah A. Denton, Sr., a businessman, and Irene Claudia (Steele) Denton. Young Jeremiah became interested in a military career at a relatively early age. In 1943 he entered the U.S. Naval Academy, from which he graduated four years later. During his third year at the academy, he married Kathryn Jane Maury, with whom he eventually had seven children.

In 1947 Denton joined the U.S. Navy. As the years passed, he climbed steadily up through the ranks and became known as a top military pilot. He also continued his education during this time, taking classes at the Armed Forces Staff College (1958–59), the Naval War College (1963), and George Washington University, where he secured a master's degree in 1964. A few months later, Denton was transferred to Southeast Asia, where U.S. military forces were fighting to prevent a Communist takeover in South Vietnam.

South Vietnam had been created only a few years earlier, when Vietnamese forces ended decades of French colonial rule. The 1954 Geneva peace agreement that ended the French-Vietnamese conflict created two countries within Vietnam. Communist forces who had led Vietnam to victory over France were given leadership of North Vietnam, while South Vietnam came under the control of a U.S.-supported government that was supposed to establish a democracy.

The Geneva agreement provided for nationwide free elections to be held in 1956 so that the two sections of Vietnam could be united under one government. But U.S. and South Vietnamese officials refused to hold the elections because they feared that the results would give the Communists control over the entire country. North Vietnam and its allies in the South—commonly known as the Viet Cong—responded by launching a guerrilla war against the South. When these attacks pushed South Vietnam to the brink of collapse in the mid-1960s, the United States escalated its involvement in the conflict. Before long, America had assumed primary responsibility for both the ground war in the South and the air war against the North.

Captured and imprisoned by the enemy

When Denton arrived in Vietnam in late 1964, he was assigned to the USS *Independence,* a massive aircraft carrier stationed in the South China Sea. On July 18, 1965, Captain Denton led a squadron of U.S. Navy planes on a bombing raid to destroy enemy positions near the city of Thanh Hoe in North Vietnam. In the middle of the mission, Denton's plane was struck by enemy fire. He bailed out of the plane before it crashed, parachuting into the nearby Ma

River. Once he landed, however, he was quickly captured by the North Vietnamese and dragged to one of their prisons.

Denton spent the next seven years and eight months as a prisoner of war in a number of North Vietnam's most notorious prison camps, including the "Hanoi Hilton," the "Zoo," and "Alcatraz." During the first four years of his captivity, he endured torture on a regular basis. On one occasion, he was tortured continuously for ten solid days and nights when he refused to give the guards some information they wanted. In addition, Denton spent month after month alone in a cold and dark coffin-sized cell, where he struggled with tremendous feelings of isolation, fear, and despair.

Denton sends important message on television

But despite the horrible conditions he was forced to endure, Denton resisted his North Vietnamese captors in a variety of ways. As one of the top-ranking U.S. officers in the POW camps, Denton helped develop a strategy of organized resistance for other prisoners to follow. He told the other captured American soldiers—most of whom were downed airmen like himself—to keep important information from the guards. "I tried to put out involved orders saying that you should die before giving the enemy classified information," he recalled in the *New York Times*. He also encouraged his fellow POWs, urging them to keep their spirits up and support one another. The prisoners passed these instructions on from cell block to cell block through use of a complicated communication code that used taps, coughs, sneezes, and other sounds as a substitute for spoken words.

As Denton's imprisonment continued, he was targeted for especially rough treatment by the North Vietnamese. They recognized that he was a strong-willed officer who exerted a great deal of influence over the other American POWs. But despite their best efforts to break his spirit with torture, starvation, and long months of solitary confinement, Denton never gave up hope that he might someday return to his family in the United States.

Many American POWs expressed admiration for Denton's patriotism and leadership in the North Vietnamese prison camps. This grit was on full display in 1966, when Den-

An American POW Recalls Torture in the Camps

In Jeremiah Denton's memoir *When Hell Was in Session,* he recalled many episodes of torture that he endured at the hands of North Vietnamese prison guards. Following is an excerpt from the book that details the sort of horrendous treatment he often experienced in the years following his capture:

> [Two guards] began roping one arm from shoulder to elbow. With each loop, one guard would put his foot on my arm and pull, another guard joining him in the effort to draw the rope as tightly as their combined strengths would permit . . . . The first pains were from the terrible pinching of flesh. After about ten minutes, an agonizing pain began to flow through the arms and shoulders as my heart struggled to pump blood through the strangled veins . . . . [One of the guards then laid a nine-foot-long iron bar] across my shins. He

> stood on it, and he and the other guards took turns jumping up and down and rolling it across my legs. Then they lifted my arms behind my back by the cuffs, raising the top part of my body off the floor and dragging me around and around. This went on for hours . . . . I began crying hysterically . . . . My only thought was the desire to be free of pain . . . . [Later, a guard nicknamed Smiley] pulled me to my feet and hit me several times . . . . He indicated that I must rise whenever he entered. Bound as I was, that was no easy matter. The next time Smiley entered, I began pushing myself against the wall until I was on my feet. He beat me anyway, slapping me hard across the face and hitting me in the stomach . . . . On the seventh day, I decided to give them something [personal information about himself]. I cried for help. Dried blood streaked my chest. Feces clung to the bottom of my pajamas, which were completely stained with urine.

ton took a particularly daring action that became the war's most famous example of American POW defiance and spirit. At that time, North Vietnamese prison officials forced Denton to take part in an interview with reporters from several other Communist countries. As the interview got underway, Denton never stated that he had been tortured. He knew that North Vietnam would destroy the film footage and inflict new punishment on him if he accused them of torturing him or the other captured airmen. But unbeknownst to his captors, Denton blinked his eyes during the interview to spell the word "torture" in Morse code. Footage of this interview, which was eventually seen by a national television audience in the United States, confirmed U.S. suspicions that American POWs were being tortured in North Vietnam. From that point on, treatment of American POWs became an important issue in press coverage of the war.

Conditions for Denton and many other American POWs finally improved in 1969, when North Vietnamese leaders recognized that their treatment of the captured pilots was hurting their efforts to garner international support for their cause. From that point on, torture became much less commonplace, and food, shelter, and medical care all improved. Still, Denton and the others remained imprisoned in generally poor conditions, thousands of miles away from their loved ones.

Denton returns home

In January 1973 the United States and North Vietnam agreed on a treaty that ended American involvement in the Vietnam War. This treaty included provisions calling for the release of all American POWs, and in February 1973 the captured U.S. soldiers finally began returning home. Denton was among the first POWs to be released, since U.S. military protocol stated that soldiers who had been imprisoned the longest should be released first.

Denton was relieved to leave his nightmarish POW experience behind him and be reunited with his family. But he repeatedly expressed pride about fulfilling his patriotic duty to his country, and he declared that America needed to continue its fight against communism.

In 1974 Denton received an appointment to serve as the commandant of the Armed Forces Staff College in Norfolk, Virginia. Two years later, he published an account of his experiences in North Vietnam POW camps called *When Hell Was in Session.* This powerful book attracted a great deal of critical attention, and it remains one of the best-known memoirs of the Vietnam War.

Denton stayed in Norfolk until 1977, when he joined the administration of Spring Hill College in his hometown of Mobile. In 1980 he won election to the United States Senate as a Republican. His victory made him the first Republican to represent Alabama in the U.S. Senate in the twentieth century. Around this same time, Denton founded the Coalition for Decency (now known as the National Forum Foundation), an organization that promotes conservative solutions to social problems facing the United States and other nations.

Denton served one term in Washington, D.C., where he became known for his conservative voting record on social issues and his deep distrust of Communist governments and organizations. In 1986 he ran for reelection but was defeated. A year later, he was appointed by President Ronald Reagan to serve as chairman of the President's Commission on Merchant Marine and Defense. He served in that role for two years before retiring from public life and returning home to Alabama. Since then, he has worked as a businessman and has founded a humanitarian aid program known as Joint Relief International Denton Operations. In 1997 this organization provided 2.8 million pounds of donated food and supplies to thirty-five countries around the world, including Vietnam.

Sources

Denton, Jeremiah A., Jr., with Edwin H. Broadt. *When Hell Was in Session.* Clover, South Carolina: Commission Press, 1976.

Howes, Craig. *Voices of the Vietnam POWs: Witnesses to Their Fight.* Oxford University Press, paperback, 1998.

Hubbell, John, with Andrew Jones and Kenneth Y. Tomlinson. *P.O.W.: A Definitive History of the American Prisoner-of-War Experience in Vietnam, 1964–1973.* New York: Reader's Digest Press, 1976.

"POW to U.S. Senator." *U.S. News and World Report,* November 24, 1980.

Daniel Ellsberg

Born April 7, 1931
Chicago, Illinois

American political scientist and government official

Daniel Ellsberg.
Reproduced by permission of Archive Photos.

D aniel Ellsberg was a high-ranking government official who helped shape American military policy during the Vietnam War. But as the war progressed, Ellsberg's early support for U.S. involvement gave way to strong antiwar feelings. This conversion led Ellsberg to leak a top-secret government study about U.S. policies in Vietnam to the *New York Times*. This study—known as the *Pentagon Papers*—revealed that the U.S. government had repeatedly misled the American public about the war in Vietnam over the previous two decades.

A brilliant young man

Daniel Ellsberg was born on April 7, 1931, in Chicago, Illinois. An excellent student, he graduated first in his high school class. He then received a scholarship to attend Harvard University, where he studied economics and political science. After graduating from Harvard with honors in 1952, he was granted a special fellowship to study advanced economics at Cambridge University in England. He then returned to Harvard in 1953, where he earned a master's degree in economics.

In 1954 Ellsberg volunteered for military service in the U.S. Marine Corps. He spent the next two years in the Marines, where he became an expert marksman and a highly regarded officer. This experience, which included an extended tour of duty in the Middle East, heightened his interest in military strategy and international politics. After leaving the service, he went back to Harvard to secure a doctoral degree in economics.

In 1959 Ellsberg accepted a job offer from the Rand Corporation, a federally funded organization that studied defense and national security issues for the U.S. government. He spent the next few years working as a military affairs consultant to the White House, conducting research on U.S. military strategy around the world. Much of his time was spent studying the fierce competition that had developed during the 1950s between the United States and the Soviet Union. In this rivalry, known as the Cold War, both nations increased their military strength and tried to expand their political influence around the world.

A key battleground

In the early 1960s Vietnam became a major focus of Ellsberg's attention. Once a colony of France, Vietnam had won its freedom in 1954 after an eight-year war with the French. But the country had been divided into two sections by the 1954 Geneva peace agreement. North Vietnam was headed by a Communist government under revolutionary leader Ho Chi Minh (see entry). South Vietnam, meanwhile, was led by a U.S.-supported government under President Ngo Dinh Diem (see entry).

The Geneva agreement provided for nationwide free elections to be held in 1956 so that the two parts of Vietnam could be united under one government. But U.S. and South Vietnamese officials refused to hold the elections because they believed that the results would give the Communists control over the entire country. American strategists thought if that happened, all of Southeast Asia might fall to communism, a development that would dramatically increase the strength of the Soviet Union.

When the South refused to hold elections, North Vietnam and its Viet Cong (Communist guerrillas) allies in the

South took up arms against Diem's government. The United States responded by sending money, weapons, and advisors to aid in South Vietnam's defense. When this assistance failed to end the Communist aggression, America sent combat troops to Vietnam. But deepening U.S. involvement in the war failed to defeat the Communists. Instead, the war settled into a bloody stalemate by the late 1960s.

Ellsberg studies Vietnam

Ellsberg visited Vietnam in both 1961 and 1962, conducting research on possible American military strategies in the region. Ellsberg enjoyed these trips tremendously, for he felt that he was making a meaningful contribution to his country. He expressed firm support for U.S. military involvement in Vietnam throughout this period.

Ellsberg soon gained a reputation as a brilliant and perceptive analyst, and his career flourished. In 1964 Assistant Secretary of Defense John McNaughton invited him to become his special assistant. Ellsberg gladly accepted the offer, reasoning that he could be of even greater service to his country as a member of President Lyndon Johnson's (see entry) administration.

Ellsberg spent a good deal of the next two years in Vietnam. At first he was excited about America's growing military buildup in the country. At one point, he even inquired about returning to Marine duty as a combat commander (authorities eventually told him that they could not risk his capture by the enemy because of his knowledge of sensitive military secrets). But by late 1965 Ellsberg's faith in the effectiveness of U.S. intervention in Vietnam faded. As he recalled in a 1998 interview at the Institute of International Studies, he gradually became convinced that "nothing lay ahead of us but frustration and stalemate and killing and dying."

During the next two years, Ellsberg submitted numerous reports and memos in which he explained his doubts about continued U.S. military involvement in Vietnam. These doubts were shared by other officials, as well as the swelling membership of the American antiwar movement. But U.S. military involvement in Vietnam continued to escalate.

"The Pentagon Papers"

In 1966 Ellsberg returned to the Rand Corporation. A year later, however, Secretary of Defense Robert McNamara (see entry) asked him to take part in an effort to compile a history of American-Vietnamese relations since 1945. Ellsberg and three dozen other researchers spent the next two years putting together the study, known as the *Pentagon Papers*. The completed forty-three-volume study included seven thousand pages of government documents and detailed analyses of the Vietnam War from both government agencies and civilian "think tanks" (institutions organized to provide intensive research into military strategy, political theory, and other subjects). The papers provided a detailed record of U.S. policy in Vietnam since the close of World War II (1939–45), when the Vietnamese first rose up against their French colonial rulers.

As work on the *Pentagon Papers* drew to a close, Ellsberg took advantage of his top-secret security clearance to review large sections of the study. As he read the compiled history, he became convinced that presidents Dwight Eisenhower, John F. Kennedy (see entry), and Lyndon B. Johnson had repeatedly misled the American public about their actions and intentions in Vietnam. "When I finished reading the *Pentagon Papers* I understood at last that the war was one war; there wasn't a French war followed by a Vietnamese war and an American war—there was one war that we had participated in from the beginning, and it was a war that we had never had any right to be in at all," Ellsberg remarked in *The Ten Thousand Day War.*

In fact, Ellsberg's review of the Pentagon documents convinced him that American involvement in the conflict had turned the war into a fight between the Vietnamese people and America's mighty military arsenal. "To call a conflict in which one army [the South Vietnamese] is financed and equipped entirely by foreigners a 'civil war' simply screens a more painful reality: that the war is, after all, a foreign aggression. Our aggression," he declared in *Papers on the War.*

Finally, Ellsberg's review of the *Pentagon Papers* led him to believe that President Richard Nixon (see entry), who had assumed office in early 1969, was following the same pattern of deceit that previous American presidents had employed regarding Vietnam. "What I particularly learned . . . from the *Pentagon Papers* was that Nixon . . . was choosing to prolong

A Daring Ride with John Paul Vann

Daniel Ellsberg became very close friends with U.S. military commander John Paul Vann during the Vietnam War. They shared an intense dedication to their jobs and a deep respect for each other's abilities and talents. Their friendship became strained, however, after Ellsberg secretly delivered the *Pentagon Papers* to *New York Times* reporter Neil Sheehan (see entry) in 1971.

In the following passage from Sheehan's book *A Bright Shining Lie,* the author relates a daring Jeep ride that Ellsberg and Vann once took through a dangerous area of Vietnam:

> Ellsberg discovered what a true companion spirit he had found one weekend in December 1965, during a drive with Vann to two of the more remote province capitals in the III Corps region . . . .Their first destination, Xuan Loc, deep in the rubber-plantation country, was about sixty road miles northeast of Saigon. They would then have another seventy-five to eighty road miles farther to go before they reached their final goal, the capital of Binh Tuy Province, a forlorn little place near the coast called Ham Tan . . . .
>
> [Vann and Ellsberg set out in the company of a young American embassy political reporter who had asked to go along.] After the turn at Bien Hoa just north of Saigon, the road became lonely. The embassy field political reporter noticed the rows of fence stakes with the bits of chopped barbed wire dangling from them. He looked at the burned militia outposts . . . ."John, I'm really not supposed to be doing this," he said. "Political reporters are not supposed to be out on the roads. We have orders not to get captured. I think I'd better try to catch a helicopter."
>
> [Vann and Ellsberg drop the embassy reporter off at a South Vietnamese military post, but the young man reconsiders and decides to continue on with them.] A short way out of Xuan Loc the road began to pass through some of the densest rain forest Ellsberg was ever to see in Vietnam. He knew precisely what to do. Vann had trained him during their previous expeditions. He glanced down at his side to be sure a grenade was handy and lifted the carbine [rifle] he had been cradling in his lap so that he could immediately open fire out the window. Vann started driving with one hand. With the other he raised the M-16 automatic [rifle] he now customarily carried to be ready to shoot out his side. Ellsberg wondered how they were going to shoot if they did encounter guerrillas. The years of neglect from the war had allowed the rain forest to encroach [grow] until the road was only wide enough for one vehicle

the war in vain hopes that he might get a better outcome than he could achieve if he'd just negotiated his way out and took what he could get and accepted, essentially, a defeat," Ellsberg claimed during his 1998 appearance at the Institute of International Studies.

to pass. The forest was so dense Ellsberg had the feeling that if he stuck his arm out the window, he wouldn't be able to get it back; the undergrowth would snatch it. Then the road began to twist through blind curves. Ellsberg decided that if his seven-year-old daughter had an automatic weapon she could ambush a whole regiment on this one-way track through the jungle.

As the road worsened and they made these preparations for action, Vann and Ellsberg kept up the conversation. Keeping up the conversation was important to them. They were enjoying the self-control and sharpening of the senses they felt in the presence of danger.

The embassy political reporter did not say a word for quite a while. About twenty minutes out of Xuan Loc, he suddenly found his voice again. "John, how's the security on this road?" he asked.

"Bad," Vann replied.

"Well, I think I'd better go back, John," the embassy man said.

Vann found a place to turn around. He did not recover his temper sufficiently to do more than curse until he had returned to Xuan Loc [where he dropped the embassy man off] and had the Scout [Jeep] back out on the one-way track through the

rain forest, now with both hands on the wheel, wrenching the vehicle through the turns to try to make up for the lost time. "You know," he said to Ellsberg, "I didn't think he'd have guts enough to get out a second time."

Ellsberg smiled. "Well, dammit, John, why did you say that about the security?"

"What could I say?" Vann said. He laughed and let go of the steering wheel for a second and swept his hands up toward the jungle that menaced from every side. "Look at it!"

At Ham Tan there was a final moment to savor. They pulled up in front of the building where the province military advisors lived and went in and introduced themselves. One of the young officers noticed the Scout parked outside. He did a double take. He looked at Vann and Ellsberg, at the vehicle, and then back at Vann and Ellsberg again.

"Did you people drive here?" he asked. They said yes as casually as they could.

"Is that road open?" another advisor asked, astounded.

"Well, it is now," Vann said.

They were the first Americans to drive to Ham Tan in nearly a year.

Ellsberg decides to leak the *Papers*

After Ellsberg finished reviewing the documents, he asked his wife to read some of the materials. He gave her selected reports that discussed various American strategies to inflict pain and misery on North Vietnam. "She came back to me after she read it with tears in her eyes," Ellsberg recalled in *The Ten Thousand Day War.* "She characterized it as [being written in] the language of torturers, and that hit me very hard."

Torn by guilt about his earlier role in Vietnam policy making, Ellsberg decided that he needed to inform the American people about the contents of the *Pentagon Papers.* He made several copies of the study and tried to deliver them to important members of Congress, even though he believed that he would probably be thrown in prison for his actions. But the lawmakers did not take any immediate action, and the documents remained a secret from the American public.

By 1970 Ellsberg had resigned from Rand and had become a vocal opponent of the war in Vietnam. He participated in antiwar rallies, wrote antiwar articles and letters, and testified at trials on behalf of draft resisters. In the meantime, President Nixon ordered two major military raids into Cambodia and Laos—Vietnam's neighbors to the west—to strike against Communist forces.

The invasions into Cambodia and Laos convinced Ellsberg that he needed to take more drastic steps to influence American policy in Vietnam. "I had the feeling that America was eating its young, was destroying some of its most dedicated, most patriotic, most concerned citizens—young Americans subject to the draft—and it was up to older people like me who had been participants to not let that burden fall entirely on their children," he explained in *The Ten Thousand Day War.*

Gives the *Pentagon Papers* to the *New York Times*

In February 1971 Ellsberg secretly gave the *Pentagon Papers* to *New York Times* reporter Neil Sheehan (see entry), a veteran Vietnam War correspondent. On June 13, 1971, the *Times* began publishing front-page reports on the contents of the *Pentagon Papers,* including excerpts from the documents themselves. The publication of these documents triggered a storm of criticism against the U.S. government. After all, the papers indicated that the nation's political leaders had repeatedly misled the American people about Vietnam over the previous two decades. For example, the *Pentagon Papers* revealed that President Johnson had planned a major increase of American troops into Vietnam during the mid-1960s, even as he assured the nation that he had no plans to escalate U.S. involvement in the war.

The leak of the *Pentagon Papers* greatly angered the Nixon administration, as well as many lawmakers and military officials. Nixon and his staff worried that the revelations of past government misconduct would hurt their own operations in Vietnam. Other officials charged that Ellsberg's actions were a betrayal of his country. The administration successfully obtained a court order that forced the *New York Times* to suspend its publication of the papers after three installments. But by this time several other American newspapers began publishing excerpts. On June 30, 1971, the U.S. Supreme Court ruled that the *Times* and other papers had the constitutional right to publish the documents. As a result, the *Pentagon Papers* were made available to the American public.

Ellsberg faces prison

Frustrated in their efforts to stop the publication of the *Pentagon Papers,* officials in the Justice Department charged Ellsberg with a variety of crimes, including conspiracy, theft, illegal possession of government documents, and violation of the U.S. Espionage Act. If convicted of all charges, he faced 115 years of imprisonment. Ellsberg surrendered to authorities on June 28, 1971. At that time, he declared that he was willing to endure prison if his actions ultimately helped end the war.

Ellsberg's trial ran for the first five months of 1973. During that time, prosecutors worked hard to portray Ellsberg as a thief who stole government property that was vital to America's national security interests. But in May 1973 Judge Matthew Byrne, Jr., learned that agents of the White House had used burglary, illegal wiretaps, and other activities in an effort to find information that might embarrass or discredit Ellsberg. The judge then decided to dismiss all charges against Ellsberg. The agents who had collected the illegal evidence, known as the "plumbers," later engaged in other illegal activities that led to the Watergate scandal and Nixon's eventual resignation from office in 1974.

Strong career as political activist

Upon gaining his release, Ellsberg became a leading figure within the American antiwar movement. When the war ended, he turned his attention to other political issues that concerned him. In the 1980s, for example, he emerged as a leading critic of nuclear weapons. He also spoke out against American foreign policy in Central America and South Africa. Ellsberg's record of political activism remained strong in the 1990s as well. In December 1998 he signed a contract to write an autobiography for Viking Press, after a spirited bidding war among several publishers.

Sources

Anderson, David L., ed. *Shadow on the White House: Presidents and the Vietnam War, 1945–1975*. Lawrence, KS: University Press of Kansas, 1993.

Ellsberg, Daniel. *Papers on the War*. New York: Simon and Schuster, 1972.

Herring, George. *The Secret Diplomacy of the Vietnam War: The Negotiating Volumes of the Pentagon Papers*. Austin: University of Texas Press, 1983.

Maclear, Michael. *The Ten Thousand Day War: Vietnam, 1945–1975*. New York: Avon, 1981.

"The Rolling Stone Interview: Dan Ellsberg." *Rolling Stone,* September 1973.

Schrag, Peter. *Test of Loyalty: Daniel Ellsberg and the Rituals of Secret Government*. New York: Simon and Schuster, 1974.

Sheehan, Neil. *A Bright Shining Lie: John Paul Vann and America in Vietnam*. New York: Random House, 1988.

Zaroulis, Nancy, and Gerald Sullivan. *Who Spoke Up? American Protest against the War in Vietnam, 1963–1975*. Garden City, NY: Doubleday, 1984.

Diane Carlson Evans

Born in 1947

U.S. Army nurse in Vietnam and founder of Vietnam Women's Memorial Project

Vietnam veteran Diane Carlson Evans has played a central role in bringing the service of U.S. women personnel in Vietnam to the attention of the American public. In 1984 she founded the Vietnam Women's Memorial Project, an organization dedicated to building a monument to the women veterans who served in Vietnam during the war. In 1993, Evans's devotion to the project was rewarded when the Vietnam Women's Memorial was dedicated in Washington, D.C.

Nursing career takes Evans to Vietnam

Diane Carlson Evans joined the U.S. Army as a registered nurse in 1966, when American military involvement in the Vietnam War was expanding rapidly. This commitment of U.S. forces stemmed from deep concerns that South Vietnam was about to be conquered by the Communist nation of North Vietnam and its guerrilla allies in the South, known as the Viet Cong. North Vietnam had been working since the 1950s to overthrow the South Vietnamese government and reunite the two countries under one Communist government. But U.S. government officials felt that a Communist government in

"Those of us who went to Vietnam practiced a lifetime of nursing in one year—our tour of duty there. We were the young, caring for the young."

Diane Carlson Evans.
Reproduced by permission of AP/Wide World Photos.

Vietnam might trigger a wave of Communist aggression around the world and threaten the security of the United States.

As a result, the United States sent money, weapons, and military advisors in the late 1950s and early 1960s to help South Vietnam defend itself against North Vietnam and the Viet Cong. Then in 1965 President Lyndon Johnson (see entry) began sending American combat troops into Vietnam. But steady increases in U.S. involvement over the next few years failed to defeat the Communists. Instead, the war dragged on inconclusively, and divisions over the conflict erupted in communities all across America.

Evans was sent to Vietnam in 1968 to serve a one-year nursing tour. For most of her year in the war-torn nation, she worked as a head nurse at a medical unit in Pleiku, a small village near the Cambodian border. This was a very violent and dangerous region of the country, so Evans and the nurses under her supervision treated large numbers of casualties (persons who are killed or severely wounded) every week. Each member of the nursing staff in Pleiku routinely worked fourteen- to sixteen-hour days trying to save the horribly wounded soldiers and Vietnamese civilians who poured into the facility. On some occasions, they had to treat young men whose limbs had been blasted off, even as enemy rockets crashed down around the medical compound.

"I became one of thousands of Army nurses doing quietly what all military and civilian nurses do: caring for the wounded and ill," Evans recalled in a May 24, 1998, speech to Vietnam veterans in Washington, D.C. "Those of us who went to Vietnam practiced a lifetime of nursing in one year—our tour of duty there. We were the young, caring for the young. The average age of the wounded soldier in Vietnam was 19.4 years. The average age of the nurse was 23. We quickly learned that the primary reason we were in Vietnam was to get each other home."

Evans performed at a high level in Pleiku, caring for wounded soldiers and attending to her many responsibilities as a nursing supervisor. But as the months passed by, the constant exposure to mutilated bodies and dying soldiers took a heavy emotional toll on her. "I couldn't stand it that we were patching them up and sending them back to the slaughter," Evans recalled in *People Weekly*. "I shut down [emotionally]."

The Wall awakens painful memories

In August 1969 Evans finished her one-year tour in Vietnam and returned to the United States. When she came home, she was shocked at the negative attitudes that many Americans seemed to have developed toward both the war and the American men and women who served in the conflict. "When I returned home from Vietnam . . . to flag burnings and antiwar, antisoldier protests, I was told that nurses were 'nothing but oil for the war machine,'" she told *People Weekly*.

Unsettled by the hostility and indifference that many Americans expressed toward Vietnam veterans in the early 1970s, Evans tried to push away her war memories and lead a normal life. In 1971 she married Army surgeon Mike Evans, with whom she started a family (they have four children). She also remained with the U.S. Army until 1972, when she left the military to continue her nursing career in the private sector. In 1975, meanwhile, North Vietnam finally conquered the South to reunite the battered nation under Communist rule.

Throughout the 1970s Evans tried not to think about her wartime experiences. "I had this anger about Vietnam, but I kept it inside and didn't show it to anyone," she told *People Weekly*. In 1982, though, Evans attended the dedication of the Vietnam Veterans Memorial in Washington, D.C. This memorial, commonly known as "the Wall," honors the 58,000 American soldiers who lost their lives in the Vietnam War. Evans's journey to the Wall stirred up many painful memories of Vietnam.

When Evans returned home, she began having flashbacks about bandaged and burned children in Vietnam. "In a split second I would be in another place and time," she told *People Weekly*. "In Vietnam we never had a wake, never had a funeral, never had time to grieve." Eventually, she joined a veterans' therapy group to help her deal with the flood of emotions that she had been holding back for so many years.

Starts the Vietnam Women's Memorial Project

As Evans learned to cope with her Vietnam memories, she developed a new-found pride about the brave service that she and other nurses had provided during the war. But as these feelings surfaced, she realized that most Ameri-

An American Nurse Recalls Arriving in Vietnam

In February 2000, The Learning Channel television network broadcast a special documentary about American women—both civilian and military—who went to Vietnam during the war. In the documentary, called *Vietnam: Women at War,* Vietnam veteran Judy Elbring recalled her feelings after she arrived in Vietnam in February 1967 as a twenty-four-year-old nurse:

> The day we arrived—oh God—it was hot, it was sticky, it was smelly, it was dangerous, there were things that were booby trapped . . . . Everything was green and dust and fences and wire and noise . . . . And I thought, what a fool I'd been . . . . This didn't look like an adventure to me; this looked very serious.
>
> I wasn't ready for seeing those kids with holes in their heads and with brains coming out of their heads and—and that they were going to die. I wasn't prepared to look in a man's face and know that he wasn't going to make it. I don't know that there's any preparation for that.

cans did not know about their contributions. Inspired by the Wall, which gave American men who fought in Vietnam the recognition that they had long deserved, Evans decided to launch an initiative that would pay tribute to the American women who served in the war.

In 1984 Evans founded the Vietnam Women's Memorial Project. Under her guidance, the organization worked to gather women veterans together and raise funds for a monument that would recognize the work of the estimated 250,000 women who served in Vietnam. She also spent countless hours seeking government approval to place the memorial near the Wall. Evans was told by some agencies that a new monument was unnecessary, since the Vietnam Veterans Memorial included the names of the eight servicewomen who had been killed in Vietnam. But this argument did not carry much weight with Evans. "I told those people that without nurses, the [Vietnam Veterans Memorial] wall would stretch for 50 miles," she recalled in *People Weekly.* "There is only one place for the women who served and that is on the same site with our brother soldiers. These women touched thousands of those names on the wall. We have to be at that spot, physically, spiritually and emotionally."

In 1988 the U.S. Congress finally authorized the construction of a Vietnam Women's Memorial near the Wall. Sculptor Glenna Goodacre was selected to design the monument. As Goodacre began work on the tribute, Evans and the other members of the Vietnam Women's Memorial Project launched a variety of fund-raising activities to cover the project's $4 million cost.

The Vietnam Women's Memorial is unveiled

The Vietnam Women's Memorial was finally dedicated on November 11, 1993, nearly a decade after Evans began work on the memorial project. An estimated 25,000 people attended the ceremony, during which Goodacre's bronze monument was finally unveiled. The statue shows a nurse comforting a fallen soldier as another nurse scans the sky for an incoming evacuation helicopter. A third woman in the sculpture stands nearby, bowing her head in sorrow. The memorial area is also bordered by eight trees that commemorate the eight servicewomen who died in Vietnam. "Welcome home, daughters of America," Evans said at the dedication. "Welcome home, my fellow sister veterans. Allow the love and pride that fill this hallowed space to enter your hearts and souls today and forever as we continue our journey in life."

Since the dedication of the Vietnam Women's Memorial in 1993, Evans has maintained her nursing career in Minnesota. But she has also remained an active member of the Vietnam veteran community. In addition, she continues to lead the Vietnam Women's Memorial Project, which is working to identify all nurses who served in Vietnam and maintain public awareness of the contributions of Vietnam-era servicewomen.

Evans often makes public appearances to talk about American nurses in Vietnam and her own wartime experiences. "When I speak in high schools and colleges about the Vietnam experience, students will come up to me and say, 'my dad served in Vietnam, but he won't talk to me about it,'" she said in a 1998 speech. "Those are the students who usually have tears in their eyes. The young women will often ask, 'What was it like for the women in the war?' Questions are being asked, and we must answer them if we are to prevent history from repeating itself."

In January 1998 Evans took part in an event called the Vietnam Challenge. This event brought dozens of American Vietnam veterans—including a number of amputees—back to Vietnam to participate in a two-week bicycling trip across the country with former Viet Cong and North Vietnamese Army soldiers. The group bicycled from Hanoi to Ho Chi Minh City (formerly Saigon), the old capital of South Vietnam. "We were each challenged physically, but the greater challenge was reconciliation," Evans recalled. "We cycled down Highway One past mountain vistas and the South China Sea—our anxiety level increased the closer we came to the former DMZ [demilitarized zone, the boundary that used to divide North and South Vietnam]. As we crossed the Ben Ha River bridge into the former South Vietnam, we became silent. We set our bikes down, hugged, cried, went off to reflect on our own or to speak the thoughts we held tight all these years. We were not riding for ourselves. We were riding for all the lives lost and missing in Vietnam."

Sources

Claflin, Terrie. "Monumental Achievement: Twenty Years after Vietnam, Invisible Vets Get Their Memorial." *Ms.,* November–December 1993.

Ellis, David. "They Also Served: A Former Army Nurse Wins Her Fight to Honor the Women of the Vietnam War." *People Weekly,* May 31, 1993.

Loose, Cindy. "Vietnam Women's Memorial Dedicated before 25,000." *Washington Post,* November 12, 1993.

Marshall, Kathryn. *In the Combat Zone: An Oral History of American Women in Vietnam.* Boston: Little, Brown, 1987.

Norman, Elizabeth M. *Women at War: The Story of Fifty Military Nurses Who Served in Vietnam.* Philadelphia: University of Pennsylvania Press, 1990.

Bernard Fall

Born November 11, 1926
Vienna, Austria
Died February 21, 1967
Near Hue, Vietnam

French journalist and historian

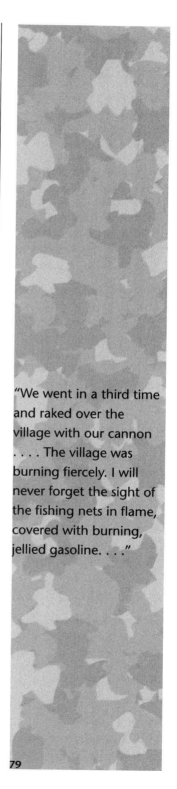

French journalist Bernard Fall covered the Vietnam War through the 1950s and 1960s, as first France and then the United States became engaged in military efforts to control the political future of Vietnam. During this time, he published several important studies of the situation in Vietnam, including *Street Without Joy, Two Viet-Nams, Hell in a Very Small Place,* and *Last Reflections on a War.* These works made Fall a recognized authority on both the French and American phases of the Vietnam War.

"We went in a third time and raked over the village with our cannon . . . . The village was burning fiercely. I will never forget the sight of the fishing nets in flame, covered with burning, jellied gasoline. . . ."

Young member of the French Underground

Bernard Fall was born in Vienna, Austria, on November 11, 1926, while his French parents were traveling in the city. After he was born, the family promptly returned to France to raise him. Fall's early childhood was comfortable and happy, but his teen years were darkened by the growing threat of Adolf Hitler and Nazi Germany. In 1939 Germany's invasion of Czechoslovakia and Poland triggered World War II (1939–45). This conflict, which lasted until 1945, eventually involved every major military power in the world. It pitted Germany,

Italy, and Japan against the United States, the Soviet Union, Great Britain, France, and other European nations.

During the summer of 1940, Germany successfully invaded France. The German army seized outright control over northern France and installed a pro-German government in the country's southern territory. When this occurred, however, a secret French rebel organization—known as the French Underground—took up the fight against the German invaders. The Underground was unable to push the Germans out of its homeland, but it repeatedly attacked German posts and installations around the country over the next several years.

Fall joined the French Underground in 1942 at the age of sixteen and took part in a number of operations against the Germans. In the meantime, however, Germany used brutal force to stamp out all resistance to its occupation. "Things got very bad," recalled Fall in 1966 on *Celebrity's Choice,* a television interview program. "My mother was deported as a hostage and she never came back and my father was tortured to death in 1943 by the Gestapo [the secret Nazi police]—we found his body in a ditch with twelve other people, two years later . . . .I hadn't known my father was in the Underground." Fall remained a member of the French Underground for more than two years before joining the Fourth Moroccan Mountain Division in 1944. He fought against Germany as a member of that army until the war came to an end a year later.

Educated in the United States

After World War II, Fall worked from 1946 to 1948 as an investigator for the Nuremberg Trials. During these proceedings, held in Nuremberg, Germany, a number of Nazi officials were convicted of committing war crimes during World War II. Fall then took classes at the University of Paris and the University of Munich before earning a Fulbright scholarship to continue his education in the United States.

Fall arrived in America in late 1951. After briefly attending classes at the University of Maryland, he enrolled at Syracuse University in New York state. Over the next few years, he earned both a master's degree (1952) and a doctorate degree (1955) at Syracuse. In 1954 he married Dorothy Winer, with whom he eventually had three children.

During this same period, meanwhile, France tried to regain its prewar control over French Indochina. This region, which included Cambodia, Laos, and Vietnam, had been under French control since the late nineteenth century. During World War II, however, France's grip over the territory had been lost. Its effort to regain colonial rule over Indochina ultimately ended in failure in 1954, when the Viet Minh—a Communist-led nationalist group that fought for Vietnamese independence from French colonial rule—handed France a decisive defeat in an area of northern Vietnam known as Dien Bien Phu.

Fall goes to Vietnam

Fall made his first visit to Indochina in 1953 to research a doctoral paper on the Viet Minh. He ended up spending eight months in Vietnam, accompanying French troops on a number of military operations. During this period, Fall developed what he later called a "bad love affair" with the troubled but beautiful region. He also established himself as an insightful and talented reporter during this visit. In fact, the letters and notes that he wrote in 1953 eventually became the basis for his first book on Vietnam, *Street Without Joy* (1961). In his introduction to a 1994 edition of this work, historian George C. Herring called *Street Without Joy* "one of a handful of truly classic accounts of the wars in Indochina . . . . It remains today perhaps the best English account of France's frustrating and ultimately unsuccessful effort to subdue the Vietminh insurgency [rebellion]."

In the mid-1950s, Fall taught Asian studies and international relations at a number of prestigious U.S. universities, including Cornell University, American University, and Howard University. In 1957, however, he returned to Southeast Asia to study the developing struggle between the newly created nations of South and North Vietnam.

North and South Vietnam had been created in 1954 by the Geneva Peace Accords. Under this treaty, which brought the French-Vietnamese conflict to a close, Vietnam was temporarily divided into Communist-led North Vietnam and U.S.-supported South Vietnam. The Geneva agreement provided for nationwide free elections to be held in 1956 so that the two parts of Vietnam could be united under one government. But

Fall Reports on an American Bombing Raid of a Fishing Village

In the following account (first published in *Ramparts* magazine in 1965 and later included in Fall's collection *Last Reflections on a War*), Bernard Fall provides readers with a powerful example of American firepower in Vietnam:

> The Viet-Nam conflict has become an impersonal, an American war. I was with an American airborne unit operating strictly on its own. There was not one Vietnamese with that unit. It was going strictly by its own mark and literally by its own light. [Fall then describes a U.S. bomber known as a "Skyraider."] It is an amazing airplane—especially in the amount of destruction it can bring to bear. You have to know an airplane like this before you can really understand the tremendous impact of American firepower

> on the Vietnamese on the ground. This airplane can carry a bombload of 7500 pounds under its wings. It can unload a variety of bombs—750-pounders, 500-pounders, 250-pounders, 100-pounder general-purpose bombs. It also can drop 260-pound fragmentation bombs, 120-pound fragmentation bombs, or 100-pound white phosphorous bombs and napalm [a jelly-like gasoline that burns everything it touches]. The "Skyraider" has four 20-millimeter cannon as well.

> This was the airplane I was to ride in on a raid on a Vietnamese fishing village . . . .

> We were airborne for one and one half hours before we reached our primary target. But as we came over the target the monsoon came down with quite incredible force and completely obscured the ground.

U.S. and South Vietnamese officials refused to hold the elections because they feared that the results would give the Communists control over the entire country. North Vietnam and its allies in the South—known as the Viet Cong—responded to this refusal by launching a guerrilla war against South Vietnam. This aggression ultimately convinced the United States to use its own military power to save South Vietnam and defeat the Communists.

Recognized as an expert on Vietnam

Fall made numerous visits to Vietnam from 1957 to 1967. During that time, he became known not only as a premier war correspondent, but also as a leading authority on the Vietnam War. He contributed hundreds of articles on politics, military affairs, and Vietnamese culture and attitudes to *For-*

Then a decision was made, in accordance with established procedures, to switch over to the alternate target which was described as a "Communist rest center" in the Camau Peninsula. A rest center may of course by anything, any group of huts, or it may be just a normal village in which Viet Cong troops have put down stakes for, perhaps, 48 hours.

As we flew over the target it looked to me very much as any normal village would look: on the edge of a river, sampans [boats] and fish nets in the water. It was a peaceful scene. Major Carson put our plane into a steep dive. I could see the napalm bombs dropping from the wings. The big bombs, first. As we peeled back from our dive, there was an incredibly bright flash of fire as napalm exploded at the tree level. The first pass had a one-two effect. The napalm was expected to force the people—

fearing the heat and the burning—out into the open. Then the second plane was to move in with heavy fragmentation bombs to hit whatever—or whomever—had rushed out into the open. So our wingman [a second U.S. bomber] followed us in and dropped his heavy explosives. Mushroom-like clouds drifted into the air. We made a second pass and dropped our remaining 500-pound napalm bombs. Our wingman followed. Then we went in a third time and raked over the village with our cannon. We came down low, flying very fast, and I could see some of the villagers trying to head away from the burning shore in their sampans. The village was burning fiercely. I will never forget the sight of the fishing nets in flame, covered with burning, jellied gasoline. Behind me I could hear—even through my padded flying helmet—the roar of our plane's 20-millimeter cannon as we flew away.

eign *Affairs, Military Review,* the *New York Times,* and other publications. In addition, he wrote several critically acclaimed books on the struggle for Vietnam. These works include *Two Viet-Nams: A Political and Military History* (1963) and *Viet-Nam Witness, 1953–1966* (1966). His best-known work, however, was *Hell in a Very Small Place* (1967), a gripping account of the French defeat at Dien Bien Phu.

Fall's reporting was praised for being both scholarly and fiercely independent. In fact, both supporters and opponents of the war respected him for his refusal to reduce the war to a simple drama of heroes versus villains. Instead, he offered balanced analysis of both the positive and negative aspects of French, American, and Vietnamese activities in Vietnam. For example, he criticized the United States for abandoning France when it tried to reestablish control over Vietnam. But he condemned many aspects of French colonialism, and he

Bernard Fall's Last Report

In February 1967 journalist Bernard Fall accompanied a group of U.S. Marines on a mission through the countryside north of Hue. This area was known as the "Street Without Joy," a title that Fall had used for one of his most famous books on the Vietnam conflict. As the patrol made its way through the area, Fall accidentally stepped on a Viet Cong land mine. The explosion killed Fall instantly. Following are the journalist's last words, preserved on a tape recorder that he was carrying:

February 19, 1967. This is Bernard Fall in the Street Without Joy, the old area where the French fought in 1953.

I am lying right now in a small stone hut near a big church in a small village with part of the 1st Battalion, 9th Marine Infantry Regiment, and we just walked across something like twelve kilometers of sand dunes and tomorrow morning we're

going to push Southeastward where supposedly there is part of a Viet Cong battalion . . . .

[The next morning, Fall and the Marines resume walking and encounter enemy fire. When the Marines counterattack, the Viet Cong disappear into the jungle.] Well, that was that for a while. It didn't look very good but we made it. They ran and since the sky was too dark for air support, we just kept on going and then we came to a church and it was a big church and was constructed in 1963 and—oh, very beautiful . . . .

I walked behind a fellow, thought I walked pretty well in his traces [tracks]. Apparently I stepped slightly aside and all of a sudden the ground gave way under me and this was one of these punji stake traps that the VC sets with very sharp points and if you fall in this you pierce your foot and go to the hospital. I was very lucky because when I felt the ground yield under my feet I threw myself forward so that my whole body weight shifted to

denounced his homeland's military strategy during the First Indochina War. Fall also disliked the Communist political philosophy. But he repeatedly expressed admiration for the intelligence and grit of North Vietnam's Ho Chi Minh (see entry) and other Communist leaders. Finally, historian George C. Herring noted that Fall's writing reflects "a deep and abiding empathy [understanding of another person's feelings and motives] for the victims of the wars in Vietnam, especially for the common soldiers who fought on all sides."

Fall reserved his most critical remarks for U.S. military strategy in Vietnam. He condemned America for trying to fight "ideology [political and social beliefs] with technology [mili-

my knees and hands and so the trap gave way and nothing happened to me but it . . . ah, shakes you up a bit and now we are sitting in a deserted farm destroyed by gunfire . . . .

Well, we're moving out again on the Street Without Joy—it's the third day now and what you heard before were the noises of the crickets and the frogs next to us where we were sleeping out in the open. It started to drizzle afterward and now we've got thick-packed fog at nine o'clock in the morning—supply chopper [helicopter] couldn't come in but we had enough food for this morning and on we go now . . . .

Afternoon of the third day. Still on the street . . . . The weather is finally cleared and we have an observation plane over our heads, turning around shepherding us. But Charlie Company [an American combat infantry unit] has fallen very badly behind now there's a big hole in our left flank and there's some people running away from us obviously getting out of the way . . . We've got to start firing if they move . . . [Sounds of gunfire, planes flying overhead, and shouted instructions.]

There's no return fire whatever but the Chieu Hois who are with us—they are former Viet Cong returned to the government side and . . . fighting now with the government forces—well, they assured us that Charlie Company is moving right through the area and by tonight we will know whether what we killed were genuine VC [Viet Cong] with weapons or simply people. I personally looked through binoculars of the platoon leader from the machine gun platoon and I saw people fleeing to the boats and waving the Vietnamese government flag with three red stripes on a yellow background. Find out more about this later . . . This is Bernard Fall on the Street Without Joy.

[Silence on the tape.] First in the afternoon about 4:30—shadows are lengthening and we've reached one of our phase lines after the fire fight and it smells bad—meaning it's a little bit suspicious . . . Could be an amb . . . . [End of Fall's tape].

tary firepower]," and repeatedly charged that the United States was underestimating its Viet Cong and North Vietnamese foes. He also claimed that America's reliance on brute force to beat the Communists turned many Vietnamese people against the U.S.-supported government in Saigon. In the following passage from *Street Without Joy*, for example, Fall bitterly criticizes American efforts to use bombing raids against Viet Cong forces in South Vietnam: "In South Vietnam, where the enemy hardly offers conventional aerial targets . . . the use of massive bomb attacks and napalm drops on villages is not only militarily stupid, but it is inhuman and is likely to backfire very badly on the psychological level. To a village which has been occupied by a VC [Viet Cong] platoon against its will and whose only suffering at the hands of the Communists was the murder of a rather unpopular village chief, 'liberation' through massive napalming and attendant losses of innocent inhabitants (not to speak of all property, stored rice, and even farm animals) will be a hollow joke, indeed."

Dies in Vietnam

In late 1963 Fall was diagnosed with retroperitoneal fibrosis, a rare incurable disease that can destroy internal organs. He underwent a couple of major operations, including surgery to remove a damaged kidney. Fall's physical problems convinced him that he did not have long to live, but he continued to pursue his journalism career.

In December 1966 Fall made his sixth trip to Vietnam. He soon joined a U.S. Marine mission outside of Hue in northern South Vietnam. On February 21, 1967, he and a Marine sergeant accidentally tripped a land mine while out on patrol in an area known as the "Street Without Joy" (this was where the title of his first book came from). The land mine exploded, killing Fall instantly. A few months after his death, his wife put together a collection of Vietnam essays and articles that Fall wrote during the mid-1960s. This collection was published in 1967 as *Last Reflections on a War: Bernard B. Fall's Last Comments on Viet-Nam.*

Sources

Fall, Bernard B. *Hell in a Very Small Place: The Siege of Dien Bien Phu.* Lippincott, 1967.

Fall, Bernard B. *Last Reflections on a War.* Doubleday, 1968.

Fall, Bernard B. *Street Without Joy: Indochina at War, 1946–54.* Harrisburg, PA: Stackpole, 1961.

Fall, Bernard B. *Two Viet-Nams: A Political and Military History.* New York: Praeger, 1963.

Fall, Bernard B. *Viet-Nam Witness, 1953–1966.* New York: Praeger, 1967.

"Death of a Scholar." *Newsweek,* March 6, 1967.

Frances FitzGerald

Born October 21, 1940
New York, New York

American journalist and author

Journalist Frances FitzGerald spent sixteen months in Southeast Asia during the height of the Vietnam War. During her time there, she became convinced that America's involvement in the conflict was having a devastating impact on Vietnamese society and that U.S. efforts to save South Vietnam were doomed to fail. After returning to the United States, she published an account of her experiences and impressions titled *Fire in the Lake: The Vietnamese and Americans in Vietnam*. This book, which examined the Vietnam War from the perspective of the Vietnamese people, received tremendous critical praise, and it is credited with increasing American opposition to the war.

Decides on career in journalism

Frances FitzGerald was born on October 21, 1940, in New York City. Her father, Desmond FitzGerald, was a prominent attorney and a deputy director of the Central Intelligence Agency (CIA). Her mother, Marietta Tree, was an urban planner and a delegate to the United Nations. FitzGerald recalls that her parents' involvement in government policy making and important world issues deeply influenced her as she was

"I thought to myself, Here's this American war being fought in a place that no one understands at all."

Frances FitzGerald.
Reproduced by permission of Corbis Corporation.

growing up. She became interested in politics at an early age, and she met many international politicians during her teen years.

FitzGerald was a top student at Foxcraft prep school in Virginia. After graduating, she enrolled at Radcliffe College, where she studied Middle Eastern history and journalism. She graduated from Radcliffe in 1962 and soon settled on a career in journalism. Before long, her work was appearing in several major newspapers and magazines.

FitzGerald turned her attention to the Vietnam War in the mid-1960s. This war had actually begun in the mid-1950s, when Vietnam was divided into two countries—North Vietnam and South Vietnam—after France surrendered its claim on the region. A short time later, South Vietnamese leaders refused to hold elections intended to reunite the two Vietnams under one government. This decision greatly angered North Vietnam's Communist leadership. It responded by launching a guerrilla war against the South with the help of Communist allies in the South known as the Viet Cong. The Communists started this campaign with the aim of eventually reuniting the country by force.

The United States, however, fiercely opposed the Communist political philosophy. It sent military and financial aid to South Vietnam to help the country defend itself from the Viet Cong and their partners in the North. But when the South continued to struggle, American political leaders decided that they needed to increase their involvement. They committed large numbers of American troops to the South's defense and launched major bombing campaigns against the North. Within a matter of months, American forces were conducting much of the war themselves.

Travels to Vietnam

FitzGerald went to Vietnam for the first time in February 1966. By this time, new U.S. forces and weaponry were pouring into the country, and American military leaders were conducting numerous military operations against the Viet Cong and North Vietnam. At first, FitzGerald intended to spend only a few weeks in Vietnam. But she changed her mind after becoming convinced that U.S. war policies and strategies in Vietnam were having a devastating impact on the Vietnamese people. "I thought to myself, Here's this American war being fought in a place that no one understands at all," she recalled in an interview in *Contemporary Authors, New Revision Series*. "It looks like there are two entirely separate enterprises going on here, the Vietnamese one and the American."

With this in mind, FitzGerald began an intensive study of the war, with a special emphasis on American-Vietnamese relations. She roamed the country for the next year, interviewing South Vietnamese officials, soldiers, and farmers and gathering her own impressions of the war. "[I wanted] to try and understand the politics of Vietnam and the effect of the American presence and the war on Vietnamese society," she later explained in *Fire in the Lake*. "At the time there was little American scholarship on Vietnam and few Americans were engaged in a serious effort to understand the political, economic, and social issues at stake for the Vietnamese."

During her travels, FitzGerald learned that America's political and military leaders had little understanding of Vietnamese culture, politics, or society. She also became convinced that U.S. military operations were destroying the lives of millions of Vietnamese people. "The physical suffering of South Vietnam is difficult to comprehend," she later wrote in *Fire in the Lake*. "But it is the social death caused by destruction of the family that is of overriding importance . . . . South Vietnam is a country shattered so that no two pieces fit together."

Fire in the Lake

FitzGerald finally returned home to the United States in 1967. At that time, she continued her study of Vietnam's culture and history with the help of French anthropologist Paul Mus (an anthropologist is a person who studies the social and cultural development of societies). She also began writing *Fire in the Lake*. In 1971 she returned to Vietnam to see how the war had affected the Vietnamese people since her departure in 1967. As she visited cities and villages throughout the South, she was stunned at the widespread destruction she witnessed. She also was saddened by the state of relations between the Americans and their South Vietnamese allies. "The relationship between the Vietnamese and the Americans, politically and personally, is incredibly bad," she stated in *Life* in 1972.

"There's a whole underlying air of mutual contempt. We cover it up, of course; we don't want to admit that."

In 1972 FitzGerald published *Fire in the Lake: The Vietnamese and the Americans in Vietnam.* The book was one of the first works to examine the conflict from the perspective of the Vietnamese people. It included a sympathetic portrait of the war-weary Vietnamese, as well as a harsh condemnation of the American presence in Vietnam. FitzGerald charged that U.S. military policies had reduced much of the nation to ruins. She also claimed that the South Vietnamese government was so corrupt and incompetent that America's mission to save the country was doomed to fail.

Fire in the Lake quickly became one of the best-selling books in the United States, which had become bitterly divided over the war in the late 1960s and early 1970s. FitzGerald's book added to the debate over the war. In fact, it is viewed by many historians as an influential book that increased the American public's opposition to the war. As Michael Mok wrote in *Publishers Weekly,* FitzGerald's book managed to "get under the skin of this ugly war which has left so many Americans feeling bewildered and morally bankrupt."

Some Americans objected to the tone of FitzGerald's book, arguing that it was too sympathetic toward the Viet Cong. These critics claimed that she emphasized the destructive impact of American military actions and minimized the war crimes committed by the Viet Cong. But most reviewers praised the work as an excellent study of American-Vietnamese relations during the war. *New York Times* reviewer Christopher Lehmann-Haupt wrote that "Miss FitzGerald's study . . . is more than just a superbly dramatic and informative account of current events on the other side of the globe. It is also a depth [detailed] analysis . . . of why events [in Vietnam] have proceeded as they have and why the drama is proving not only a tragedy for the people of Vietnam but also for the American people." Historian Arthur Schlesinger, Jr., added that "If Americans read only one book to understand what we have done to the Vietnamese and to ourselves, let it be this one." *Fire in the Lake* eventually won the Pulitzer Prize, a National Book Award, and the Bancroft Prize for historical writing. Today, it continues to be regarded as one of the finest books on the Vietnam War.

Since *Fire in the Lake* was published, FitzGerald's journalism career has continued to flourish. She has provided coverage of political events around the world and has written a number of books on various aspects of American society. In 2000 she published *Way Out There in the Blue: Reagan, Star Wars and the End of the Cold War,* an examination of President Ronald Reagan and his administration (1981–88).

Sources

Elwood-Akers, Virginia. *Women Correspondents in the Vietnam War, 1961–1975.* Metuchen, NJ: Scarecrow Press, 1988.

FitzGerald, Frances. "The End Is the Beginning." *New Republic,* May 3, 1975.

FitzGerald, Frances. *Fire in the Lake: The Vietnamese and Americans in Vietnam.* New York: Atlantic/Little, Brown, 1972.

FitzGerald, Frances. "Life and Death of a Vietnamese Village." *New York Times Magazine,* September 4, 1966.

FitzGerald, Frances. "The Tragedy of Saigon." *Atlantic Monthly,* December 1966.

Howard, Jane. "Frankie's Fire." *Life,* October 27, 1972.

Mok, Michael. "Frances FitzGerald." *Publishers Weekly,* October 16, 1972.

Ross, Jean W. An Interview with Frances FitzGerald. *Contemporary Authors, New Revision Series,* Vol. 32. Detroit: Gale Research, 1991.

Jane Fonda

Born December 21, 1937
New York, New York

American actress and political activist

Jane Fonda.
Reproduced by permission of Archive Photos.

Actress Jane Fonda was one of the most prominent celebrity antiwar activists during the Vietnam War. But she took her antiwar stance a step further than all but the most radical activists. Rather than simply opposing U.S. policies, she actively supported America's enemy—the Communist government of North Vietnam. During a highly controversial visit to North Vietnam in 1972, Fonda angered many Americans by posing for pictures with an antiaircraft gun, criticizing U.S. soldiers on Radio Hanoi, and insisting that American prisoners of war were being treated well by the Communists. She continued to defend the North Vietnamese government even after the United States ended its involvement in the conflict.

Builds a career as an actress

Jane Seymour Fonda was born on December 21, 1937, in New York City. She was the daughter of Henry Fonda, a popular stage and movie actor of the time, and his second wife, Frances Seymour Brokaw Fonda. Jane's mother suffered from mental illness and committed suicide when Jane was a teenager. Since she never got along well with her father, she depended on her younger brother, Peter Fonda, for emotional support.

Her father's career as an actor meant that the Fonda family often moved back and forth between New York and Los Angeles. Jane attended private schools on both U.S. coasts during her childhood. In 1955 she completed her high school education at Emma Willard Academy in Troy, New York. She then attended Vassar College for two years. Insecure and lonely, Fonda made few close friends and struggled with the eating disorder bulimia during her student days. In 1957 she convinced her father to send her to Paris to study art, but she spent most of her time there partying instead.

After returning from Paris, Fonda studied acting at Lee Strasberg's Actors' Studio in New York City. In 1959 she made her Broadway debut in the play *There Was a Little Girl.* She made her film debut the following year in *Tall Story,* which co-starred Anthony Perkins. Throughout the 1960s Fonda built a promising career as an actress. Some of her early movies included *Barefoot in the Park, Cat Ballou, The Chase, Barbarella,* and *They Shoot Horses, Don't They?* She also married director Roger Vadim and lived in France for several years. In 1971 she won an Academy Award as best actress for her portrayal of a prostitute in *Klute.*

Becomes an antiwar activist

As her acting career took off, Fonda also was experiencing a political awakening. She became interested in feminism and other social causes. She also got involved in the growing protests against the Vietnam War, which pitted the Communist nation of North Vietnam and its secret allies, the South Vietnamese Communists known as the Viet Cong, against the U.S.-supported nation of South Vietnam. North Vietnam wanted to overthrow the South Vietnamese government and reunite the two countries under one Communist government. But U.S. government officials felt that a Communist government in Vietnam would increase the power of the Soviet Union and threaten the security of the United States.

In the late 1950s and early 1960s the U.S. government sent money, weapons, and military advisors to help South Vietnam defend itself. In 1965 President Lyndon Johnson (see entry) sent American combat troops to join the fight on the side of South Vietnam. But increased U.S. involvement in the war failed to defeat the Communists. Instead, the war turned into a bloody stalemate. The American public was bitterly divided about how to proceed in Vietnam, and antiwar demonstrations took place across the country.

Fonda first became concerned about the Vietnam War when she was living in France. She recalled seeing French television coverage of the destruction that American bombing caused in Vietnam. She was also affected by news coverage of antiwar demonstrations in the United States, including the 1967 March on the Pentagon. "I watched women walking up to the bayonets that were surrounding the Pentagon and they were not afraid," she is quoted as saying in *Jane Fonda: An Intimate Biography*. "I'll never forget that experience. It completely changed me. It began all my searching for what was behind it all."

By the early 1970s Fonda had become one of the most visible celebrities involved in the antiwar movement. She often appeared at antiwar rallies, and she became romantically involved with the radical antiwar activist Tom Hayden (see entry). In 1971 Fonda organized a show that toured coffeehouses and theaters near American military bases. The show included skits and songs that made fun of the government and questioned American military involvement in Vietnam. Fonda intended it to provide a counterpoint to the patriotic shows put on by Bob Hope and other celebrities to entertain the American troops.

Since she was a well-known actress, Fonda attracted a great deal of publicity with her antiwar activities. Before long, she ended up on President Richard Nixon's (see entry) list of enemies of the U.S. government. Agents for the Federal Bureau of Investigation (FBI) tapped her telephone, broke into her bank safe-deposit box, and harassed her friends and family. But Fonda continued to speak out against the war and the U.S. government's policies.

Makes a controversial visit to North Vietnam

In July 1972 Fonda made a highly controversial two-week visit to North Vietnam, whose military had been fighting

U.S. forces for nearly a decade. Her Communist hosts gave her a tour of the damage that American bombing campaigns had caused in the capital city of Hanoi and the surrounding countryside. During this tour, Fonda posed with a North Vietnamese antiaircraft gun that was used to shoot down U.S. planes. She also met with several American soldiers who were being held by the Communists as prisoners of war (POWs). The North Vietnamese arranged these meetings carefully and controlled the POWs with threats of torture. But Fonda ignored this possibility and announced to the world that the American prisoners were being treated well.

During her visit to North Vietnam, Fonda also broadcast a series of statements on Radio Hanoi in which she criticized American soldiers and the U.S. government and demanded an end to the bombing. Her words angered the U.S. soldiers and POWs who heard them. "It's difficult to put into words how terrible it is to hear that siren song that is so absolutely rotten and wrong," said American POW George Day in *Citizen Jane*. He went on to charge that Fonda "caused the deaths of unknown numbers of Americans by buoying up the enemy's spirits and keeping them in the fight."

Upon returning to the United States, Fonda came under harsh criticism for her public support of North Vietnam. People who approved of American involvement in Vietnam were furious. Some people claimed that she should be put on trial for treason (betraying the country). One conservative newspaper even printed an editorial suggesting that she should be shot. Many people who opposed the Vietnam War resented Fonda's actions as well. They said that her radical position in support of the enemy made the antiwar movement look bad. "Fonda did irreparable damage to the antiwar movement," antiwar veteran Dean Phillips told Myra MacPherson in *Long Time Passing*. "She [ticked] off 80 percent of Americans not on the fringes [of radical pro-war or antiwar feelings]."

Continues her defense of the Communists

Following her visit to North Vietnam, Fonda was so unpopular in the United States that her movie career ended for several years. In fact, she became known by the derogatory nickname "Hanoi Jane" (after the North Vietnam capital city of Hanoi). Fonda devoted her time to antiwar activities during these years. She married Tom Hayden in 1972, and together they formed the Indochina Peace Campaign (IPC). Fonda also sued the U.S. government for harassing her, claiming that the FBI had engaged in illegal activities and violated her rights. She eventually settled the lawsuit when the FBI admitted its wrongdoing.

In early 1973 the United States and North Vietnam reached an agreement to end American involvement in the war. As part of the agreement, the Communists agreed to return all American POWs. When the POWs returned home, people across the country put aside their differences over the war and gave them a heroes' welcome. Over the next few months, the public learned about the terrible abuse and torture the POWs had endured at the hands of the North Vietnamese. But Fonda refused to believe the American soldiers and continued to defend the Communists. In fact, she called the American POWs liars and killers. These comments led to further criticism in the media and made her even more unpopular in American society.

In 1975 North Vietnam took control of South Vietnam to win the Vietnam War. At this time, thousands of South Vietnamese citizens who were considered threats to the new government were executed or sent to labor camps. But Fonda refused to join singer Joan Baez (see entry) and other well-known antiwar activists in urging Vietnam's government to end the violence. Instead, she criticized the activists and continued to defend the Communists.

Apologizes for her wartime actions

In the late 1970s Fonda revived her film career. She organized her own movie production company, called IPC Films, in order to make socially responsible movies that would be both "thought-provoking and commercial." In 1978 IPC released *Coming Home,* a film about a disabled Vietnam veteran who struggles to readjust to American society. Fonda earned a second Academy Award for her portrayal of the veteran's love interest. In 1979 she appeared in *The China Syndrome,* a critically acclaimed film about an accident at a nuclear power plant. Two years later she shared the screen with her famous father for the first time in *On Golden Pond.*

During the 1980s Fonda became one of the first celebrities to offer advice on fitness. She opened a chain of health clubs, published several best-selling diet books, and launched a series of popular home-exercise videotapes. The proceeds from these fitness enterprises helped finance her husband's political campaign for the California legislature. In the early 1990s Fonda divorced Tom Hayden and married Ted Turner, the owner of a huge cable-television and entertainment empire. At this time, she retreated from her earlier careers as an actress and activist and instead seemed content to be a supportive wife. In 2000, however, Fonda announced that she and her third husband were separating.

Fonda remains a controversial figure for her activities during and after the Vietnam War. Many American veterans still hold deep resentment toward her for her public support of North Vietnam. Looking back on her wartime activities years later, Fonda admitted that she had made some mistakes and caused some pain. "I am proud of most of what I did and I am very sorry for some of what I did," she said in an interview with Barbara Walters for the ABC network. "My intentions were never to hurt [the American soldiers and POWs] or make their situation worse. It was the contrary. I was trying to help end the killing, end the war, but there were times when I was thoughtless and careless about it."

Sources

Anderson, Christopher. *Citizen Jane: The Turbulent Life of Jane Fonda.* New York: Henry Holt, 1990.

Davidson, Bill. *Jane Fonda: An Intimate Biography.* London: Sidgwick and Jackson, 1990.

Freedland, Michael. *Jane Fonda: A Biography.* London: Weidenfeld and Nicolson, 1988.

MacPherson, Myra. *Long Time Passing: Vietnam and the Haunted Generation.* New York: Doubleday, 1984.

J. William Fulbright

Born April 9, 1905
Sumner, Missouri
Died February 9, 1995
Washington, D.C.

U.S. senator from Arkansas, 1945–1974

"When I look back on [my sponsorship of the Gulf of Tonkin Resolution], I couldn't have made a greater mistake. I consider that as my greatest mistake in the Senate . . . ."

J. William Fulbright.
Reproduced by permission of AP/Wide World Photos.

J. William Fulbright was the U.S. Senate's best-known critic of American policies in Vietnam during the mid-to-late 1960s, when U.S. troop commitments reached their peak. His views, which received added attention because of his chairmanship of the powerful Senate Foreign Relations Committee, made him one of the most controversial members of Congress during the Vietnam War era.

From professor to politician

J. William Fulbright was born April 9, 1905, in Sumner, Missouri. The son of a prominent farmer and a journalist, he was an excellent student and athlete in high school and at the University of Arkansas. After graduating from Arkansas in 1925, he earned a Rhodes Scholarship to study at Pembroke College at Oxford University in England. He earned a master's degree at Oxford in 1931 before returning to the United States. In 1932 he married Elizabeth Williams, with whom he eventually had two daughters. Two years later he received a law degree from George Washington University.

After briefly working as an attorney for the U.S. Department of Justice, Fulbright accepted a teaching position at George Washington University. In 1936 he moved to the faculty of the University of Arkansas, where he quickly emerged as one of the school's most respected professors. In 1939 Fulbright was named president of the University of Arkansas, but his time as president was marked by internal disagreements over university policies. He lost his position at Arkansas in 1941.

In 1943 Fulbright entered Congress as a Democratic representative from Arkansas. The young politician made his mark soon after his arrival in Washington, D.C. He impressed his colleagues with the depth of his knowledge and his style. In September 1943, he introduced landmark legislation that led to the formation of the United Nations. Fulbright's role in the creation of the United Nations transformed him into "an instant celebrity" in Washington, D.C., noted Haynes B. Johnson and Bernard M. Gwertzman in *Fulbright: The Dissenter.*

Makes his mark in U.S. Senate

After serving one two-year term in the House of Representatives, Fulbright used his national reputation to win an open seat in the U.S. Senate. The Arkansas Democrat assumed his Senate seat in 1945 and kept it for the next three decades.

During his early Senate career, Fulbright continued to concentrate much of his time and energy on U.S. foreign policy and international relations. In 1946, for example, he established an international fellowship program to encourage the exchange of scholars between America and other nations. This initiative, known as the Mutual Educational Exchange Program or the Fulbright Program, provides grants for American students to study overseas and for foreign students to continue their education in the United States. Since its inception, an estimated two hundred thousand students have participated in the program, including such famous figures as poet Maya Angelou, former United Nations secretary-general Boutros Boutros-Ghali, and Greek prime minister Andreas Papandreou. Today, the Fulbright Program continues to provide students in America and around the world with opportunities to visit and study in foreign lands.

In the 1950s Fulbright's influence over American foreign policy continued to grow. Unlike many of his colleagues, he adopted a moderate position on "Cold War" issues. (The Cold War was a period of intense rivalry between the United States and the Soviet Union in which both nations competed to spread their political philosophies and influence around the world.) Fulbright disagreed with other politicians who regarded the Communist political philosophy as a terrible and immediate threat to the security of the United States. But at the same time he supported U.S. efforts to protect itself from the Soviet Union, the world's greatest Communist power.

By the late 1950s Fulbright was known as one of the Senate's leading scholars on international relations. But he also became known during this time as an opponent of civil rights legislation that aimed to eliminate segregation (separation by race) and other laws that discriminated against blacks. In fact, Fulbright became an important member of a group of Southern lawmakers who worked for years to defeat the civil rights movement. For example, he signed the 1956 "Southern Manifesto," a document in which Southern politicians bitterly condemned efforts to end segregation. In addition, he voted against the Civil Rights Act of 1964 and the Voting Rights Act of 1965. But despite the resistance of Fulbright and other southern lawmakers these landmark pieces of civil rights legislation were passed into law. Today, Fulbright's opposition to the civil rights movement is regarded by many historians as a dark stain on an otherwise distinguished Senate career.

Awarded chairmanship of important committee

In 1959 Fulbright was named chairman of the Senate Foreign Relations Committee, a powerful committee that helped shape American foreign policy around the world. As chairman, the Arkansas senator exerted great influence over the committee's activities on a wide range of policy issues. Fulbright's responsibilities in this regard soon led him to turn his attention to events in Vietnam.

A long-time colony of France, Vietnam had won its freedom in 1954 after an eight-year war with the French. But the country had been divided into two sections by the 1954

Geneva Peace Accords. North Vietnam was headed by a Communist government under revolutionary leader Ho Chi Minh (see entry). Leadership of South Vietnam, on the other hand, was given to politicians who promised to build a democracy.

The Geneva agreement provided for nationwide free elections to be held in 1956 so that the two sections of Vietnam could be united under one government. But South Vietnamese officials refused to hold the elections because they believed that the results would give the Communists control over the entire country. This stand was supported by the United States. American strategists believed that if South Vietnam fell to communism, Communist movements might sweep through all of Southeast Asia and increase the international influence and prestige of Communist China and the Soviet Union.

When the South refused to hold elections, North Vietnam joined with Viet Cong guerrillas in the South to overthrow the South Vietnamese government by force. The United States responded by sending money, weapons, and advisors to aid in South Vietnam's defense. In the early 1960s this assistance increased at a very rapid rate. But despite growing U.S. involvement, South Vietnam continued to teeter on the brink of collapse.

Fulbright and Vietnam

In 1964 Fulbright and most other American lawmakers expressed firm support for President Lyndon Johnson's (see entry) introduction of U.S. forces into South Vietnam. In fact, the Arkansas senator sponsored the Gulf of Tonkin Resolution, which Johnson later used as his legal authority for waging war against North Vietnam and its Viet Cong allies. This resolution was passed by Congress in August 1964, after U.S. Navy ships based in Vietnam allegedly came under attack from North Vietnamese forces. It authorized Johnson to take "all necessary measures" against further attacks. Today, however, most historians believe that the U.S. Navy vessels were never attacked.

"When I look back on [my sponsorship of the Gulf of Tonkin Resolution], I couldn't have made a greater mistake," Fulbright stated in *The Bad War: An Oral History of the Vietnam War.* "I consider that as my greatest mistake in the Senate, to believe what they [the Johnson administration] said and not take it skeptically and examine it. They made it appear that this was very important to support the President and that if he had the backing of this great country, that we could make North Vietnam understand that the United States couldn't be pushed around in this fashion and that they would in effect sue for peace, and it would end the thing [the war] there . . . . There's no excuse for my stupidity in going along with the administration. I shouldn't have . . . . I was mistaken and I'm sorry and that's all I can say."

In 1965 the Johnson administration began pouring U.S. troops and weaponry into Vietnam at a furious rate. Around this same time, Fulbright began to express private doubts about the wisdom of America's growing military presence in the conflict and its ability to win the war quickly. He also rejected the Johnson administration's description of the war as a Cold War clash of great strategic importance to the United States. Instead, Fulbright came to regard the war as a regional struggle that should be settled by the Vietnamese people without outside interference.

In late 1965 Fulbright reluctantly decided that he needed to express his growing concerns about the Vietnam War in public. "Fulbright dreaded the thought of bringing on himself the firestorm of pressure and controversy that would certainly be triggered by publicly criticizing the war policies of a still-popular president," wrote Eugene Brown in *J. William Fulbright: Advice and Dissent*. "Yet, he could not much longer suppress his own gnawing doubts about the wisdom of committing America's power and prestige to the military determination of what he was coming to view as a localized political conflict."

Fulbright holds Senate hearings on the war

In January and February of 1966 Fulbright arranged for the Senate Foreign Relations Committee to hold public hearings on American military involvement in Vietnam. These televised hearings, which featured testimony from both critics and supporters of U.S. war policies, attracted considerable attention all across the United States. In fact, the hearings are widely credited with increasing public skepticism about the Johnson administration's handling of the Vietnam War.

Over the next few years, Fulbright became one of the Senate's most visible critics of American intervention in Vietnam. He repeatedly charged that Vietnam's future should be determined by its people and argued that the country's form of government simply was not that important to America's own future. "The war in Indochina is a bad investment of our resources and our talents," declared the senator, who called for negotiations that would enable the U.S. to withdraw from the conflict.

Fulbright's outspoken criticism deeply angered Johnson, his administration, and millions of Americans who supported U.S. intervention in Vietnam. But his stand made him a hero to the nation's fast-growing antiwar movement and helped convince other lawmakers to oppose the war. In the meantime, Fulbright detailed his views on Vietnam and other foreign policy issues in several books, including the 1967 bestseller *The Arrogance of Power.*

Fulbright's condemnation of the Johnson administration's policies in Vietnam became even stronger during the late 1960s, when escalating U.S. intervention triggered massive protests and divisions in America's streets and neighborhoods. "By committing half a million of our young men to bloody and endless combat in these distant jungles our leaders have converted a struggle between Vietnamese for possession of the Vietnamese land into a struggle between Americans for possession of the American spirit," Fulbright declared in a March 1968 speech on the Senate floor.

In January 1969 Richard M. Nixon (see entry) succeeded Johnson as president. After Nixon assumed office, Fulbright continued his calls for a quick withdrawal of U.S. forces from Vietnam. In addition, he urged his Senate colleagues to increase the Senate's involvement in shaping America's relations with other nations. He believed that if the Senate assumed a more active role in American foreign policy decisions, America would be less likely to get involved in conflicts like the Vietnam War in the future.

In 1974 Fulbright lost his bid for a sixth term as senator. This defeat ended his fifteen-year chairmanship of the Senate Foreign Relations Committee and convinced him to retire from public life. In 1988 he suffered the first of a series of strokes that put him in poor health. In 1993 President Bill

Clinton—who had worked as an intern in Fulbright's Senate office in the early 1960s—presented the former Arkansas senator with the Presidential Medal of Freedom in recognition of his distinguished Senate career. He died two years later in Washington, D.C., of complications from a final stroke.

Sources

Berman, William C. *William Fulbright and the Vietnam War: The Dissent of a Political Realist.* Kent, OH: Kent State University Press, 1988.

Brown, Eugene. *J. William Fulbright: Advice and Dissent.* Iowa City: University of Iowa Press, 1985.

Fulbright, J. William. *The Arrogance of Power.* New York: Random House, 1967.

Johnson, Haynes Bonner, and Bernard M. Gwertzman. *Fulbright: The Dissenter.* New York: Doubleday, 1968.

The Vietnam Hearings. Introduction by J. William Fulbright. New York: Random House, 1966.

Woods, Randall Bennett. *Fulbright: A Biography.* New York: Cambridge University Press, 1995.

Barry Goldwater

Born January 1, 1909
Phoenix, Arizona Territory
Died May 29, 1998
Phoenix, Arizona

U.S. senator from Arizona, 1952–1964 and 1968–1987; Republican presidential nominee in 1964

A rizona Senator Barry Goldwater became a national leader in the Republican Party in the 1950s and early 1960s. In 1964 he captured the Republican nomination for the presidency on the strength of his conservative political beliefs and fierce opposition to communism. But the American public rejected the Arizona senator as a potentially dangerous leader. They worried that he might deepen U.S. involvement in Vietnam or start a nuclear war with the Soviet Union. American voters turned instead to Democrat Lyndon B. Johnson (see entry), who easily defeated Goldwater for the presidency.

"I would remind you that extremism in the defense of liberty is no vice. And let me remind you also that moderation in the pursuit of justice is no virtue."

Childhood in Arizona

Barry Morris Goldwater was born in Phoenix on January 1, 1909, two years before Arizona became a state. His parents were Baron M. Goldwater, a clothing store owner, and Josephine (Williams) Goldwater. Goldwater was a high-spirited boy who showed more interest in athletics and exploring Arizona's outdoors than he did in his schoolwork (although he did become fascinated with Arizona's history and geography at an early age). As a teen, he attended Virginia's Staunton Mili-

Barry Goldwater.
Reproduced by permission of Corbis Corporation.

tary Academy. Goldwater enjoyed academy life and began to consider a future career in the military. But after graduation he enrolled in the University of Arizona so that he could be closer to his family.

Goldwater took classes at the University of Arizona for one year. But in 1929 his father died. Goldwater then left school to work in the family business. Over the next several years he built the company into one of the most successful in the Phoenix area. He started a family around this time as well. In September 1934 he married Margaret Johnson, with whom he eventually had four children.

Serves in World War II

When the United States became involved in World War II in 1941, Goldwater enlisted in the U.S. Army. A licensed pilot, he was assigned to the army's air force. He spent the next four years flying cargo planes and serving as a pilot instructor in the war's Asian theater (a region of the Pacific Ocean in which America and its allies fought against Japan). By the time the war ended in 1945, Goldwater had risen to the rank of lieutenant colonel.

Goldwater's involvement with the military did not end after World War II. Instead, he remained active in the Air National Guard Reserve, where he attained the rank of major general. Goldwater combined the black and white soldiers under his command into integrated units, despite strong criticism from opponents who wanted to keep all U.S. armed forces segregated.

Enters politics

Goldwater also became involved in state politics after returning to Arizona. In 1946 he was appointed to serve on an important commission studying Colorado River water use in Arizona and neighboring states. Three years later, he was elected to the Phoenix City Council.

In 1952 Goldwater upset Democratic incumbent (the current office-holder) Ernest McFarland to claim a seat in the United States Senate. He kept the seat for the next twelve years, winning reelection to a second six-year term in 1958. During this period, Goldwater became known as one of the Republican Party's most conservative members. He was a passionate supporter of "states' rights"—the belief that each state has the right to determine its own response to issues without interference from the national government. Not surprisingly, then, he also proposed sharp reductions in the size and influence of the federal government. This meant that he opposed many popular federal programs that provided funding for education, farming, and senior citizen care.

Goldwater's conservative beliefs also extended to American foreign policy. He regarded the Soviet Union and other Communist countries as a dangerous threat to the future of the United States. For this reason, he became a strong supporter of Republican Senator Joseph McCarthy, who accused many U.S. officials—as well as artists, writers, and movie stars—of being Communist agents during the early 1950s. McCarthy's crusade to root out Communists in the U.S. government and military eventually crumbled. The American public and its leaders became convinced that the McCarthy-led investigations were treating innocent people very unfairly. But Goldwater continued to support him. He was one of twenty-two Republicans who refused to vote for a Senate measure that censured (officially criticized) McCarthy for his conduct.

Growing crisis in Vietnam

As a strong opponent of communism, Goldwater watched events unfold in Vietnam with great concern during the 1950s. In 1954 Vietnam broke free of French colonial rule after eight years of war. But when the war ended, America and other nations pressured the Vietnamese to accept the terms of a peace agreement that temporarily divided the country into two sections. North Vietnam was led by a Communist government under Ho Chi Minh (see entry), while South Vietnam was headed by a U.S.-supported government under Ngo Dinh Diem (see entry).

The Geneva Accords of 1954 provided for nationwide free elections to be held in 1956, with a goal of reuniting the two halves of Vietnam under one government. At this time, however, the United States and the Communist-led Soviet Union were involved in a fierce rivalry known as the Cold War, in which both nations tried to spread their political views and influence around the world. U.S. government officials worried that free elections in Vietnam would result in a Communist victory. They expressed concern that if all of Vietnam fell into Communist hands, other countries in Asia might also turn Communist and increase the international power of the Soviets. For this reason, the U.S. government and South Vietnam refused to hold the agreed-upon elections.

This decision angered supporters of communism in both North and South Vietnam. Determined to unite the country under Communist rule, they launched a military campaign to topple Diem's government. The United States responded by approving massive quantities of military and financial aid to South Vietnam. This assistance helped Diem but failed to stop his enemies, and during the early 1960s the conflict developed into a full-blown war.

Runs for president

Goldwater believed deeply that the United States needed to keep South Vietnam out of Communist hands. He urged both President Dwight Eisenhower (who served from 1953 to 1961) and President John F. Kennedy (who served from 1961 to 1963; see entry) to use American military might to keep Diem in power. This outspoken advocacy of military force contributed to the Arizona senator's growing reputation as one of the nation's leading conservative voices.

During the early 1960s Goldwater became the favored presidential candidate of Republican conservatives all around the country. They urged him to run for the Republican nomination for the upcoming 1964 presidential election, which would pit the Republican nominee against Kennedy, a Democrat. Goldwater reluctantly agreed. But in November 1963 Kennedy was assassinated, and Vice President Lyndon B. Johnson became president.

Goldwater and many other Republicans knew that Johnson would be a very difficult candidate to defeat in the 1964 election. They believed that America's grief over losing Kennedy would lead many voters to support Johnson, who promised to carry out the slain president's policies. But Goldwater agreed to continue battling for the Republican nomination.

Goldwater battles Johnson

Goldwater eventually defeated New York Governor Nelson Rockefeller for the Republican presidential nomination in a bitterly fought contest. Goldwater's victory angered and disappointed many "moderate" Republicans who did not share the nominee's very conservative views. But Goldwater refused to soften his positions in order to gain their support. In fact, on July 16, 1964, he delivered a famous nomination acceptance speech that emphasized his determination to keep South Vietnam out of Communist hands at all costs. "We are at war in Vietnam," he declared. "I would remind you that extremism in the defense of liberty is no vice. And let me remind you also that moderation in the pursuit of justice is no virtue."

On July 24, 1964, Goldwater and Johnson met and agreed not to use the conflict in Vietnam as a major campaign issue. But the candidates' respective attitudes toward Vietnam and the Cold War still became a big factor in the presidential race. Goldwater repeatedly urged the Johnson administration to "carry the war to North Vietnam" (attack North Vietnam) and publicly speculated about using nuclear weapons to destroy Communist bases in Vietnam. These remarks alarmed many Americans.

President Johnson took advantage of public concerns about Goldwater's willingness to go to war and use nuclear weapons. Johnson cast himself as the "peace" candidate who would make sure that America did not get drawn into a costly conflict in Vietnam. The president and his advisors, meanwhile, suggested that Goldwater would plunge the United States into war if elected. "Some others are eager to enlarge the conflict [in Vietnam]," said Johnson, referring to Goldwater. "They call upon us to supply American boys to do the job that Asian boys should do. They ask us to take reckless actions, which might risk the lives of millions and engulf much of Asia." Johnson's campaign also ran a famous television commercial that emphasized Goldwater's "pro-war" reputation. In the commercial, a peaceful scene of a child picking daisies is suddenly obliterated by a rising mushroom cloud, a symbol of nuclear destruction.

In November 1964 Goldwater lost to Johnson in one of the most lopsided presidential elections in American history. The Republican candidate won only six states and 39 percent of the popular vote. His landslide defeat was blamed on many factors, including his opposition to the Civil Rights Bill of 1964 and his criticisms of farm subsidies (financial aid to farmers), Medicare, and poverty programs (he opposed all of these measures because they increased the role of the federal government). But most people agree that Goldwater's "trigger-happy" reputation was the biggest factor in his defeat.

Returns to Senate

Goldwater spent the next four years in retirement in Arizona. In the meantime, the United States increased its involvement in the Vietnam War under President Johnson. In 1968 Goldwater returned to Washington, D.C., reclaiming his Arizona Senate seat. He renewed his call for increased military pressure on North Vietnam during this time, arguing that the war could not be won without a commitment to use all-out force.

In the early 1970s America was rocked by the Watergate political scandal, which ultimately forced Republican President Richard Nixon (see entry) to resign in 1974. This scandal concerned revelations that members of Nixon's reelection organization broke into the Democratic campaign headquarters in the Watergate Hotel in Washington, D.C., in 1972 to gather secret information. Nixon and several members of his administration attempted to cover up the burglary.

When the Watergate scandal first erupted, Goldwater stood as one of President Richard Nixon's strongest early supporters. But when it became clear that Nixon had lied about his role in the scandal, Goldwater called on the president to resign. He later called Nixon the "most dishonest man" he ever met.

Looking back on Vietnam

In April 1975 the long war in Vietnam finally ended with a Communist victory. Goldwater expressed great anger and regret about the loss of South Vietnam. He blamed America's antiwar movement and timid political leadership for the defeat. He also strongly opposed the government's decision to grant amnesty [official pardon] to "draft dodgers" (Americans who avoided the Vietnam-era military draft by illegal means).

Years later, Goldwater continued to insist that the United States could have been victorious in Vietnam if American political leaders had adopted a more punishing military strategy against the North. "If I had inherited the mess that Johnson got into, I would have said to North Vietnam, by dropping leaflets out of B-52s [American bomber planes that were used extensively in the war], 'You quit the war in three days or the next times these babies come over, they're going to drop some big bombs on you,'" he said in one interview in the late 1980s. "And I'd make a swamp out of North Vietnam . . . . I'd rather kill a hell of a lot of North Vietnamese than one American and we've lost enough of them."

Retires from Senate

In the early 1980s the United States underwent a significant political shift toward conservatism. As this shift took place, many observers credited Goldwater as one of the movement's early pioneers. They noted that many popular elements of 1980s-era conservatism—such as reducing the power of the federal government—were first championed by the Arizona senator.

Goldwater's political career ended in 1987, when he decided not to seek reelection for a sixth term in the Senate. He retired from public life but remained outspoken on issues that concerned him. For example, he voiced strong support for gay rights, reasoning that neither the government nor other people had any right to interfere in the private lives of citizens. This position infuriated some conservatives who opposed homosexuality on religious grounds. But defenders pointed out that Goldwater's stand was consistent with his lifelong political philosophy, which emphasized individual freedom and liberty.

Goldwater's health began to fail in the late 1990s. In 1996 he suffered a stroke, and one year later he was diagnosed with Alzheimer's disease. He died on May 12, 1998, of natural causes at his home in suburban Phoenix.

Sources
Edwards, Lee. *Goldwater: The Man Who Made a Revolution*. Washington, D.C.: Regnery, 1995.

Goldberg, Robert Alan. *Barry Goldwater*. New Haven, CT: Yale University Press, 1995.

Goldwater, Barry. *The Conscience of a Conservative*. Shepherdsville, KY: Victor Publishing, 1960.

Goldwater, Barry, with Jack Casserly. *Goldwater*. New York: Doubleday, 1988.

Goldwater, Barry. *With No Apologies: The Personal and Political Memoirs of United States Senator Barry M. Goldwater*. New York: Morrow, 1979.

White, Theodore H. *The Making of the President 1964*. 1965.

David Halberstam

Born April 10, 1934
New York, New York

American journalist and author

David Halberstam.
Reproduced by permission of Archive Photos.

David Halberstam was one of the best-known journalists of the Vietnam War. He spent fifteen months covering the war for the *New York Times* in late 1962 and 1963. During this time, he became known for his hard-hitting stories, which often contradicted official accounts provided by the U.S. government and military. Although Halberstam came under intense criticism for his war reporting in some circles, it also earned him the prestigious Pulitzer Prize for journalism in 1964. After returning to the United States, Halberstam published several books about the Vietnam era, including *The Best and the Brightest.* He is also the author of numerous other books on American history and sports.

"I believed in the cause that was at stake and in the men who were fighting it."

A brilliant young reporter

David Halberstam was born on April 10, 1934, in New York City. He was the second of two sons born to Charles and Blanche Halberstam. His father was a surgeon in the U.S. military, so the family moved around a lot when David was young. After living in Texas, Minnesota, and Connecticut, they ended up in Yonkers, New York. At Yonkers High School, Halberstam wrote for the school newspaper and ran track. His grades were good enough to earn him admission to Harvard University, where he became the managing editor of the daily student newspaper, the *Harvard Crimson.* He earned a bachelor's degree in journalism from Harvard in 1955.

After graduating from college, Halberstam surprised many of his Harvard classmates by accepting a job as a reporter at a small-town Mississippi newspaper called the *Daily Times Leader.* At that time, African Americans in the South were just beginning to protest against segregation (the forced separation of people by race) and other forms of discrimination. Halberstam hoped to use his position to influence the growing debate about civil rights. But he became frustrated and left the paper when it became clear that his editor and many local white citizens were not interested in his antisegregation perspective. He then took a job with the *Nashville Tennessean,* where he did get an opportunity to report on the civil rights movement.

In 1960 Halberstam became a staff writer in the Washington bureau of the *New York Times,* one of the largest and most respected newspapers in the country. A year later, he was sent to the Congo (which became Zaire and is now known as the Democratic Republic of the Congo) in Africa, where United Nations forces were trying to stop a bloody tribal war. The young reporter jumped into his new position as a foreign correspondent with enthusiasm. He put himself in dangerous situations many times, and several of his vivid stories made it to the front page of the *New York Times.* Before long, Halberstam had earned a reputation as a daring and talented journalist.

Covers the Vietnam War

In September 1962 the *New York Times* sent Halberstam to Southeast Asia to report on an ongoing conflict in Vietnam. A longtime colony of France, Vietnam had won its freedom in 1954 after an eight-year war with the French. But the country had been divided into two sections by the 1954 Geneva Peace Accords. North Vietnam was headed by a Communist government under revolutionary leader Ho Chi Minh (see entry). Leadership of South Vietnam was given to Ngo Dinh Diem (see entry), who promised to build a democracy.

The Geneva Accords provided for nationwide free elections to be held in 1956 so that the two sections of Vietnam could be united under one government. But South Vietnamese officials refused to hold the elections because they believed that the results would give the Communists control over the entire country. This stand was supported by the United States. American leaders believed that if South Vietnam fell to communism, Communist movements might sweep through all of Southeast Asia and increase the international influence and prestige of China and the Soviet Union.

When South Vietnam refused to hold elections, North Vietnam joined with Viet Cong guerrillas in the South to overthrow the South Vietnamese government by force. The United States responded by sending money, weapons, and advisors to aid in South Vietnam's defense. In the early 1960s this assistance increased at a very rapid rate. But despite growing U.S. involvement, South Vietnam continued to teeter on the brink of collapse. During this period, the U.S. government provided optimistic accounts of events in Vietnam in order to maintain public support for their efforts there. They wanted the American people to believe that the Diem government was popular and strong, and that the extent of U.S. military assistance was limited. Many reporters filed stories that reflected the U.S. government's description of events. But some members of the American and international press corps based in South Vietnam suggested that the country was in serious trouble.

When Halberstam first arrived in Vietnam, he supported American involvement in the conflict. He believed that the U.S. government had a responsibility to help other countries stand firm against communism. "We were there to help another country against encroachment [invasion] from within, and I did not dissent [disagree]," he told Christopher Anderson in *People*. "I believed in the cause that was at stake and in the men who were fighting it." But within a short time, Halberstam began to realize that the official version of events did not always match reality. "It was all lies and lies and lies," he told William Prochnau in *Once Upon a Distant War*. Halberstam began to question the word of official sources and instead tried to obtain firsthand information.

Against the wishes of the U.S. military advisors in South Vietnam, Halberstam began filing reports that contradicted the official version of events. For example, he wrote that Diem's government was corrupt and unpopular. He noted that significant sections of the country were controlled by the Viet Cong. He also reported that the South Vietnamese army—known as the Army of the Republic of Vietnam or ARVN—was weak and dependent on U.S. military equipment and intelligence. Even though these reports were mostly accurate, they angered American government and military leaders. The officials wanted the press to repeat their reassuring public statements that the Diem government was prospering and the Viet Cong threat was fading away. But Halberstam continued to submit stories that gave his own impressions of the situation in South Vietnam throughout his time there.

Turns Vietnam experience into best-selling books

During his fifteen months in Vietnam, Halberstam gained a reputation for using the real experiences of soldiers in the field to expose the true story behind the U.S. government's statements. In January 1963, for example, he reported on the Battle of Ap Bac. In this operation, South Vietnamese troops and their U.S. military advisors set out to destroy a Viet Cong radio transmitter in the village of Ap Bac. They believed it was guarded by only a hundred Viet Cong guerillas. But the Communist forces intercepted radio messages about the plan and were able to prepare a strong defense. During the battle that followed, the South Vietnamese forces fought poorly and made a series of strategic errors. In the end, eighty ARVN soldiers were killed and a hundred wounded, while the Viet Cong guerillas slipped away without suffering many casualties.

Afterward, some American and South Vietnamese officials claimed that they had won the Battle of Ap Bac. But Halberstam and several other journalists uncovered the truth about the Viet Cong's strength and the ARVN's poor performance. These reports became front-page news in the United States and greatly raised public awareness of the real situation in Vietnam. In 1964 Halberstam received the prestigious Pulitzer Prize for his coverage of the war. At the same time, however, he became the subject of criticism from many U.S. government and military officials. These officials blamed the media for increasing opposition to U.S. involvement in Vietnam among the American people. They claimed that journalists like Halberstam inspired the Communists to continue fighting and made it impossible for U.S. forces to win the war.

After returning from Vietnam in December 1963, Halberstam continued to write about his experiences in a series of books and magazine articles. In 1965 he published *The Making of a Quagmire: America and Vietnam during the Kennedy Era.* This influential book, which traces the history of U.S. involvement in the conflict, helped establish Halberstam as an expert on the war. With its success, Halberstam left the *New York Times* in 1967 in order to concentrate on building a career as an author. He looked at the Vietnam War from a different perspective in his 1971 book *Ho,* which is a biography of North Vietnamese Communist leader Ho Chi Minh.

Halberstam's best-known book about the Vietnam era is *The Best and the Brightest,* published in 1972. In this book he looks at early American involvement in the war through the actions of key decision makers in the U.S. government. Halberstam draws highly critical profiles of several important figures in the John F. Kennedy (see entry) and Lyndon B. Johnson (see entry) administrations, including National Security Advisor McGeorge Bundy (see entry), Secretary of State Dean Rusk (see entry), and Secretary of Defense Robert McNamara (see entry). Halberstam explained that he wrote the book in order to find out how these men—who "had been praised as the best and the brightest men of a generation"—could have become "the architects of a war which I and many others thought the worst tragedy to befall this country since the Civil War." *The Best and the Brightest* became a best-seller and remains a classic in Vietnam War literature.

Continues writing about American history and sports

In the years since he became a full-time author, Halberstam produced a number of well-regarded books on American history and culture. In 1979 he published *The Powers That Be,* which examines how the American news media helped shape politics and society. In 1986 he wrote *The Reckoning,* which contrasts the history and business approach of the U.S. automaker Ford Motor Company with that of the Japanese automaker Nissan. These two books, along with *The Best and the Brightest,* are often considered to be Halberstam's three-part series about power in America.

In 1997 Halberstam returned to his early work on the civil rights movement in his book *The Children.* He contacted several of the young African American protestors he had interviewed in 1960, when he was a reporter for the *Nashville Tennessean,* and followed their life stories to the present day. In between his more serious projects, Halberstam has often turned his reporter's eye to the world of sports. He has published several books about baseball and its links to American culture, including *The Summer of '49* and *October 1964.* One of his favorites among his own books is *The Amateurs,* which follows an American crew team as they train for the Olympics. In 1999 Halberstam published *Playing for Keeps: Michael Jordan and the World He Made,* a biography of the Chicago Bulls star.

Sources

Anderson, Christopher. "David Halberstam." *People Weekly,* November 4, 1985.

Contemporary Authors New Revision Series. Vol. 45. Detroit: Gale, 1995.

Downie, Leonard, Jr. *The New Muckrakers: An Inside Look at America's Investigative Reporters.* New York: New Republic Books, 1976.

Dygert, James H. *The Investigative Journalist: Folk Heroes of a New Era.* Englewood Cliffs, NJ: Prentice-Hall, 1976.

Encyclopedia of World Biography. Detroit: Gale, 1998.

Prochnau, William W. *Once Upon a Distant War: David Halberstam, Neil Sheehan, Peter Arnett—Young War Correspondents and Their Early Vietnam Battles.* New York: Times Books, 1995.

Tom Hayden

**Born December 12, 1940
Royal Oak, Michigan**

**American political activist; cofounder
of the radical antiwar group Students
for a Democratic Society (SDS)**

T om Hayden became a political activist during his college
days, when he co-founded Students for a Democratic Society (SDS). Through this organization, he was involved in the
social protests of the 1960s, including the civil rights movement and the antiwar movement. In 1968 Hayden helped
organize a major demonstration against the Vietnam War during the Democratic National Convention in Chicago. The
demonstration turned into a violent confrontation between
protestors and Chicago police. Afterward, Hayden and seven
other activists—who became known as the Chicago Eight—
were put on trial for causing the riot. Once the war ended,
Hayden became active in politics in California.

Becomes a student activist

Thomas Emmett Hayden was born on December 12,
1940, in Royal Oak, Michigan, a suburb of Detroit. He was the
only child in a working-class Catholic family. His father, an
accountant, left the family when Tom was a child. From that
time on, his mother supported him by working as a librarian.
Hayden first showed his rebellious nature in high school. As

"I became a
revolutionary in bits
and pieces. It was a
cumulative process in
which one commitment
led to another."

Tom Hayden.
*Courtesy of the Library
of Congress.*

119

editor of the student newspaper, he often got in trouble for criticizing school officials and policies in his editorials.

In 1957 Hayden enrolled at the University of Michigan as a journalism major. He became a writer for the student newspaper, the *Michigan Daily.* Within a short time, however, Hayden grew frustrated with the rules guiding student conduct, which he viewed as unclear and strict. "You couldn't find out what the rules were or how to change them," he recalled. He felt that the students should have more say in their own education, but he was not sure how they could achieve this.

In the summer of 1960 Hayden hitchhiked to California. He was unhappy with many aspects of American life at this time. He thought that Americans placed too much importance on material possessions and felt that everyone seemed to want to look and act like everyone else. Longing to be different, he at first intended to become a dropout rebel like the hero of Jack Kerouac's novel *On the Road.* But his experiences in California helped direct him toward radical politics as a way to bring social change.

During his trip Hayden witnessed the poverty of migrant farm workers. He learned about the nuclear weapons research that was taking place because of the military rivalry between the United States and the Soviet Union. And he met student radicals who led protests at the University of California at Berkeley and interviewed civil rights protesters who held demonstrations at the Democratic National Convention in Los Angeles. All of these experiences added to Hayden's determination to work toward change in American society. "I became a revolutionary in bits and pieces," he stated. "It was a cumulative process in which one commitment led to another."

Forms Students for a Democratic Society (SDS)

When he returned to the University of Michigan for his senior year, Hayden joined a group of fellow students in forming Students for a Democratic Society (SDS). SDS was intended to be a national organization that would coordinate the political involvement of college students around the country. As editor of the *Michigan Daily* during his senior year, Hayden began encouraging other students to become activists. He urged them to work to end poverty, racism, the military arms race, and other problems in American society.

Hayden graduated from college in 1961 and spent the next year working as a volunteer for the Student Nonviolent Coordinating Committee (SNCC). This organization was dedicated to helping African Americans in their fight for civil rights and social justice. In 1962 he wrote the first draft of the Port Huron Manifesto, a document outlining the basic principles of SDS. The document began, "We are people of this generation, bred in at least modest comfort, housed in universities, looking uncomfortably to the world we inherit." It went on to call for a more democratic American government that would represent individuals and communities, rather than business interests and the upper class.

Later that year, Hayden returned to the University of Michigan to complete a master's degree in sociology. He also served as the president of SDS during this time. In 1964 he established the Economic Research and Action Project (ERAP). This special SDS program was intended to help poor people in the nation's inner cities. As part of ERAP, Hayden lived in an all-black area of Newark, New Jersey. Along with other activists, he tried to organize the local people to pressure the city government for changes. For example, they worked to convince the city to build playgrounds, repair roads, and provide jobs for local residents. Hayden found his job difficult, however, because many residents tended to be suspicious of him and the other SDS members.

Leads protests against the Vietnam War

By the mid-1960s Hayden had begun to turn his attention to protesting against American involvement in the Vietnam War. This conflict pitted the Communist nation of North Vietnam and its secret allies, the South Vietnamese Communists known as the Viet Cong, against the U.S.-supported nation of South Vietnam. North Vietnam wanted to overthrow the South Vietnamese government and reunite the two countries under one Communist government. But U.S. government officials felt that a Communist government in Vietnam would increase the power of the Soviet Union and threaten the security of the United States.

In the late 1950s and early 1960s the U.S. government sent money, weapons, and military advisors to help South Vietnam defend itself against North Vietnam and the Viet

Bobby Seale (1936–)

Black activist Bobby Seale was one of the members of the Chicago Eight. Born on October 22, 1936, Robert George Seale grew up in a poor area of Oakland, California. After dropping out of high school in his senior year, he joined the U.S. Air Force, where he was trained as an aircraft sheet-metal mechanic. But he received a dishonorable discharge after three years of service when he disobeyed an officer. Seale then completed his high school education at night while holding a day job as a sheet-metal mechanic. In 1959, he entered Merritt College in Oakland. It was during his time as a college student that he became involved in the civil rights movement.

During his college years, Seale joined a student group called the Afro-American Association. Through this group he met Huey Newton, who introduced him to the writings of black nationalist leaders like Malcolm X. Over time, Seale grew increasingly angry about the unfair treatment of blacks in American society. He eventually came to believe that blacks could not rely on the U.S. justice system to protect them from violence and discrimination at the hands of whites. Instead, he felt that African Americans should band together and use armed resistance to gain equal rights.

In October 1966, Seale and Newton founded the Black Panther Party. The goal of this radical organization was to defy white authority and demand representation for blacks in the American political system. The Black Panthers also fought to improve living conditions for blacks and to end police brutality in black neighborhoods. In May 1967, they came to national attention by staging a protest in the California State Legislature. The legislature was debating a proposal that would prohibit carrying guns in public. But the Black Panthers believed that African Americans needed to arm themselves against white authority. They protested against the proposal by showing up at a legislative session heavily armed with rifles and handguns. Seale was arrested for disrupting the legislature and spent six months in jail. The protest increased the Black Panthers' popularity among African Americans, but also made it a controversial and feared organization among many whites.

In 1968, Seale began trying to form alliances with radical white leaders, many of whom were involved in protests against the Vietnam War. Some black activists wanted African Americans to fight their own battles, separately from whites. But Seale felt that joining forces with other protest groups could only help his cause. As he told Wallace Terry in *Time*, "You don't fight racism with racism. The best way to fight racism is with solidarity [joining together]." Under his guidance, the Black Panthers joined several other radical organizations in forming the Peace and Freedom Party. Newton became the party's candidate for president in the 1968 elections.

The Democratic Party held a convention in Chicago that year to select its candidate for the presidency. Antiwar

Bobby Seale (left) and Huey Newton.
Reproduced by permission of AP/Wide World Photos.

activists organized a major demonstration outside the convention hall. Seale appeared at the demonstration and gave an emotional speech about the treatment of blacks in American society. As the protests deteriorated into a violent struggle with Chicago police, Seale was arrested. He and seven prominent antiwar activists were put on trial in September 1969 on charges of inciting (causing) a riot. The American media dubbed the group—which also included David Dellinger (see entry), Tom Hayden, and Abbie Hoffman (see entry)— the Chicago Eight.

Shortly before the trial began, Seale's attorney underwent surgery. Seale asked Judge Julius Hoffman to delay the trial until his lawyer could recover, but the judge refused. Then Seale requested that he be allowed to represent himself, but the

judge ordered him to use the same attorney as the other seven defendants. Feeling that his rights had been violated, Seale refused to cooperate with the court proceedings. The other defendants viewed the trial—and the media attention it attracted—as an opportunity to present their views about the Vietnam War. They continually disrupted the proceedings with outbursts and angry speeches. The judge responded by repeatedly finding them in contempt of court.

Finally, Judge Hoffman declared a mistrial in Seale's case and agreed to try him separately from the other defendants, who then became known as the Chicago Seven. Seale was later found guilty of 16 counts of contempt of court and sentenced to four years in prison. But the charges were dropped in 1972, after he had served two years of his term.

By the 1970s, Seale led the Black Panthers away from armed confrontation. He concentrated the organization's efforts on community assistance programs, like building health clinics in poor neighborhoods and providing breakfast for inner-city children. In 1973, he ran for mayor of Oakland as a Democrat and finished second out of nine candidates. The following year, Seale left the Black Panthers and formed Advocates Scene, a group dedicated to helping poor people and minorities become involved in grassroots politics. He published his autobiography, *A Lonely Rage,* in 1978.

Cong. In 1965 President Lyndon Johnson (see entry) sent American combat troops to join the fight on the side of South Vietnam. But deepening U.S. involvement in the war failed to defeat the Communists. Instead, the war turned into a bloody stalemate. As the war dragged on, the American public became bitterly divided about U.S. involvement in Vietnam.

Like many other Americans, Hayden felt that the U.S. government's actions were wrong. He did not think that the United States should interfere with the reunification of Vietnam. Instead, he believed that the Vietnamese people should be allowed to decide their own future. In 1965 Hayden visited North Vietnam with a group of other antiwar activists. The idea behind his visit was to establish a connection between the American peace movement and the North Vietnamese government. Hayden knew that some people would view him as a traitor for meeting with the enemy. But he believed that the best way to support the U.S. troops was to end the war as quickly as possible.

During his visit to the capital city of Hanoi, Hayden was deeply moved by the destruction and suffering caused by American bombing. Upon returning to the United States, he expressed admiration for the strength and revolutionary spirit of the North Vietnamese people. He wrote a book about his experiences, *The Other Side,* to try to inform the American people about "what our government was doing in this small country eight thousand miles away."

Member of the Chicago Eight

By 1966 Hayden had become a leading figure in the radical antiwar movement. He made speeches on college campuses and appeared at antiwar demonstrations across the country. In 1967 he left the ERAP program in Newark after the city was rocked by a series of riots. At this point, Hayden dedicated all his time and energy to the antiwar movement.

Hayden began working with the leaders of other antiwar groups, including the National Mobilization Committee to End the War in Vietnam (MOBE), to organize a huge protest at the 1968 Democratic National Convention in Chicago. At this convention, representatives of the Democratic political party planned to select their candidate for the presidency and formulate the Vietnam policy they would present in their upcoming campaign.

When the Democrats met in the summer of 1968, thousands of protestors showed up outside the convention hall. Many people—including Hayden—made angry, antigovernment speeches. In *Chicago '68* he is quoted as calling the U.S. government "an outlaw institution under the control of war criminals." As the protests went on, Chicago Mayor Richard J. Daley (see entry) sent his police force to control the demonstrators. But many law officers used brutal force against the protestors, and the confrontations escalated into an ugly riot. Scenes of fights between antiwar activists and police officers dominated television newscasts and overshadowed the convention.

Instead of trying to stop the violence, Hayden urged the people of Chicago to rise up against the police and the city government. "The city and the military machinery it has aimed at us won't permit us to protest in an organized fashion," he stated. "We must turn this overheated military machine against itself. Let us make sure if blood flows, it flows all over the city." In the end, more than a thousand protestors and two hundred police officers were injured in the fighting.

A year later, Hayden and seven other organizers of the demonstrations—known in the media as the Chicago Eight—were put on trial for conspiracy to cause a riot. But the antiwar activists repeatedly disrupted the trial with loud outbursts and disobedient behavior. At one point, they even draped a Viet Cong flag over their table. In addition, they used the trial to present their political views. As the six-month trial progressed, it turned into a chaotic media circus.

In February 1970 Hayden was found guilty on several charges and sentenced to five years in prison. But he appealed the judge's decision, and his conviction was overturned. Later that year, he wrote a popular book, *Trial,* about his experience as a member of the Chicago Eight.

Works for change from within the government

At its peak, Hayden's SDS organization had around four hundred campus chapters and was very active in the civil rights and antiwar movements. In the early 1970s, however,

SDS split into smaller groups as its members argued over the organization's main focus. When this happened, Hayden continued protesting against the Vietnam War outside of SDS, writing wrote several books and articles expressing his views of the U.S. government and its policies.

In 1973 Hayden married actress Jane Fonda (see entry), who had also become a well-known antiwar activist. Together they formed a new organization, the Indochina Peace Campaign, to work toward ending the war. When the U.S. troops withdrew from Vietnam later that year, Hayden continued pressuring the government to reduce its financial support for South Vietnam.

After the Vietnam War ended in victory for North Vietnam in 1975, Hayden changed the focus of his activism. Rather than trying to change the government from the outside, he decided to run for public office in order to try to make the government more democratic from within. He joined the Democratic political party and ran for the U.S. Senate from California in 1976, but he lost in the primary. He was elected to the California state legislature a short time later and served throughout the 1980s and into the 1990s. In 1997 he launched an unsuccessful campaign to become mayor of Los Angeles.

Sources

Farber, David. *Chicago '68.* Chicago: University of Chicago Press, 1988.

Findley, Tom. "Tom Hayden Rolling Stone Interview." *Rolling Stone,* October 26, 1972 (Part 1), November 9, 1972 (Part 2).

Garfinkle, Adam. *Telltale Hearts: The Origins and Impact of the Vietnam Antiwar Movement.* New York: St. Martin's Press, 1995.

Hayden, Tom. *Reunion: A Memoir.* New York: Random House, 1988.

Wells, Tom. *The War Within: America's Battle over Vietnam.* Berkeley: University of California Press, 1994.

Zaroulis, Nancy, and Gerald Sullivan.*Who Spoke Up? American Protest against the War in Vietnam, 1963–1975.* Garden City, NY: Doubleday, 1984.

Michael Herr

Born 1940
Syracuse, New York

American journalist

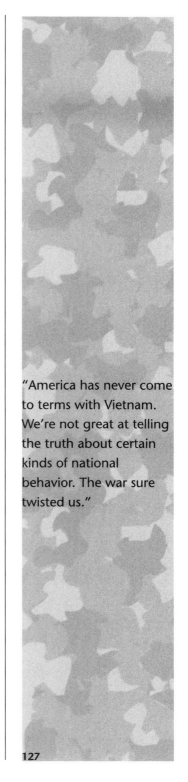

Writer Michael Herr is best known as the author of *Dispatches,* a nonfiction account of the Vietnam War that received tremendous critical acclaim when it was published in 1977. The memoir, which was based on Herr's experiences in Vietnam in 1967 and 1968 as a correspondent for *Esquire* magazine, provided readers with a vivid picture of the war and its impact on young American soldiers. More than two decades later, the book continues to be viewed as a classic work of war literature. As Stewart O'Nan wrote in *The Vietnam Reader,* "of all the books to come out of the Vietnam War, journalist Michael Herr's *Dispatches* . . . is most often cited as the best, capturing the thrills, terror, and madness of the war."

"America has never come to terms with Vietnam. We're not great at telling the truth about certain kinds of national behavior. The war sure twisted us."

Early career in journalism

Michael Herr was born and raised in a middle-class neighborhood in Syracuse, New York. He studied journalism at Syracuse University before securing work in the early 1960s as a writer for *Holiday* magazine and other periodicals. By the mid-1960s, however, he recognized that the biggest story in American journalism was the growing war in Vietnam.

The Vietnam War pitted the U.S.-supported nation of South Vietnam against the Communist nation of North Vietnam and its guerrilla allies—known as the Viet Cong—in the South. The Communists wanted to overthrow the South Vietnamese government and unite the two countries under one Communist government. In the late 1950s and early 1960s the United States sent money, weapons, and advisors to South Vietnam to help it fend off the Viet Cong. In 1965 the United States began using thousands of American combat troops and extensive air bombing missions to crush the Communists. But deepening U.S. involvement in the war failed to defeat the Viet Cong or the North Vietnamese. Instead, the war settled into a bloody stalemate that eventually claimed the lives of more than 58,000 U.S. soldiers. As disillusionment over the war increased, the American public became bitterly divided over the nation's involvement in Vietnam.

Herr's efforts to secure a reporting assignment that would take him to the war-torn country eventually paid off. In 1967 he reached an agreement with *Esquire* magazine to go to Vietnam and provide monthly reports on the war. Soon after his arrival, however, Herr convinced the magazine to suspend the monthly columns in favor of longer articles that would allow him to explore the true nature of the conflict. "Something [about the war] wasn't even being asked," he explained in *Dispatches*. "Hiding low under the fact-figure crossfire [statistical analysis of the war] there was a secret history, and not a lot of people felt like running in there to bring it out."

Time in Vietnam

Herr spent the next eleven months traveling across South Vietnam. During that time, he personally witnessed many of the war's most famous events. He reported on the massive Communist invasion known as the Tet Offensive, in which Viet Cong and North Vietnamese forces simultaneously attacked dozens of South Vietnamese cities. He also provided coverage of the siege of Khe Sanh (a siege is a military strategy in which an army attempts to capture a city or military base by surrounding and blockading it). This remote American-South Vietnamese military base endured weeks of deadly sniper, artillery, and mortar attacks from Communist forces before the siege was finally broken.

Herr also spent large blocks of time in the company of American soldiers as they went about their duties. He joined them on dangerous patrols deep into the Vietnam jungle and ate and drank with them at base camps. These experiences enabled Herr to develop a deep understanding of the dark and violent world the soldiers inhabited and the emotions they struggled with on a daily basis. "After a year I felt so plugged in to all the stories and the images and the fear that even the dead started telling me stories," Herr recalled in *Dispatches*. "However many times it happened, whether I'd known them or not, no matter what I'd felt about them or the way they died, their story was always there and it was always the same: it went, 'Put yourself in my place.'"

As the months passed by, Herr recognized that the possibility of death haunted every soldier he met. Moreover, his constant exposure to death and violence made him frighteningly aware of his own vulnerability. "You could die in a sudden bloodburning crunch as your chopper hit the ground like dead weight," he wrote in *Dispatches*. "You could fly apart so that your pieces would never be gathered, you could take one neat round [bullet] in the lung and go out hearing only the bubble of the last few breaths, you could die in the last stage of malaria with that faint tapping in your ears, and that could happen to you after months of firefights and rockets and machine guns . . . . You could be shot, mined, grenaded, rocketed, mortared, sniped at, blown up and away so that your leavings [remains] had to be dropped into a sagging poncho and carried to Graves Registration."

By the time Herr left Vietnam in 1968 to return to the United States, he felt a great sympathy for the American soldiers who remained. "Humanly I was on their side because they were in a real [terrible situation] and you'd have to be some kind of monster not to be on their side," he told Eric James Schroeder in *Vietnam, We've All Been There*. In addition, he felt a deep obligation to write about the war's violence and brutality on behalf of the American soldiers who were trapped in the conflict. As he wrote in *Dispatches,* the soldiers would "ask you with an emotion whose intensity would shock you to please tell it [tell about the war], because they really did have the feeling that it wasn't being told for them, that they were going through all of this and that somehow no one back in the World [America] knew about it."

Herr Recalls the Atmosphere in Vietnam

In the following excerpt from *Dispatches,* journalist Michael Herr writes about the atmosphere of fear and menace that he experienced during his travels in Vietnam. In the first paragraph, he talks about all the different ways in which people died in the war. In the second paragraph, he recounts how it felt to hitch rides on the American military helicopters that transported troops to and from combat zones and military bases throughout South Vietnam.

All the same, one place or another it was always going on, rock around the clock, we had the days and he [the enemy] had the nights. You could be in the most protected space in Vietnam and still know that your safety was provisional [temporary], that early death, blindness, loss of legs, arms or . . . major and lasting disfigurement—the whole rotten deal—could come in on the freaky-fluky as easily as in the so-called expected ways, you heard so many of those stories it was a wonder anyone was left alive to die in firefights and mortar-rocket attacks. After a few weeks, when . . . I saw that everyone around me was carrying a gun, I also saw that any one of them could go off at any time, putting you where it wouldn't matter whether it had been an accident or not. The roads were mined, the trails booby-trapped, satchel charges and grenades blew up jeeps and movie theaters, the VC [Viet Cong] got work inside all the camps as shoeshine boys and laundresses and honey-dippers, they'd starch your fatigues and

Writing *Dispatches*

After returning to America, Herr resumed his journalism career. He also began putting together a book about his time in Vietnam. But writing about his wartime experiences proved to be an emotionally exhausting task. In addition, Herr learned that three of his closest friends from Vietnam—all photographers—had been killed or reported missing in action. These factors combined to push Herr into what he later called "a massive physical and psychological collapse." He subsequently underwent intensive therapy to come to terms with his experiences in Vietnam. Herr gradually recovered, and in the mid-1970s he resumed writing.

In 1977 Herr finally published the book, nearly ten years after he left Vietnam. The book, called *Dispatches,* was a brilliant and original work of literature that blended his own wartime experiences and impressions with an intense examination of the

[dispose of your garbage] and then go home and mortar your area. Saigon and Cholon and Danang [cities in South Vietnam] held such hostile vibes that you felt you were being dry-sniped every time someone looked at you, and choppers fell out of the sky like fat poisoned birds a hundred times a day. After a while I couldn't get on one without thinking that I must be out of my . . . mind.

Fear and motion, fear and standstill, no preferred cut there, no way even to be clear about which was really worse, the wait or the delivery. Combat spared far more men than it wasted, but everyone suffered the time between contact [battle with the enemy], especially when they were going out every day looking for it; bad going on foot, terrible in trucks and APCs [armored personnel carriers], awful in helicopters, the worst, traveling so fast toward something so frightening. I can remember times when I went half dead with my fear of the motion, the speed and direction already fixed and pointed one way. It was painful enough just flying "safe" hops between firebases and LZ's [landing zones]; if you were ever on a helicopter that had been hit by ground fire your deep, perpetual chopper anxiety was guaranteed. At least actual contact when it was happening would draw long ragged strands of energy out of you, it was juicy, fast and refining, and traveling toward it was hollow, dry, cold and steady, it never let you alone. All you could do was look around at the other people on board and see if they were as scared and numbed out as you were. If it looked like they weren't you thought they were insane, if it looked like they were it made you feel a lot worse.

horror, insanity, and dark excitement of the Vietnam War. The work caused an immediate sensation among historians, critics, and general readers alike. It was both a best-seller and a nominee for the 1978 National Book Award in nonfiction. More than two decades later, it continues to be regarded as one of the true masterpieces of Vietnam War literature. "Major literary scholars of war are unanimous in their judgments that this rock 'n' roll work of literary journalism is perhaps the single most powerful book to come out of that [the Vietnam] war, and the book is almost universally considered a landmark," wrote Donald J. Ringnalda in *Dictionary of Literary Biography*.

Screenwriter for Vietnam films

After completing *Dispatches*, Herr helped write the screenplays for two major films about Vietnam, *Apocalypse Now* (1979) and *Full Metal Jacket* (1987). In the early 1980s he

relocated to England with his wife, Valerie, and two daughters. The Herr family remained in Europe for the next decade before returning to the United States and settling in upstate New York in the early 1990s.

In the years since *Dispatches,* Herr has produced few other literary works. In fact, his only other full-length book to appear over the past two decades was *Walter Winchell: A Novel,* a 1990 novel-screenplay about a famous American newspaper columnist of the 1940s.

Herr is also known as an intensely private person. He dislikes being photographed and rarely gives interviews. In 1992, however, he granted an interview to Eric James Schroeder for the book *Vietnam, We've All Been There.* During their conversation, Herr expressed doubt about the United States' ability to ever completely recover from the wounds it suffered during the Vietnam War. "America has never come to terms with Vietnam," he told Schroeder. "We're not great at telling the truth about certain kinds of national behavior. The war sure twisted us. We haven't felt the same about ourselves since Vietnam. We're haunted by it, but we won't name the shape of the ghost; we won't say what it is."

Sources

Ciotti, P. "Michael Herr: A Man of Few Words." *Los Angeles Times Magazine,* April 15, 1990.

Herr, Michael. *Dispatches.* New York: Knopf, 1977.

Morgan, Thomas B. "Reporters on the Lost War." *Esquire,* July 1984.

Myers, Thomas. *Walking Point: American Narratives of Vietnam.* Oxford University Press, 1988.

Ringnalda, Donald J. "Michael Herr." *Dictionary of Literary Biography,* Vol. 185: *American Literary Journalists, 1945–1995, First Series.* Detroit: Gale, 1997.

Schroeder, Eric James. *Vietnam, We've All Been There: Interviews with American Writers.* Westport, CT: Praeger, 1992.

Ho Chi Minh

Born May 19, 1890
Nghe An Province, Vietnam
Died September 2, 1969
Hanoi, North Vietnam

President of North Vietnam, 1945–1969

"We will expose all those who serve as lackeys [servants] for the U.S. imperialists to coerce, deceive, and divide our people . . . . We are still laboring under great difficulties but victory will certainly be ours."

Ho Chi Minh.

H o Chi Minh is probably the most influential figure in modern Vietnamese history. A committed revolutionary throughout his life, Ho led Vietnamese Communist forces fighting for the independence of his country. He became the first president of the Democratic Republic of Vietnam (which later became known as North Vietnam) in 1945, when the Communist-led Viet Minh revolutionary group took control of Vietnam following World War II. He continued to lead the Viet Minh against French colonial forces during the Indochina War. He remained president of North Vietnam during the early years of the Vietnam War, when Communist forces fought for control of U.S.-supported South Vietnam. Ho died in 1969, six years before North Vietnam finally won the war, but many people still consider him the father of Vietnamese independence.

Becomes a revolutionary leader

The man who became known around the world as Ho Chi Minh was born on May 19, 1890, in the small village of Kim Lien in Nghe An province in central Vietnam. According to many reports, his name at birth was Nguyen That Thanh, which means "Nguyen Who Will Be Victorious" in Vietnamese. He went by a variety of other names during his career as a revolutionary, but he became best known under the name Ho Chi Minh, which means "He Who Enlightens."

At the time of Ho's birth, Vietnam was a colony of France known as French Indochina. His father, Nguyen Sinh Sac, was a local government official who resigned from his job in protest against French colonial policies. The youngest of three children in his family, Ho inherited a strong patriotic spirit from his father. In fact, he began carrying messages for an anti-French resistance group at the age of nine.

Ho received his education at the National Academy in Hue, which was known as one of the top schools in Vietnam. After teaching and studying in Saigon for a short time, he left Vietnam around 1912. By this time, he had begun to feel threatened by the colonial government due to his anti-French activities. He also hoped to gain firsthand knowledge of political systems around the world. He would not return to Vietnam for thirty years.

Ho spent several years at sea, working as a cook's helper on a French steamship. After visiting New York, London, and other cities, he settled in Paris around 1917. Ho soon became involved in the political debates surrounding the negotiations to end World War I. Calling himself Nguyen Ai Quoc ("Nguyen the Patriot"), he wrote a petition demanding self-rule for the colonies held by European nations. He attempted to deliver this petition to American President Woodrow Wilson at the peace conference, but he was unsuccessful.

Over the next few years, Ho's reputation in political circles continued to grow. In 1920 he joined the French Communist Party. He also wrote a series of pamphlets and articles protesting French rule in Indochina. He demanded that the Vietnamese people be allowed to elect their own leaders and receive representation in the French government. Some of these works were published under the name Nguyen O Phap ("Nguyen Who Hates the French"). When copies of his writings made their way to resistance leaders in Vietnam, Ho was hailed as a hero in his homeland.

In 1923 Ho traveled to Moscow, where he received training to become a revolutionary leader. The Communist government of the Soviet Union supported his plans to organize groups of Vietnamese nationalists (people with strong feelings of loyalty for their country) to fight for Vietnam's independence from France. Toward this end, Ho and other young anticolonial activists formed the Vietnamese Revolutionary Youth League in 1925.

Leads the Viet Minh fight for independence

In 1930 Ho met with a group of fellow Vietnamese revolutionaries in Hong Kong, including future North Vietnamese political leaders Le Duc Tho (see entry) and Pham Van Dong (see entry). They joined forces to create the Indochinese Communist Party. Some members of the party returned to Vietnam, where they encouraged peasants to protest against the French colonial government. The French reacted violently to one such protest, sending fighter planes to fire upon a crowd of demonstrators. Over a hundred Vietnamese people were killed. Ho used such instances of French brutality to attract support to the Indochinese Communist Party. In 1931 Ho was arrested in Hong Kong and spent some time in prison. Upon his release, he continued organizing uprisings against the French from hideouts in southern China.

During World War II (1939–45), France suffered a series of military defeats and surrendered to Germany. Unable to protect its colonies in Indochina, the French government allowed Japan to occupy Vietnam and set up military bases there in 1940. The following year, Ho returned to Vietnam for the first time in many years. He and other nationalists viewed the Japanese occupation as an opportunity to regain control of the country from France.

At this time, Ho and his supporters formed the Vietnam Doc Lap Dong Minh Hoa (League for the Independence of Vietnam). This Communist-led nationalist group, usually known by the shortened name Viet Minh, was determined to fight for Vietnamese independence from both the French and the Japanese. In order to attract support from the broadest range of people, they downplayed their Communist roots and instead emphasized the ideals of patriotism and freedom from foreign control. The Viet Minh helped the American forces that were fighting against the Japanese during World War II. They hoped that the U.S. government would reward their efforts by supporting their bid for independence.

In 1945 the Allied forces (which mainly consisted of the United States, Great Britain, and the Soviet Union) defeated both Germany and Japan to win World War II. As soon as Japan was defeated, the Viet Minh launched a revolution to regain control of Vietnam. This so-called August Revolution was successful, as the Viet Minh took control of large areas of the country. In September 1945 Ho formally declared Vietnam's independence from both the French and the Japanese. He announced that the nation would be known as the Democratic Republic of Vietnam, with a capital in the northern city of Hanoi. He also stated that he would serve as the first president of the newly independent nation.

But it soon became clear that France—which had suffered a great deal of damage to its land, economy, and reputation as a world leader during World War II—was not willing to give up its former colony. After a year of negotiations between Ho and the French government, war erupted between the French and the Viet Minh in late 1946. Nine years later, the

Ho Chi Minh was a beloved symbol of patriotism and freedom to the North Vietnamese people.
Reproduced by permission of AP/Wide World Photos.

Ho Chi Minh Complains about U.S. Interference in Vietnam's Affairs

In 1950 the United States provided military aid to France in its war against the Viet Minh. This decision infuriated Viet Minh leader Ho Chi Minh. In the following excerpt from a 1950 interview, Ho charges that America's decision was part of a U.S. plot to gain control of Vietnam and the other nations of Indochina (Cambodia and Laos):

The U.S. imperialists [people who try to establish authority over other nations] have of late openly interfered in Indochina's affairs. It is with their money and weapons and their instructions that the French colonialists have been waging war in Viet-Nam, Cambodia, and Laos.

However, the U.S. imperialists are intensifying their plot to discard the French colonialists so as to gain complete control over Indochina. That is why they do their utmost to redouble their direct intervention in every field—military, political, and economic . . . . The U.S. imperialists supply

their henchmen [thugs] with armaments [weapons] to massacre the Indochinese people. They dump their goods in Indochina to prevent the development of local handicrafts. Their pornographic culture contaminates the youth in areas placed under their control. They follow the policy of buying up, deluding [fooling], and dividing our people. They drag some bad elements into becoming their tools and use them to invade our country . . . .

To gain independence, we, the Indochinese people, must defeat the French colonialists, our number one enemy. At the same time, we will struggle against the U.S. interventionists. The deeper their interference, the more powerful are our solidarity [unity] and our struggle. We will expose their maneuvers before all our people, especially those living in areas under their control. We will expose all those who serve as lackeys [servants] for the U.S. imperialists to coerce, deceive, and divide our people . . . . We are still laboring under great difficulties but victory will certainly be ours.

Viet Minh finally defeated the French. The Geneva Accords of 1954, which ended the Indochina War, divided Vietnam into two sections. Ho Chi Minh and his Communist government led the northern section, which was officially known as the Democratic Republic of Vietnam but was usually called North Vietnam. The southern section, which was known as the Republic of South Vietnam, was led by a U.S.-supported government under Ngo Dinh Diem (see entry).

The peace agreement provided for nationwide free elections to be held in 1956, with a goal of reuniting the two sections of Vietnam under one government. But U.S. government officials worried that holding free elections in Vietnam would bring power to Ho and the Viet Minh, who had led the nation's war for independence from France. They felt that a Communist government in Vietnam would increase the power of China and the Soviet Union and threaten the security of the United States. As a result, South Vietnamese President Diem and his American advisors refused to hold the elections.

Encourages his people during the Vietnam War

Ho and the other North Vietnamese leaders grew very angry when the elections did not take place as scheduled. They remained determined to reunite the two parts of the country under a Communist government, by force if necessary. Within a short time, a new war began between the two sections of Vietnam. North Vietnam's main weapon during the early years of this war was a group of South Vietnamese Communist rebels known as the Viet Cong. Using tactics of guerilla warfare, the Viet Cong gradually gained control of large areas of the South Vietnamese countryside.

In the late 1950s and early 1960s the U.S. government sent money, weapons, and military advisors to help South Vietnam defend itself against North Vietnam and the Viet Cong. In 1965 President Lyndon Johnson (see entry) authorized U.S. bombing missions over North Vietnam and sent American combat troops to South Vietnam. But deepening U.S. involvement failed to defeat the Communists. Instead, the Vietnam War turned into a bloody stalemate.

During the 1960s Ho's health began to fail. His role in the North Vietnamese government gradually decreased. But he remained a beloved symbol of patriotism and freedom to the North Vietnamese people. In the early years of the Vietnam War, "Uncle Ho" repeatedly expressed his determination to fight on until the Communists gained a complete victory. He characterized the war as a fight for Vietnamese independence from foreign control. He claimed that the U.S. government was controlled by imperialists (people who seek to extend their power or influence over others) who were interfering in the national affairs of Vietnam. Many Vietnamese rallied around Ho and found him to be a source of inspiration in their struggles.

Ho Chi Minh died of a heart attack on September 2, 1969, exactly twenty-four years after he had declared Vietnamese independence following World War II. He still expressed confidence in the Communists' mission at the time of his death. "Our compatriots in the North and in the South shall be reunited under the same roof," he wrote in his final statement. "We, a small nation, will have earned the unique honor of defeating, through a heroic struggle, two big imperialisms—the French and the American—and making a worthy contribution to the national liberation movement."

Ho's death in the middle of the war was a difficult blow for North Vietnam. But the Communists continued fighting. In 1975 North Vietnamese forces captured the South Vietnamese capital city of Saigon to win the Vietnam War. They finally achieved Ho's dream of reuniting the two parts of Vietnam under one Communist government. Many Vietnamese people view Ho Chi Minh as the father of Vietnamese independence, and historians have recognized his gifts as a leader, organizer, and motivator in the Vietnamese revolutionary movement.

Sources

Duiker, William J. *Ho Chi Minh*. New York: Hyperion, 2000.

Fall, Bernard B., ed. *Ho Chi Minh on Revolution: Selected Writings, 1920–1966*. New York: Praeger, 1967.

Fenn, Charles. *Ho Chi Minh: A Biographical Introduction*. New York: Scribner's, 1973.

Halberstam, David. *Ho*. New York: Random House, 1971.

Ho Chi Minh. *Against U.S. Aggression, for National Salvation*. Hanoi, Vietnam: Foreign Languages Publishing House, 1967.

Sainteny, Jean. *Ho Chi Minh and His Vietnam: A Personal Memoir*. Chicago: Cowles, 1972.

Abbie Hoffman

Born November 30, 1936
Worcester, Massachusetts
Died April 12, 1989
Bucks County, New York

American social activist and
radical political leader

A bbie Hoffman was a colorful and controversial political activist who led numerous outrageous demonstrations against the Vietnam War during the 1960s. He also cofounded the Youth International Party, or Yippies, a group that rejected many traditional elements of American society in favor of a lifestyle of "sex, drugs, and rock 'n' roll."

Early rebel

Abbot Hoffman was born November 30, 1936, in Worcester, Massachusetts. He grew up in a middle-class neighborhood with his parents, John Hoffman and Florence (Schanberg) Hoffman, and two younger siblings. In high school he was a smart but rebellious student who repeatedly got into trouble with teachers. After being expelled from his public high school, Hoffman entered Worcester Academy, a private school. He then enrolled at Brandeis University, from which he graduated in 1959. He continued his education at the University of California at Berkeley, earning a master's degree in psychology in 1960.

"I am first and foremost . . . a guy who loves action who hates the dullness of regular life."

Abbie Hoffman.
Courtesy of the Library of Congress.

Hoffman became interested in political activism during his years at Brandeis and Berkeley, and he participated in a wide array of peace and civil rights activities after returning to Worcester in 1961. "I am first and foremost as you know a guy who loves action who hates the dullness of regular life—the boredom of this fat system," he wrote to one acquaintance during this time. In 1963 he took a job as a salesman of medicine and other pharmaceutical products. But he devoted most of his free time to working on behalf of civil rights groups and other organizations that were trying to make changes in American society. In 1965 he became even more active in the civil rights movement. He traveled to the American South, where he joined the effort to end segregation (the enforced separation of people by race) and racial discrimination against black Americans.

Protesting the Vietnam War

In 1966 Hoffman's commitment to his political activities became so all-consuming that his employer fired him from his sales job. Hoffman responded by moving to New York City and devoting all of his time to political activism. At the same time, he shifted much of his activist focus to the growing war in Vietnam.

The Vietnam War was a conflict that pitted the U.S.-supported nation of South Vietnam against the Communist nation of North Vietnam and its Viet Cong allies in the South. The Viet Cong were guerrilla fighters who wanted to overthrow the South Vietnamese government and unite the two countries under one Communist government. In the late 1950s and early 1960s the United States sent money, weapons, and advisors to South Vietnam to help it fend off the Viet Cong. In 1965 President Lyndon Johnson (see entry) sent American combat troops to fight on the side of South Vietnam. But deepening U.S. involvement in the war failed to defeat the Communists. Instead, the war settled into a bloody stalemate, and the American public became bitterly divided about how to proceed in Vietnam.

After arriving in New York, Hoffman quickly emerged as a leader of the city's thriving hippie, antiestablishment culture. These people—primarily young men and women from middle-class backgrounds—rejected the economic and social foundations of American culture as spiritually corrupt. Instead, they embraced a lifestyle in which sex, drug use (especially marijuana and LSD), tolerance for others, and community sharing were all celebrated. Hoffman enjoyed being a part of this environment, but it did not affect his continued passion for social activism. In fact, he wrote in *Soon to Be a Major Motion Picture* that "I was determined to bring the hippie movement into a broader protest."

March on the Pentagon

In 1967 Hoffman organized a variety of "happenings" to protest various aspects of American society and gain publicity for the countercultural lifestyle. In April 1967 Hoffman and a few followers threw dollar bills onto the floor of the New York Stock Exchange from the visitors gallery. The action created chaos on the floor of the exchange when many of the traders stopped working in order to chase after the floating bills. Hoffman and his allies viewed the traders' response as evidence that American society was ruled by greed and selfishness. On another occasion he sent 3,000 marijuana cigarettes, with directions on how to smoke them, to randomly selected people throughout the New York area.

Hoffman became even better known to the American public in October 1967, when he participated in a huge antiwar demonstration in Washington, D.C. This protest, which had been organized by the National Mobilization Committee to End the War in Vietnam (MOBE), was scheduled to conclude with a protest march on the Pentagon, the headquarters of the Department of Defense. "There's nothing to explain about the war in Vietnam," said Hoffman. "Those days are over. The time has come for resistance."

Most of the weekend protest passed peacefully, as hundreds of thousands of antiwar Americans gathered together at the Lincoln Memorial for a rally that included music and speeches. The march on the Pentagon, however, ended up being far more chaotic. Fewer than 50,000 protestors took part in the march, but many of the march participants were radicals who liked to use confrontational tactics to express their opposition to the war. Once the marchers reached the Pentagon, they engaged in a tense standoff with U.S. troops who had been assigned to defend the facility. At one point, Hoffman led the protestors in

Jerry Rubin helped create the Youth International Party, or "Yippies," along with Abbie Hoffman.
Reproduced by permission of Archive Photos.

a highly publicized effort to use their combined mental willpower to levitate [raise] the Pentagon and rid it of evil spirits. The levitation effort failed, and violence broke out when soldiers tried to break up the demonstration. Nearly 700 people were arrested in the clash, and dozens of others were injured.

The Yippies

On January 1, 1968, Hoffman and another radical activist named Jerry Rubin announced the creation of a new group called the Youth International Party or "Yippies." Hoffman and Rubin boasted that the group had "no leaders, no members, and no organization," but in reality, they served as the group's guiding force. Over the next several months, the Yippies used a wide variety of publicity stunts to register their dissatisfaction with American society. These activities included burning money in public and nominating a pig for president.

In August 1968 the Yippies joined other antiwar demonstrators in Chicago, where the Democratic Presidential Convention was being held. They gathered in the city to rally against the party's leadership, which they blamed for the continuation of the war in Vietnam. As the convention got underway, Hoffman and other radical leaders launched a series of antiwar protests that ended in violent clashes between demonstrators and Chicago police. Televised coverage of the street battles shocked Americans all across the country, for much of the footage indicated that Chicago police reacted with excessive force and brutality. Some people blamed the demonstrators for the police violence. But Hoffman did not agree. "Being accused of inciting [starting] a police riot makes no sense at all to me," he told Tom Wells, author of *The War Within*. "A good police force cannot be incited to riot. It's just that simple."

In the months following the Chicago incident, legal authorities charged Hoffman and several other antiwar leaders with conspiracy to riot and crossing state lines to incite a riot. Their trial—known as the "Trial of the Chicago Seven"—became a national spectacle. Hoffman and the other defendants repeatedly clashed with Judge Julius J. Hoffman (who was no relation to Abbie Hoffman) during the trial, which lasted from September 1969 to February 1970. The defendants openly mocked the judge and the American justice system, and Judge Hoffman responded by issuing numerous rulings that were hostile to the defendants. At one point, he even ordered one of the defendants—Black Panther leader Bobby Seale—to be bound and gagged for his outbursts.

Hoffman and the others eventually received short jail sentences. But the trial turned the defendants into national celebrities, and Hoffman became a regular guest on television talk shows. He also established himself as a popular writer during this time, advancing his antiestablishment message in books like *Woodstock Nation* (1969) and *Steal This Book!* (1971). In 1972 his conviction in the Chicago case was overturned on appeal.

A Yippie follower of Abbie Hoffman attends an anti-Vietnam War demonstration.
Reproduced by permission of Corbis Corporation.

Controversial within the antiwar movement

By the late 1960s Hoffman had emerged as one of the most visible leaders of America's antiwar movement. But he also became very controversial during this time. Hoffman's supporters claimed that he provided energy and enthusiasm to the antiwar movement. They also argued that he had a knack for devising demonstrations and "happenings" that attracted media attention.

But some people within the antiwar movement believed that Hoffman hurt their cause. They charged that his antics made a bad impression on the millions of Americans who were still trying to decide how they felt about the war. Some critics also claimed that he was a publicity hound whose critical attitudes toward American society alienated mainstream antiwar groups and reduced the movement's overall effectiveness. These concerns eventually led some antiwar leaders to distance themselves from Hoffman and other radical protestors. For example, organizers of the October 1969 Moratorium Against the War demonstrations refused to let either Hoffman or Rubin give a speech during the event.

Hoffman continued to speak out against the war from 1969 through the early 1970s. He was arrested numerous times and was under constant surveillance from law enforcement agencies during this time. In May 1971 he suffered a broken nose at the hands of Washington, D.C., police during an antiwar demonstration in the city. After this injury, Hoffman withdrew from public view for several months.

Goes into hiding

In early 1974 Hoffman disappeared from public view after being charged with selling cocaine. He lived in hiding for the next six years, spending time in the United States, Canada, and Mexico. He suffered two nervous breakdowns during this time but always managed to avoid capture. In fact, he spent a few years living in New York state as a freelance writer named "Barry Freed." In 1976 his wife, Anita Krushner Hoffman, published some letters from Hoffman to his young son in *To america with Love: Letters from the Underground* (Hoffman and his wife named their son "america").

In 1980 Hoffman finally emerged from hiding and turned himself in to authorities. In 1981 he pleaded guilty to reduced charges and spent about a year in prison. After gaining his release, Hoffman worked as an environmental activist and supported himself by organizing speaking tours throughout the United States. On these tours Hoffman described the 1960s protest era as a very important part of American history. "In the sixties apartheid [racial segregation] was driven out of America," he said in his last public speech before he died. "We didn't end racism, but we ended legal segregation. We ended the idea that you can send a million soldiers ten thousand miles away to fight in a war that people do not support. We ended the idea that women are second-class citizens . . . . We were young, we were reckless, arrogant, silly, and headstrong—and we were right."

The 1980s proved to be an unhappy time for the activist. As the decade progressed, Hoffman expressed great frustration with the state of American politics and society. In the late 1980s he struggled with severe depression and injuries suffered in a serious car accident. In April 1989 he committed suicide by taking an overdose of drugs.

Sources

DeBenedetti, Charles, with Charles Chatfield. *An American Ordeal. The Antiwar Movement of the Vietnam Era*. Syracuse, NY: Syracuse University Press, 1990.

Farber, David. *Chicago '68*. Chicago: University of Chicago Press, 1988.

Gitlin, Todd. *The Sixties: Years of Hope, Days of Rage*. New York: Bantam Books, 1987.

Hoffman, Abbie, and Anita Hoffman. *To america with Love: Letters from the Underground*. New York: Stonehill Press, 1976.

Hoffman, Abbie. *The Best of Abbie Hoffman*. New York: Four Walls, Eight Windows, 1990.

Hoffman, Abbie. *Soon to Be a Major Motion Picture*. New York: Perigree Books, 1980.

Jezer, Marty. *Abbie Hoffman: American Rebel*. New Brunswick, NJ: Rutgers University Press, 1992.

Mailer, Norman. *Armies of the Night*. New York: New American Library, 1968.

Wells, Tom. *The War Within: America's Battle Over Vietnam*. Berkeley: University of California Press, 1994.

Lyndon B. Johnson

**Born August 27, 1908
Stonewall, Texas
Died January 22, 1973
Austin, Texas**

**Thirty-sixth president of the United States,
1963–1969**

"America can and America will meet any wider challenge from others, but our aim in Vietnam, as in the rest of the world, is to help restore the peace and to reestablish a decent order."

Lyndon B. Johnson—or "LBJ," as he was commonly known—endured one of the most difficult presidencies in American history. As successor to President John F. Kennedy (see entry) after his tragic and shocking assassination in 1963, Johnson tried to carry on Kennedy's policies. He also launched ambitious new programs of his own to address civil rights, education, and poverty problems in the United States. These programs were important parts of Johnson's dream of building a "Great Society." But the Vietnam War destroyed his presidency. He supervised America's direct entry into the conflict. But his policies failed to produce victory in Vietnam, and the war triggered great unrest throughout the United States. The unpopularity of his Vietnam policies eventually convinced Johnson to end his presidency voluntarily, as he refused to run for reelection in 1968.

A Texas childhood

Lyndon Baines Johnson was born near Stonewall, Texas, on August 27, 1908. He and his one brother and three sisters grew up in economic circumstances that sometimes bor-

*Lyndon B. Johnson.
Reproduced by permission of AP/Wide World Photos.*

dered on poverty. Their father, Sam Ealy Johnson, Jr., worked as a farmer, cattle trader, and local politician. Both he and his wife, Rebekah (Baines) Johnson, labored hard to provide for their family with basic necessities. This modest upbringing had a tremendous influence on Lyndon Johnson's personality. He developed a great sympathy for hardworking people who faced economic insecurity.

The Johnson family's fortunes improved in 1919, when Sam Johnson won an election returning him to the Texas state legislature after an absence of a dozen years. He eventually served five terms as a member of the state House of Representatives. As he grew older, young Lyndon became a common sight in the halls of the building where his father worked. He enjoyed being in the company of his father, but he was also fascinated with the hustle and bustle of the legislature, with its speeches, ceremonial activities, and aura of importance. This early exposure to politics made a deep and favorable impression on Johnson.

After graduating from high school in 1924, Johnson spent a couple of years working at a variety of jobs. He then enrolled at Southwest Texas State Teachers College, from which he earned a teaching degree in 1930. Before earning his degree, however, he spent a year teaching Hispanic children in Cotulla, Texas. This experience deepened his conviction that American society should do more to help its poor and disadvantaged members.

Enters the world of politics

Johnson taught briefly in the Texas school system in the 1930s. But he was soon drawn to the political world that had charmed him since childhood. In 1931 Johnson became a special assistant to Texas Congressman Richard Kleberg. He devoted the next four years to learning all that he could about the lawmaking process and political strategy. He also became friendly with several influential lawmakers, including Speaker of the House Sam Rayburn, a fellow Texan. In 1934 Johnson married Claudia Alta "Lady Bird" Taylor, the daughter of a prominent Texas businessman.

Meanwhile, America struggled in the grip of the Great Depression. This was a grim period of factory closings, farm failures, and high unemployment that swept through the United States and the rest of the world in the 1930s. Before long, Johnson became directly involved in U.S. government efforts to combat this terrible economic downturn. In 1935 President Franklin D. Roosevelt appointed Johnson to direct the Texas office of the National Youth Administration (NYA). This agency was established to provide jobs and vocational training to unemployed youths. Johnson excelled in this challenging position. He put together a program that successfully placed thousands of young Texans in jobs building new roads and schools.

After two years with the NYA, Johnson moved on to the U.S. House of Representatives. He defeated a crowded field of contenders to win an open seat in the legislature in 1937. Upon assuming office, Johnson took advantage of his familiarity with the legislative process and his friendships with key lawmakers to make himself a powerful presence in Washington, D.C. He held the seat until 1948, winning reelection six straight times. During that period, Johnson became known as a steady Roosevelt ally and an effective lawmaker who successfully channeled many federal programs and funds to his home district. He also served in the U.S. Navy for six months during World War II, but in July 1942 Roosevelt ordered Johnson and all other members of Congress to return to their lawmaking duties.

An impressive career in the Senate

In 1948 Johnson switched to the U.S. Senate. At this time, Texas was a strongly Democratic state, and everyone knew that the Democratic nominee for the Senate would win the general election. Johnson mounted a strong campaign for his party's nomination, and he earned the spot by a margin of eighty-seven votes (out of nearly one million votes cast) over his nearest competitor.

Johnson quickly gained a reputation as one of the Senate's most energetic and effective members. In 1951 his fellow Democrats elected him "party whip," an important leadership position within the party. Four years later, the Democrats took control of the Senate, and Johnson became the youngest majority leader in the nation's history. A heart attack in 1955 temporarily slowed him down, but he returned to his leadership position within a matter of weeks. He remained the Senate's majority leader until January 1961, when he was sworn in as President John F. Kennedy's vice president.

During Johnson's Senate career, some observers criticized him for making excessive compromises and bargains with other lawmakers in order to get laws passed. But many other legislators praised him for his knowledge of Senate rules, his ability to guide bills into law, and his dedication (he sometimes forced the Senate to work late into the night to conclude important business). He also became known as a strong anti-Communist and, after 1957, as a supporter of early civil rights legislation.

Kennedy's vice president

In 1960 Democratic presidential nominee John F. Kennedy invited Johnson to be his running mate in the upcoming fall elections. Johnson accepted the offer, even though he was disappointed that he had not been able to secure the presidential nomination for himself. In November 1960 Kennedy defeated his Republican opponent, Richard M. Nixon (see entry), to win the presidency. Many historians believe that Kennedy's decision to make Johnson his vice-presidential choice helped lift the Democrats to victory in several important Southern states.

Johnson served as vice president from January 1961 to November 1963. During that time, he remained loyal to Kennedy, who responded by giving Johnson a number of important responsibilities. For example, he served as chairman of the National Aeronautics and Space Council, which was in charge of America's new space program. Johnson also chaired the President's Committee on Equal Employment Opportunity, which worked to eliminate discrimination in hiring practices at the federal level.

As time passed, however, the former Texas senator found many aspects of his new job to be quite frustrating. He got along well with Kennedy, but clashed with many of the president's key advisors. These officials had little in common with Johnson and were not sure that he truly supported Kennedy's policies. In addition, Johnson felt less useful as vice president than he had as a leader of the Senate.

Lyndon Johnson signs the 1964 Civil Rights Act into law.
Reproduced by permission of Corbis Corporation.

Kennedy is assassinated

Johnson's days as vice president ended suddenly on November 22, 1963, when Kennedy was assassinated while riding in a motorcade (a ceremonial parade of automobiles) through Dallas, Texas. Johnson was riding two cars behind the president when he was shot and killed. The death of Kennedy meant that Johnson was now the president of the United States.

Kennedy's violent death stunned the nation, but Johnson acted decisively to reassure the American people that the government's leadership remained in capable hands. He announced that he would retain key members of the Kennedy administration in the Johnson White House and declared his intention to work hard to fulfill Kennedy's major policy goals. Most importantly, Johnson behaved in a calm and steady manner that encouraged people throughout the mourning nation.

Over the next year, Johnson kept his promise to guide many of Kennedy's policy proposals into law. The most impor-

152   Vietnam War: Biographies

tant of these was the 1964 Civil Rights Act, which forbade employers, hotels, restaurants, and other public businesses from discriminating against blacks and other minorities. But Johnson also signed notable laws designed to improve education, economic opportunity, and community health in poor areas of America.

Johnson defeats Goldwater

In November 1964 Johnson easily defeated Republican presidential nominee Barry Goldwater (see entry) to win another four years in the White House. Many Americans voted for Johnson because they liked his vision of the country's future. "We have the opportunity to move not only toward the rich society and the powerful society, but upward to the Great Society," he declared in a May 22, 1964, speech at the University of Michigan. "The Great Society rests on abundance and liberty for all. It demands an end to poverty and injustice, to which we are totally committed in our time."

But Johnson's landslide triumph was also due in part to doubts about Goldwater's temperament. Many voters feared that Goldwater's fierce anti-Communist feelings might lead him to make dangerous foreign policy decisions as president. They worried that he might start a nuclear war with the Communist-led Soviet Union. They also worried that he might deepen U.S. military involvement in Vietnam, where pro- and anti-Communist factions were engaged in a war for control of the country.

Vietnam had been a colony of France until 1954, when it won its freedom after an eight-year war with the French. But the country had been divided into two sections by the 1954 Geneva peace agreement. North Vietnam was headed by a Communist government under revolutionary leader Ho Chi Minh (see entry). South Vietnam, meanwhile, was led by an anti-Communist government that talked about creating a democracy. As a result, the United States threw its support behind the South's political leadership.

The Geneva agreement provided for nationwide free elections to be held in 1956 so that the two sections of Vietnam could be united under one government. But U.S. and South Vietnamese officials refused to hold the elections because they believed that the results would give the Communists control over the entire country. American strategists

Hubert H. Humphrey (1911–1978)

Hubert Humphrey was one of the national leaders of the Democratic Party for nearly three decades, from the 1950s through his death in 1978. During that time, he built a record of distinguished public service that was highlighted by his leadership in the realm of civil rights. But the Vietnam War cast a dark shadow over his career during the 1960s. As vice president to President Lyndon Johnson, Humphrey struggled to find a balance between his loyalty to Johnson and his growing doubts about the war. And in 1968 his inability to separate himself from Johnson's unpopular Vietnam policies cost him the presidency.

Humphrey was born in Wallace, South Dakota, on May 27, 1911. He attended college at the Denver College of Pharmacy, the University of Minnesota, and Louisiana State University. In the early 1940s he taught political science at a college in Minnesota, and in 1945 he became the youngest mayor ever to lead the city of Minneapolis.

In 1948 Humphrey entered the national spotlight when he fought to add a strong civil rights position to the Democratic Party's national platform. "The time has arrived for the Democratic party to get out of the shadow of states' rights and walk forthrightly into the bright sunshine of human rights," he said. One year later, he won election to the U.S. Senate. He spent the next sixteen years representing Minnesota in the Senate, where he became known for his strong support of civil rights and education legislation.

In 1964 Humphrey agreed to serve as vice president in the Johnson administration. But his years in the Johnson White House turned out to be frustrating and unhappy ones. In 1965 Humphrey suggested that the United States call a halt to the bombing of North Vietnam and negotiate a settlement to end the war. Johnson interpreted the vice president's remarks as disloyal. In fact, he angrily excluded Humphrey from Vietnam policy discussions for the next year. Humphrey responded by becoming a vocal defender of Johnson's Vietnam strategy. But his support angered Democratic opponents of the war, and it failed to repair his relationship with Johnson. In fact, many historians have noted that the president often bullied or mistreated Humphrey.

believed if that happened, all of Southeast Asia might fall to communism, a development that would dramatically increase the strength of the Communist regimes in the Soviet Union and China.

Hubert H. Humphrey.
Reproduced by permission of AP/Wide World Photos.

In 1968 Humphrey won the Democratic nomination for the presidency. But that year's Democratic convention badly tarnished his campaign. Inside the Chicago convention hall, differences over Vietnam policy triggered bitter splits within the party. Outside, ugly and violent clashes erupted between antiwar demonstrators and Chicago police officers.

Over the next several months, Humphrey tried to close the gap between himself and his Republican opponent, Richard Nixon (see entry). This effort, though, was hindered by the independent candidacy of George Wallace, who attracted some traditional Democratic voters. Humphrey's campaign also was hurt by the fact that many voters associated him with Johnson's failed policies. Humphrey finally distanced himself from LBJ a few weeks before the election. His announcement that he was willing to scale back U.S. military involvement in Vietnam and pursue new peace talks was greeted very favorably, and the gap between Humphrey and Nixon narrowed dramatically. But Humphrey's rally fell short, as Nixon defeated him by less than one percent of the national vote.

After failing in his quest for the presidency, Humphrey returned to the Senate. He made another bid for the job in 1972, but he lost the Democratic nomination to George McGovern (see entry). In 1976 Minnesota voters returned him to the U.S. Senate, even though he had recently been diagnosed with bladder cancer. Humphrey resumed his Senate duties for a time, but his cancer gradually worsened. He died on January 13, 1978, in Waverly, Minnesota.

When the South refused to hold elections, North Vietnam and its Viet Cong (Communist guerrillas) allies in the South took up arms against the South Vietnamese government. The United States responded during the late 1950s and early 1960s by sending money, weapons, and advisors to aid in South Vietnam's defense. By late 1964, when Johnson won election, America was regularly shipping weaponry, airplanes, financial aid, and support (noncombat) personnel to the struggling nation.

Johnson dreams of building a "Great Society"

As Johnson began his first full term as president in early 1965, he worked very hard to fulfill his dream of creating a "Great Society" in the United States. In Johnson's mind, this meant that his administration needed to tackle a wide range of problems in American life, including poverty, racial discrimination, inadequate medical care, and pollution.

Armed with Democratic majorities in both the U.S. Senate and the U.S. House of Representatives and the support of the American people, Johnson guided numerous "Great Society" bills into law in 1965 and 1966. The Voting Rights Act of 1965 eliminated voting laws that discriminated against minorities. The Education Act of 1965, meanwhile, set aside additional funding to school systems, provided preschool programs for young children, and created financial aid programs and scholarships for needy college students. Another Johnson triumph was the creation of the Medicare and Medicaid programs, which provided health insurance for elderly and poor people.

In addition, Johnson emerged as a strong protector of the environment in the months following his election victory. He signed several major antipollution measures, including the Water Quality Act of 1965, the Clean Air Act of 1965, and the Clean Water Restoration Act of 1966. Finally, Johnson fulfilled his promise to declare a "War on Poverty" as president. He signed a series of laws that provided Americans in poor and minority communities with greater assistance in such areas as job training, housing, day care, and education.

Johnson's success in 1965 increased his confidence that he could successfully treat many of American society's greatest ills. He knew that eliminating poverty, prejudice, pollution, and other problems would require great determination and dedication. But he repeatedly expressed his belief that his vision of a "Great Society" was within reach. Unfortunately, the Vietnam War destroyed Johnson's dream.

President Johnson Defends American Intervention in Vietnam

Throughout his presidency, Lyndon Johnson strongly defended his decision to send American troops into Vietnam. In the following excerpt from a July 28, 1965, press conference, Johnson explained his belief that Vietnam was a key to preventing the expansion of Communism throughout Southeast Asia:

> This is a different kind of war. There are no marching armies or solemn declarations. Some citizens of South Vietnam, at times with understandable grievances, have joined in the attack on their own government. But we must not let this mask the central fact that this is really war. It is guided by North Vietnam, and it is spurred by Communist China. Its goal is to conquer the South, to defeat American power, and to extend the Asiatic dominion of communism.
>
> There are great stakes in the balance. Most of the non-Communist nations of Asia cannot, by themselves and alone, resist the growing might and the grasping ambition of Asian communism. Our power, therefore, is a very vital shield. If we are driven from the field in Vietnam, then no nation can ever again have the same confidence in American promises or in American protection.

Johnson increases the U.S. commitment in Vietnam

When Johnson first became president, he vowed to help South Vietnam defend itself from the Viet Cong. He was certain that if the United States let the Communists take over in Vietnam, then the Communist governments of China and the Soviet Union would view it as a signal that they could threaten other parts of the world without U.S. interference. "I felt sure they would *not* stay their hand," Johnson recalled in his memoir *The Vantage Point: Perspectives of the Presidency, 1963–1969*. "If we ran out on Southeast Asia, I could see trouble ahead in every part of the globe—not just in Asia but in the Middle East and in Europe, in Africa and in Latin America. I was convinced that our retreat from this challenge would open the path to World War III."

Despite increased U.S. aid, however, the situation in South Vietnam continued to worsen throughout 1964. Widespread corruption and a series of military coups took a heavy toll on the nation's political leadership and stability. Meanwhile, the Viet Cong seized control of ever-larger sections of the countryside. These grim developments convinced Johnson to increase America's military commitment in the region.

In August 1964 Johnson announced that two North Vietnamese torpedo boats had on two recent occasions attacked U.S. destroyers in the Gulf of Tonkin, an area of the South China Sea bordering Vietnam. Johnson used reports of the second attack as an excuse to expand U.S. military involvement in the conflict, even though doubts were raised about whether an attack actually took place (historians now believe that North Vietnamese forces probably did not launch a second attack). He asked Congress for a resolution that would give him authority to escalate military activity in Vietnam. The Gulf of Tonkin Resolution passed overwhelmingly.

The Gulf of Tonkin vote symbolized strong support for increased military operations in Vietnam. After all, Johnson's desire to keep South Vietnam out of Communist control was shared by a majority of lawmakers and ordinary Americans alike. But as the fall 1964 presidential election approached, he assured the nation that he would not introduce U.S. combat troops into the war. "Some others are eager to enlarge the conflict," Johnson said in August 1964. "They call upon us to supply American boys to do the job that Asian boys should do . . . . Such action would offer no solution at all to the real problem of Vietnam. America can and America will meet any wider challenge from others, but our aim in Vietnam, as in the rest of the world, is to help restore the peace and to reestablish a decent order."

Johnson sends U.S. combat troops into Vietnam

In early 1965 the situation in South Vietnam continued to deteriorate. Johnson responded by ordering a sustained bombing campaign against North Vietnam. This operation, nicknamed Rolling Thunder, started in March 1965 and continued with only brief interruptions for the next three-and-a-half years. Johnson hoped that the Rolling Thunder campaign would force the Communists to end their activities against the South. But the Viet Cong and North Vietnamese remained defiant, and in the spring of 1965 Johnson ordered American ground troops into South Vietnam. He decided that America's political interests and international reputation would not allow him to pull out of the war-torn country.

Johnson and his political and military advisors hoped that by increasing American military involvement in Vietnam, they could eliminate the Communist threat and stabilize the South Vietnamese government. But the dedicated Viet Cong and North Vietnamese forces refused to give up, and Johnson was forced to steadily increase the size of the U.S. commitment. He instituted a military draft to expand the size of the armed forces and sent thousands of American soldiers to serve in the war. In 1965 the number of American soldiers in Vietnam increased from 23,000 to 181,000. This number continued to swell throughout Johnson's term, reaching 535,000 in 1968. And still the war dragged on.

By 1966 the war had become a major problem for Johnson. Some lawmakers, advisors, and military experts assured him that he was taking the right course of action in Vietnam. But others harshly criticized his war policies. Some claimed that he needed to order more punishing military measures against North Vietnam in order to claim victory. Others argued that he should withdraw all American troops from the divided country and let the Vietnamese people decide things for themselves.

Johnson faced even greater criticism from America's antiwar movement. The membership of this movement expanded dramatically from 1965 to 1967, as Americans learned more and more about the brutal, deadly war. Antiwar protest was especially strong on college campuses, where student activists charged that the United States was waging an immoral war against the Vietnamese people. By the end of 1966, "Hey, hey, LBJ, how many kids did you kill today?" was a common chant at many antiwar rallies across the country.

Johnson struggles to pay for the war

Johnson refused to consider withdrawal from Vietnam. "The road ahead is going to be difficult," he stated in a May 1966 press conference. "There will be some 'Nervous Nellies' and some who will become frustrated and bothered and break ranks under the strain, and some will turn on their leaders, and on their country, and on our fighting men. There will be times of trial and tension in the days ahead that will exact the best that is in all of us. But I have not the slightest doubt that the courage and the dedication and the good sense of the wise American people will ultimately prevail. They will stand united until every boy is brought home safely, until the gallant people of South Vietnam have their own choice of their own government."

Johnson's decision to continue expanding America's military involvement in Vietnam soon triggered another big problem at home. The U.S. military effort cost billions of dollars in new airplanes, helicopters, military salaries, supplies, and other expenses. But Johnson refused to cut funding for his "Great Society" programs so that he could pay for the new military expenses. Instead he tried to support both his war policies and his social programs. This decision triggered an economic phenomenon known as inflation. During periods of inflation, the cost of food, clothing, and other goods and services rise sharply, making them less affordable. Johnson eventually called for tax increases so that the government could cover both its domestic and military spending. But this move failed to calm the country's economic troubles and increased the public's opposition to the war.

Years later, Johnson wrote that he felt that the nature of the Vietnam War left him without any good strategic options. "I knew from the start that I was bound to be crucified either way I moved," he told Doris Kearns, author of *Lyndon Johnson and the American Dream.* "If I left the woman I really loved—the Great Society—in order to get involved with that [terrible] war on the other side of the world, then I would lose everything at home. All my programs. All my hopes to feed the hungry and shelter the homeless. All my dreams to provide education and medical care to the browns and the blacks and the lame and the poor. But if I left that war and let the Communists take over South Vietnam, then I would be seen as a coward and my nation would be seen as an appeaser [someone who gives in or surrenders to demands]."

A crippled presidency

In 1967 Johnson continued to express public confidence about his Vietnam policies. In fact, he joined military and political officials in declaring that U.S. forces were finally on the verge of victory in Vietnam. In private, however, he expressed great frustration about the war and its impact on his presidency. Indeed, the war had become so expensive and controversial that other issues, like education and antipoverty programs, fell by the wayside. In the meantime, his efforts to persuade North Vietnam to enter into peace negotiations were repeatedly brushed aside.

Johnson also confessed to feeling anger and sadness about the deep hatred that many Americans had come to feel for him. This animosity was due not only to the Vietnam War itself, but also to Johnson's conduct. Many Americans—and almost all opponents of U.S. involvement in Vietnam—believed that Johnson had misled the public about his intentions and actions throughout the conflict. "To some extent . . . LBJ was the victim of his own considerable political acumen [skill]," said George C. Herring, author of *LBJ and Vietnam: A Different Kind of War.* "He took the nation to war so quietly, with such consummate [great] skill (and without getting a popular mandate) that when things turned sour the anger was inevitably directed at him."

In early 1968 North Vietnam launched a massive invasion of the South. This attack, called the Tet Offensive, failed to produce a lasting Communist victory. Instead, U.S. and South Vietnamese forces pushed back the enemy offensive. But Tet further increased public distrust of Johnson, for it showed that the president and other key officials had either lied or completely underestimated the strength and determination of the Communists.

On March 31, 1968, Johnson announced that he had ordered a halt to the bombing of North Vietnam. He explained that he called the halt in hopes of spurring peace discussions with the North's leadership. He then stunned the American public by announcing that he would not seek reelection in the upcoming 1968 presidential elections. He declared that he made this decision so that he could devote all of his time to ending the war in Vietnam.

Public reaction to Johnson's retirement announcement was very positive. "Johnson's colleagues, friends, and political observers unanimously viewed his decision as a positive, forward, and constructive step for national unity and

Johnson Announces His Decision Not to Seek Reelection

On March 31, 1968, President Lyndon Johnson gave a historic television address in which he announced a temporary halt to the bombing of North Vietnam. He then shocked the American people by declaring that he had decided not to seek reelection in the upcoming fall presidential elections.

Tonight I want to speak to you of peace in Vietnam and Southeast Asia.

No other question so preoccupies our people. No other dream so absorbs the 250 million human beings who live in that part of the world. No other goal motivates American policy in Southeast Asia.

For years, representatives of our government and others have traveled the world—seeking to find a basis for peace talks . . . . There is no need to delay the talks that could bring an end to this long and this bloody war.

Tonight, I renew the offer I made last August—to stop the bombardment of North Vietnam. We ask that talks begin promptly, that they be serious talks on the substance of peace. We assume that during those talks Hanoi will not take advantage of our restraint. We are prepared to move immediately toward peace through negotiations.

So, tonight, in the hope that this action will lead to early talks, I am taking the first step to de-escalate the conflict. We are reducing—substantially reducing—the present level of hostilities. And we are doing so unilaterally, and at once . . . .

Throughout my entire public career I have followed the personal philosophy that I am a free man, an American, a public servant, and a member of my party, in that

peace in Vietnam," observed Larry Berman in *Lyndon Johnson's War.* "Stepping aside brought Johnson more praise than any of his actions in the past year . . . . Johnson's decision to remove himself from the renomination race represented the ultimate recognition that the Vietnam War had become interwoven with his personality and his presidency."

Final years

During Johnson's last few months in office, he canceled the Rolling Thunder bombing campaign for good in hopes that the action would help bring peace. He left the presidency in January 1969, hopeful that ongoing negotiations might finally be bringing the vicious war to a close. But U.S. military involvement in Vietnam continued for another four

order always and only. For thirty-seven years in the service of our nation, first as a congressman, as a senator, and as vice president, and now as your president, I have put the unity of the people first. I have put it ahead of any divisive partisanship [radical support for one's own political party]. And in these times as in times before, it is true that a house divided against itself by the spirit of faction, of party, of region, of religion, of race, is a house that cannot stand.

There is division in the American house now. There is divisiveness among us all tonight. And holding the trust that is mine, as president of all the people, I cannot disregard the peril to the progress of the American people and the hope and prospect of peace for all peoples . . . .

I have concluded that I should not permit the presidency to become involved in the partisan divisions that are developing in this political years. With America's sons in the fields far away, with America's future under challenge right here at home, with our hopes and the world's hopes for peace in the balance every day, I do not believe that I should devote an hour or a day of my time to any personal partisan causes or to any duties other than the awesome duties of this office—the presidency of your country.

Accordingly, I shall not seek, and I will not accept, the nomination of my party for another term as your president.

But let men everywhere know, however, that a strong, confident, and a vigilant America stands ready tonight to seek an honorable peace—and stands ready tonight to defend an honored cause—whatever the price, whatever the burden, whatever the sacrifice that duty may require.

years, and the war itself did not end until 1975, when the Communists seized control of the South.

After leaving office, Johnson retired to his ranch in Texas. In late 1969 and early 1970 he agreed to a series of television interviews with news journalist Walter Cronkite, but he stayed out of the public eye for the most part. In 1971 he published a memoir of his White House years, called *The Vantage Point: Perspectives on the Presidency, 1963–1969*. He died on January 22, 1973, of a severe heart attack.

Sources

Berman, Larry. *Lyndon Johnson's War.* New York: W. W. Norton, 1989.

Bernstein, Irving. *Guns or Butter: The Presidency of Lyndon Johnson.* New York, 1996.

Califano, Joseph A., Jr. *The Triumph and Tragedy of Lyndon Johnson.* New York: Simon and Schuster, 1991.

Conkin, Paul K. *Big Daddy from the Pedernales: Lyndon Baines Johnson.* Boston: Twayne Publishers, 1986.

Herring, George C. *LBJ and Vietnam: A Different Kind of War.* Austin: University of Texas Press, 1994.

Johnson, Lady Bird. *A White House Diary.* New York: Holt, Rinehart and Winston, 1970.

Johnson, Lyndon B. *The Vantage Point: Perspectives of the Presidency, 1963–1969.* New York: Holt, Rinehart and Winston, 1971.

Kaye, Tony. *Lyndon B. Johnson.* New York: Chelsea House, 1987.

Kearns, Doris. *Lyndon Johnson and the American Dream.* New York: Signet Books, 1976.

John F. Kennedy

Born May 29, 1917
Brookline, Massachusetts
Died November 22, 1963
Dallas, Texas

Thirty-fifth president of the United States, 1961–1963

During his term as president of the United States in the early 1960s, John F. Kennedy became very concerned about South Vietnam's ability to withstand Communist forces and establish a stable democratic government. As a result, he approved a significant increase in American assistance to South Vietnam. He sent both financial aid and thousands of U.S. military advisors to the troubled nation. But when the administration of President Ngo Dinh Diem (see entry) refused to institute reforms to increase its popularity with the South Vietnamese people, Kennedy decided that the country needed new leadership. A few months later, a group of South Vietnamese military leaders overthrew Diem and took control of the government with the blessing of the Kennedy administration. But Kennedy's plans to work with these new leaders ended abruptly on November 22, 1963, when he was assassinated in Texas.

A childhood marked by privilege and illness

John Fitzgerald Kennedy, known as "Jack" to friends and family, was born May 29, 1917, in Brookline, Massachu-

"In the final analysis, it is [Vietnam's] war. They are the ones who have to win it or lose it. We can help them, we can give them equipment, we can send them our men out there as advisors, but they have to win it, the people of Vietnam against the Communists."

John F. Kennedy.
Courtesy of the Library of Congress.

setts. He was the second of four sons born to Joseph P. Kennedy, a wealthy businessman and diplomat, and Rose Fitzgerald Kennedy, daughter of Boston Mayor John F. Fitzgerald. As they grew older, all the Kennedy boys were taught that their financial security and social status obligated them to seek careers in which they could help guide America's future and serve its citizens.

Jack Kennedy grew up in Massachusetts and New York, where he studied at several exclusive schools. He posted average grades during his early years, but he was a natural leader who was very popular with his classmates. He was also a fine athlete, even though he suffered from a wide range of physical ailments—including scarlet fever, jaundice, whooping cough, bronchitis, asthma, appendicitis, and recurring back pain—during much of his childhood and young adulthood. Many biographers believe that Kennedy's early struggles with illness gave him a lifelong appreciation for people who displayed courage and determination in difficult circumstances.

In 1936 Kennedy enrolled at Harvard University in Cambridge, Massachusetts. He graduated four years later with a bachelor's degree in political science. During his time at Harvard, Kennedy began to take his studies more seriously. In fact, he wrote a thesis paper (a detailed research paper that must be completed in order to graduate) during his senior year that received considerable critical praise. In that paper Kennedy examined Great Britain's failure to anticipate the threat of Adolf Hitler and Germany in the years leading up to World War II (1939–45). Kennedy's thesis was so impressive that it was published later in 1940 under the title *Why England Slept*.

World War II heroism

After leaving Harvard, Kennedy volunteered for the U.S. Army. The army rejected him because of his chronic back problems, but he refused to give up on his goal of serving in the military. After completing an intense five-month training program that he devised for himself, Kennedy managed to gain acceptance into the U.S. Navy in September 1941. A few months later, in December 1941, the United States formally entered World War II after Japan bombed America's Pearl Harbor military base in Hawaii.

In early 1943 Kennedy was given command of the *PT–109*, a Navy patrol boat. He skippered the boat through the waters of the South Pacific Ocean for the next several months. On August 2, 1943, the *PT–109* was rammed and sliced in two by a Japanese destroyer while on patrol off the Solomon Islands. The attack killed two members of the boat's twelve-man crew. Kennedy and the other survivors bobbed in the wreckage for the next several hours. When rescue vessels failed to show up, Kennedy ordered everyone to swim to a small island that was about three miles away. During this difficult swim, Kennedy towed a wounded sailor by gripping a strap of the injured man's life jacket between his teeth.

After the *PT–109* crew was safely ashore, Kennedy spent the next few days swimming along a water route that was sometimes used by American ships. His efforts to gain help for his men finally paid off when he encountered friendly islanders who passed along his message to military authorities. Kennedy and his men were subsequently rescued. Kennedy received the U.S. Navy and Marine Corps Medal for heroism for his bravery and leadership during the ordeal.

Widespread press coverage of this episode made Kennedy a hero back in America. But the physical toll of the experience worsened his back problems. Troubled by terrible back pain and a bout with a tropical disease called malaria, Kennedy was transferred back to the United States in December 1943. After a lengthy hospitalization he was released, but he never returned to active combat duty. He was honorably discharged in 1945, when World War II ended.

Begins political career

After World War II, Kennedy concentrated on building a political career for himself in his native Massachusetts. A Democrat, he decided to run for the U.S. House of Representatives in a working-class district of Boston that had a large Irish Roman Catholic population. Kennedy's war hero reputation, Irish Catholic background, and friendly manner all combined to make him a formidable contender. He won the Democratic Party's nomination for the seat, and in late 1946 he cruised to victory over his Republican challenger in the general election.

Kennedy served in the House of Representatives from 1947 to 1953. During this period, he became known as a skilled and intelligent lawmaker with moderate political views. In 1952 Kennedy decided to make a bid for the U.S. Senate seat held by Republican Henry Cabot Lodge, Jr. (see entry). Using a focused and energetic campaign that relied heavily on his World War II record and his appealing personality, Kennedy achieved a narrow victory over Lodge.

Kennedy served Massachusetts as a senator for the next eight years. During that time he started a family with Jacqueline L. Bouvier, whom he married on September 12, 1953. He also wrote *Profiles in Courage* (1956), a book that told the life stories of American politicians who risked their careers by taking courageous but unpopular positions in various eras of U.S. history. In 1957 *Profiles in Courage* received the prestigious Pulitzer Prize literary award.

As his Senate career progressed, Kennedy became known to his colleagues as a bright and independent lawmaker. He regularly supported legislation that he thought would benefit the people of Massachusetts. But he also showed a willingness to support bills that might be unpopular with Massachusetts voters when he believed that the legislation was good for the nation. For example, he was the only legislator from Massachusetts who voted for President Dwight Eisenhower's proposal to build the St. Lawrence Seaway, a canal connecting the East Coast to the Great Lakes. Boston-area businesses believed that the project would hurt them because the Seaway would enable foreign ships to bypass Boston and trade far up the passageway with cities located all along the Great Lakes. But Kennedy supported the measure because he believed it would provide an economic boost to the United States as a whole.

On foreign policy issues, Kennedy held moderate views. He advocated increased aid to poor countries and became known as a tough critic of European colonialism in Asia and Africa. (Colonialism is a practice in which one country assumes political, economic, and military control over another country; many European countries established colonial governments in various regions of the world in the eighteenth and nineteenth centuries.) Like most other politicians, he also viewed the Soviet Union and other Communist nations as potentially serious threats to the United States.

With this in mind, he called for increased defense spending and urged the Eisenhower administration to work actively against communism around the world.

In 1956 Kennedy made a strong bid for the Democratic vice-presidential nomination, but he was edged out by Tennessee Senator Estes Kefauver. In 1958 Kennedy was reelected to his seat in the U.S. Senate with an amazing 74 percent of the vote. This triumph convinced the Massachusetts lawmaker to run for the presidency in the upcoming 1960 elections.

Wins the presidency

Kennedy won the 1960 Democratic presidential nomination, defeating Senator Hubert Humphrey of Minnesota and Senator Lyndon B. Johnson (see entry) of Texas. He then selected Johnson to be his vice-presidential running mate. In the general election, Kennedy faced Republican nominee Richard M. Nixon (see entry), who had been President Eisenhower's vice president.

As the fall presidential campaign progressed, Kennedy knew that he had to talk to the American people about his Roman Catholic background. The United States had never had a Catholic president before, and many political observers believed that prejudice against Catholicism might cripple his candidacy. But Kennedy reassured Protestant voters that his presidency would be based on careful analysis of the issues confronting the nation. He urged Americans to cast their votes based on the issues rather than prejudice. "If this election is decided on the basis that forty million Americans lost their chance of being president on the day they were baptized, then it is the whole nation that will be the loser in the eyes of Catholics and non-Catholics around the world, in the eyes of history, and in the eyes of our own people," he declared during one campaign speech. Kennedy's blunt discussion of his religious background reassured most American voters and contributed to his eventual victory.

As the election drew near, Kennedy's confident manner and likable personality strengthened his candidacy. In addition, his calls for increased defense spending, new medical programs, environmental protection, and expansion of the U.S. space program appealed to many voters. And on September 26, 1960, Kennedy scored a dramatic victory over Nixon in America's first-ever nationally televised presidential debate. As the debate progressed, Kennedy showed that he was knowledgeable about the issues that concerned American voters. Even more importantly, he looked relaxed and confident on the television screen. Nixon, on the other hand, looked pale and grumpy. Many historians believe that the contrast in appearance between the two candidates ultimately convinced many voters to support Kennedy.

Kennedy and the "Cold War"

On November 8, 1960, Kennedy barely defeated Nixon in the national election to become the thirty-fifth president of the United States. His victory made him the youngest person ever elected president.

As Kennedy prepared to take office, he convinced many of the country's brightest young executives and scholars to join his administration. He also made it clear that the United States would continue to play a vital role in world affairs during his administration. "Let every nation know, whether it wishes us well or ill, that we shall pay any price, bear any burden, meet any hardship, support any friend, oppose any foe in order to assure the survival and success of liberty," he stated in his January 20, 1961, inauguration speech. "In the long history of the world, only a few generations have been granted the role of defending freedom in its hour of maximum danger. I do not shrink from this responsibility. I welcome it. I do not believe that any of us would exchange places with any other people or any other generation. The energy, the faith, the devotion which we bring to this endeavor will light our country and all who serve it—and the glow from that fire can truly light the world."

During the first two years of Kennedy's presidency, the "Cold War"—an intense rivalry between the United States and the Soviet Union, the world's leading Communist power—dominated the young president's attention. During this time, the Kennedy administration engaged in a number of tense confrontations with the Soviets. The most serious crisis occurred in October 1962, when the United States learned that the Soviet Union was installing nuclear missiles in Cuba, a country located ninety miles off the coast of Florida. This move greatly alarmed the United States because the missile bases would give the Soviets the ability to strike targets all across America.

Kennedy responded to the crisis by ordering a naval blockade of Cuba and initiating secret negotiations with Soviet leader Nikita Khrushchev. During these talks, Kennedy combined diplomacy and patience with a stern message that he was willing to use military force to defend U.S. interests. After thirteen tense days, the Soviet Union agreed to remove the missiles from Cuba. In exchange, the United States promised not to take up arms against Cuba's Communist government and agreed to remove some missiles from Turkey.

Kennedy and Vietnam

Episodes such as the "Cuban Missile Crisis" further convinced Kennedy and most other American lawmakers and officials that communism posed a serious threat to the United States. As a result, America became even more determined to keep the young Southeast Asian nation of South Vietnam out of Communist hands.

South Vietnam had been created in 1954 by the Geneva Peace Accords, which had ended French colonial rule in Vietnam. Under this treaty, Vietnam was temporarily divided into Communist-led North Vietnam and U.S.-supported South Vietnam. The treaty included an agreement that these two sections of Vietnam would be united under one government by national elections to be held in 1956. But South Vietnam and the United States refused to honor this part of the agreement because they feared that the Communists—who had led the fight to end French rule—would win the elections. As a result, North Vietnam and South Vietnamese guerrillas known as the Viet Cong joined together to overthrow South Vietnam and reunite the country under one Communist government.

From 1961 to 1963, the Kennedy administration poured financial aid and governmental advisors into South Vietnam in an effort to help the new nation establish a strong economy and a democratic government. Kennedy also increased the number of U.S. military advisors in South Vietnam from 700 to 15,000 in hopes that they could help stamp out the Communist threat.

Despite massive U.S. assistance, however, the situation in South Vietnam continued to deteriorate. President Ngo Dinh Diem led a government that was terribly corrupt and unpopular, but he refused to make reforms that might increase support for his regime. In fact, Diem approved brutal crackdowns against Buddhists and other citizens who protested against his government's unfair policies and corrupt practices. In addition, Diem and his military leaders were unable or unwilling to mount any effective measures to stop the Viet Cong guerrillas that roamed South Vietnam's countryside. By mid-1963 the ineffectiveness of the South's military and the unpopularity of the Diem regime had enabled the Viet Cong to gain control over large regions of the country.

In May 1963 South Vietnamese forces opened fire on unarmed Buddhist demonstrators in the city of Hue. This murderous police action convinced Kennedy that Diem was more interested in maintaining his political power than in rallying the South Vietnamese people against the Communist threat. As a result, the Kennedy administration secretly told several South Vietnamese generals that it would prefer to see new leadership in South Vietnam. Assured that the United States would not interfere in a coup attempt, the generals seized control of the government from Diem in November 1963. Kennedy reacted favorably to the coup, although he was reportedly shocked to learn that Diem and his brother were executed after their capture.

Kennedy is assassinated

On November 22, 1963, Kennedy was shot and killed while riding in a motorcade through Dallas, Texas. A man named Lee Harvey Oswald was quickly arrested for the murder, but he was himself killed on November 24 by Jack Ruby, a nightclub owner who was reportedly outraged over Kennedy's death. A government investigation led by Chief Supreme Court Justice Earl Warren later determined that Oswald acted alone, but many Americans remain suspicious that other people were involved in the assassination.

Kennedy's sudden and violent death shocked America and the world. It triggered a period of intense national mourning and helped create an enduring image of Kennedy as a romantic figure who was unfairly taken from his country just as he was about to guide America into a new era of prosperity. After Kennedy's death, vice president Lyndon B. Johnson was sworn in as the new president of the United States. As president from 1963 to 1969, Johnson supervised a dramatic escalation in U.S. involvement in the Vietnam War.

Many Americans have wondered how the conflict in Vietnam would have unfolded had Kennedy remained alive. Some historians believe that he would not have approved the commitment of U.S. ground troops into Vietnam (more than 58,000 American soldiers eventually died in the war). They note that Kennedy refused to approve direct U.S. military action against the Viet Cong or North Vietnam during his presidency. They also point out that less than two months before his death, Kennedy stated that "in the final analysis, it is their war. They are the ones who have to win it or lose it. We can help them, we can give them equipment, we can send them our men out there as advisors, but they have to win it, the people of Vietnam against the Communists." Finally, some former aides have claimed that Kennedy planned to end U.S. involvement in Vietnam if he had been reelected in 1964.

But other scholars believe that American involvement in Vietnam probably would have increased under Kennedy. They argue that Kennedy remained staunchly anti-Communist at the time of his death. In addition, they note that Kennedy's closest advisors were the same men who counseled President Johnson to expand U.S. involvement in Vietnam during the mid-1960s.

Sources

Halberstam, David. *The Making of a Quagmire: America and Vietnam during the Kennedy Era.* Rev. ed. New York: Knopf, 1988.

Hammer, Ellen J. *A Death in November: America in Vietnam, 1963.* New York: Oxford University Press, 1987.

Manchester, William. *Portrait of a President: JFK in Profile.* Boston: Little, Brown, 1967.

Newman, John M. *JFK and Vietnam: Deception, Intrigue, and the Struggle for Power.* New York: Warner Books, 1992

Schlesinger, Arthur, Jr. *A Thousand Days: John F. Kennedy in the White House.* Boston: Houghton Mifflin, 1965.

Sorenson, Theodore. *The Kennedy Legacy.* New York: Macmillan, 1969.

Robert F. Kennedy

Born November 20, 1925
Brookline, Massachusetts
Died June 6, 1968
Los Angeles, California

U.S. attorney general, 1961–1964; U.S. senator
from Washington, D.C., 1964–1968

"I am concerned that, at the end of it all, there will only be more Americans killed, more of our treasure spilled out; and . . . more hundreds of thousands of Vietnamese slaughtered . . . ."

Robert F. Kennedy.
Courtesy of the Library of Congress.

Robert F. Kennedy was a close advisor to President John F. Kennedy (his older brother; see entry) in the early 1960s, and he emerged as a powerful force in American politics in his own right as the decade unfolded. By 1968 Kennedy's strong criticism of U.S. involvement in the Vietnam War and America's high regard for his family established him as a leading presidential candidate. But his bid for the Democratic nomination for the presidency ended in June 1968, when he fell to an assassin's bullet, just as his brother had five years earlier.

Part of a famous family

Robert Francis Kennedy was born November 20, 1925, in Brookline, Massachusetts. He was the seventh of nine children born to Joseph Patrick Kennedy, Sr., a wealthy business executive who served for a time as U.S. ambassador to Great Britain, and Rose Fitzgerald Kennedy. As he grew up, Robert—or "Bobby," as he was often called—was sometimes overshadowed by his older brothers, Joseph Jr., and John, and his famous father. But rather than meekly accept this position, he developed into a fiercely competitive and ambitious young man.

In 1936 Joseph Kennedy, Sr., was named ambassador to Great Britain, and he moved his family to London. When World War II (1939–45) broke out three years later, however, he sent his family back to the United States. After graduating from prep school, Kennedy enrolled at Harvard University in Massachusetts in 1944. A short time later, however, his oldest brother Joe was killed while flying a bombing mission over Germany. Bobby Kennedy subsequently left Harvard and joined the U.S. Navy, where he became a lieutenant. He served in the Navy until World War II ended a year later.

In 1946 Kennedy resumed his studies at Harvard, earning a bachelor of arts degree two years later. In 1950 he married Ethel Skakel, with whom he eventually had eleven children. The last of these children was born after Kennedy's death in 1968. In 1951 he graduated from the University of Virginia with a law degree.

Special counsel for the government

After earning his law degree, Kennedy became an attorney with the Criminal Division of the U.S. Department of Justice. He resigned a year later, though, in order to manage John F. Kennedy's successful U.S. Senate campaign. In 1953 Robert Kennedy returned to law, accepting a position as a special counsel (lawyer) for Senator Joseph McCarthy's famous committee on "un-American activities."

McCarthy was one of the most famous political figures in America in the early 1950s. During this time, he charged that many Americans—including some employees of the State Department—were Communist sympathizers. These charges were very serious, for Communism was a political philosophy, favored by the Soviet Union, that alarmed most Americans. McCarthy subsequently led Senate investigations into alleged Communist activities in the United States.

Robert Kennedy was a firm anti-Communist, but he and many other Americans became concerned about McCarthy's bullying probe. They felt that his threatening methods and stern warnings about Communist spies were creating an atmosphere of fear and distrust in communities all across the country. Finally, Democratic members of McCarthy's committee walked out of the hearings to protest his methods. Kennedy resigned from the committee a short time later in support of their action. McCarthy, meanwhile, was formally censured (severely criticized) by the U.S. Senate for his actions, and he soon faded from public prominence.

Attorney general in the Kennedy White House

In 1954 Kennedy became a special counsel for the Democrats in the U.S. Senate. Three years later, he was named chief counsel to the Senate Select Committee on Improper Activities in Labor and Management. Kennedy and his staff of sixty-five soon launched a major investigation into corruption in the International Brotherhood of Teamsters, a powerful labor union. During the ensuing investigation, Kennedy helped expose a variety of criminal activities within the union. He also repeatedly clashed with Teamster leader James Hoffa, who was later imprisoned for misusing union funds and jury tampering. The battles between Kennedy and Hoffa received extensive coverage across the country and earned the young attorney a reputation as a crusading crime fighter.

In 1960 Kennedy returned to politics, managing his brother's successful presidential campaign victory over Republican nominee Richard Nixon (see entry). After the election, John Kennedy asked his brother to join his administration as attorney general, the highest law enforcement office in the United States. Robert accepted the offer, even though it was harshly criticized by some observers as "nepotism" (favoritism shown by a powerful politician or executive to close friends or relatives).

Robert Kennedy ignored those who criticized his appointment, concentrating instead on fulfilling the duties of his office. Over the next few years, he aggressively pursued investigations against organized crime organizations. He also used his position to protect civil rights activists who were working to end discriminatory laws and practices against blacks in the American South and across the country. His efforts in this area earned him a reputation as an early supporter of the civil rights movement.

Kennedy proved to be an effective attorney general. But he became even better known for the very close relationship he had with his brother. In fact, he emerged as President Kennedy's most trusted advisor on both domestic and foreign policy issues. In recognition of Kennedy's influence in the White House, reporters even began describing him as an unofficial "assistant president."

Robert Kennedy and Vietnam

One foreign policy issue that concerned both of the Kennedys in the early 1960s was the troubled state of South Vietnam. This nation had been created in 1954 by the Geneva Peace Accords, which ended French colonial rule in Vietnam. Under this treaty, Vietnam was temporarily divided into Communist-led North Vietnam and U.S.-supported South Vietnam. The treaty included an agreement that these two sections of Vietnam would be united under one government by national elections to be held in 1956. But South Vietnam and the United States refused to honor this part of the agreement because they feared that the Communists would be victorious and gain control over the entire country. As a result, North Vietnam and South Vietnamese guerrillas known as the Viet Cong joined together to overthrow South Vietnam and reunite the country under one Communist government.

From 1961 to 1963 the Kennedy administration's involvement in Vietnam increased dramatically. It sent big packages of financial aid and thousands of military advisors and public officials to South Vietnam in an effort to help the new nation establish a strong economy and a democratic government. Robert Kennedy fully supported his brother's decision to provide military and financial aid to South Vietnam. But despite this assistance, the government continued to suffer from widespread corruption, political instability, and a lack of popular support.

Becomes senator after his brother's assassination

On November 22, 1963, President Kennedy was assassinated in Dallas, Texas. His violent death shocked the American people and plunged Robert Kennedy into an extended period of mourning and depression. He continued to serve as attorney general under new president Lyndon B. Johnson (see entry), however, until September 1964. At that time, he resigned to run for a U.S. Senate seat in New York as a Democrat.

Kennedy's campaign for the U.S. Senate was successful, and over the next few years he became known as one of Washington, D.C.'s most outspoken and serious-minded senators. He built a strong record as a lawmaker with a special interest in ending poverty and discrimination in America. In fact, Kennedy became known as a tireless advocate for blacks, migrant farm workers, Native Americans, and other politically powerless Americans at a time when few other politicians pursued these causes.

When Kennedy first became a senator, he expressed support for President Lyndon Johnson and many of his policies. Johnson was a fellow Democrat who shared Kennedy's convictions that the government needed to address poverty, racism, poor schools, and other problems in American society. But the relationship between Johnson and Kennedy soon became strained. Johnson knew that many Americans looked favorably upon Kennedy. They respected his record of public service and associated him with his slain brother, whom they continued to mourn. These factors led Johnson to view Kennedy as a potential political threat to his leadership of the country and the Democratic Party.

Kennedy, meanwhile, became concerned about Johnson administration policies in a number of areas, most notably Vietnam. In 1965 Johnson had ordered a massive escalation of U.S. military involvement in Vietnam. He sent American ground troops to fight in the war and approved major bombing campaigns against North Vietnam. When these steps failed to defeat the Communists, he poured additional soldiers, weapons, and money into the conflict. But the North Vietnamese and their Viet Cong allies continued to resist, and by 1967 the war had become a grim "battle of attrition" (a fight that continues until one side gives up out of exhaustion).

Speaks out against the war

In 1965 and 1966 Kennedy expressed growing concern about the Vietnam War's toll on both the American and the Vietnamese people. He also voiced doubts about South Vietnam's political leadership and the effectiveness of U.S. military strategies. But he refrained from publicly criticizing the Johnson administration's conduct of the war until February 1966. At that time, he called for a negotiated settlement to the war.

In 1967 Kennedy began to criticize Johnson's Vietnam policies more frequently. By this time, he had come to believe that the administration's decision to use massive air strikes and ground troops to overpower North Vietnam was an immoral and ineffective policy, and that the war was wasting the lives of thousands of young American soldiers. Finally, Kennedy saw that continued U.S. involvement in the conflict was creating deep and bitter divisions in many areas of American society. These factors convinced Kennedy that "the time has come to take a new look at the war in Vietnam."

Kennedy's outspoken criticism of the war continued into early 1968. In March he gave a speech at Kansas State University in which he urged Johnson to end the war before all of Vietnam was destroyed: "I am concerned that, at the end of it all, there will only be more Americans killed, more of our treasure spilled out; and because of the bitterness and hatred on every side of this war, more hundreds of thousands of Vietnamese slaughtered, so that they may say, as Tacitus said of Rome: 'They made a desert, and called it peace.'"

Launches campaign for the presidency

By early 1968 the uproar over the Vietnam War had badly damaged Johnson's presidency. On March 31, 1968, he announced that he was not going to run for reelection. This stunning decision convinced Kennedy to run for the Democratic Party's presidential nomination. His leading opponents for the nomination were Minnesota Senator Eugene McCarthy and Vice President Hubert Humphrey.

Kennedy was a strong candidate, although he was not popular with all Americans. Many whites in the South disliked him for his support for civil rights, and some business leaders and middle-class Democrats thought that he was too liberal. But his candidacy received enthusiastic support among blacks and Catholics, some antiwar Americans, and younger Americans. Over the next few months, Kennedy traveled around the country to talk about the issues that concerned him. He vowed to end American involvement in Vietnam, reduce crime, and improve the lives of the nation's poor. His emotional message drew huge crowds and convinced many political observers that he would eventually win his party's nomination. On June 5, 1968, though, Kennedy was shot by an assassin in a Los

Angeles hotel, only hours after learning that he had won the all-important California Democratic primary (a special election held by political parties to select candidates for political office). One day later, he died of his wounds. He was later buried at Arlington National Cemetery in Virginia, approximately fifty feet from the grave of his brother John.

Robert Kennedy's violent death plunged the United States into another period of national mourning. It also contributed to the widespread feeling that differences over Vietnam and other issues seemed to be tearing the country apart. Finally, his assassination triggered genuine despair among many Americans who had seen Kennedy as the nation's best hope for ending the war and bringing the country back together again.

Sources

Halberstam, David. *The Unfinished Odyssey of Robert Kennedy.* New York: Random House, 1969.

Hilty, James W. *Robert Kennedy, Brother Protector.* Philadelphia: Temple University Press, 1997.

Kennedy, Robert F. *To Seek a Newer World.* Garden City, NY: Doubleday, 1967.

Schlesinger, Arthur M., Jr. *Robert Kennedy and His Times.* 1978.

Sorenson, Theodore C. *The Kennedy Legacy.* New York: Macmillan, 1969.

Steel, Ronald. *In Love with Night: The American Romance with Robert Kennedy.* New York: Simon and Schuster, 2000.

Vanden Heuvel, William J. *On His Own: Robert F. Kennedy, 1964–1968.* Garden City, NY: Doubleday, 1970.

Martin Luther King, Jr.

Born January 15, 1929
Atlanta, Georgia
Died April 4, 1968
Memphis, Tennessee

American civil rights leader

M artin Luther King, Jr., was America's most influential leader in the civil rights movement of the 1950s and 1960s. His campaign of nonviolent protest helped usher in a new era of equality and opportunity for blacks and other minorities across America. But King's deep desire to bring about peace and social justice in the United States and around the world also led him to turn his attention to the Vietnam War. In fact, by 1967 he had become an outspoken critic of American involvement in Vietnam. He charged that U.S. military policies in the war-torn country were immoral, and claimed that the war had terrible economic and social consequences for America's black communities. King's stand was bitterly criticized by Americans who supported the war and even by some members of the civil rights movement. But the civil rights leader maintained his public opposition to the Vietnam War until his death in April 1968.

"The bombs in Vietnam explode at home; they destroy hopes and possibilities for a decent America."

Religious upbringing leads to the ministry

Martin Luther King, Jr., was born January 15, 1929, in Atlanta, Georgia. He was the oldest son of Martin Luther King,

Martin Luther King, Jr.
National Archives and Records Administration.

Sr., a minister at Atlanta's Ebenezer Baptist Church, and Alberta Williams King. As a youngster, King attended local schools in which students were legally segregated (separated) by race. This system of segregation, which extended into all areas of American society, discriminated against blacks and placed them in an inferior position.

King was an excellent student who took a great interest in the world around him. He enrolled at Georgia's Morehouse College when he was fifteen years old and graduated four years later with a bachelor's degree in sociology. During this same time, he was ordained as a Baptist minister. After leaving Morehouse, he continued his education at Crozer Theological Seminary in Pennsylvania, where he earned a master's degree in theology in 1951. From there he went to Boston University, where he met Coretta Scott. They married in 1954 and eventually had four children. King, meanwhile, secured his doctoral degree in theology from Boston University in 1955.

During King's years in school, he developed a great belief in the power of nonviolent protest as a tool to bring about change in American society. By 1954, when he became minister of the Dexter Avenue Baptist Church in Montgomery, Alabama, he had become convinced that nonviolent protests could be used to combat segregation and other forms of racism in America.

Becomes a prominent civil rights activist

King's involvement in the American civil rights movement began in 1955, when a black woman from Montgomery named Rosa Parks was arrested and jailed after she refused to give up her bus seat to a white passenger. The National Association for the Advancement of Colored People (NAACP) quickly organized a boycott (a refusal to use as a means of protest) of the city bus service among the city's black community. NAACP leaders then selected King, who was already known as an inspiring public speaker, to lead the boycott effort.

The Montgomery bus boycott lasted until November 1956, when the U.S. Supreme Court upheld a ruling that called for the city's bus service to be desegregated. This triumph delighted blacks across the South and vaulted King into national prominence. In fact, his eloquent speeches against racial injustice energized Southern blacks and brought many new faces into the still-developing civil rights movement. Moreover, King's bravery in the face of threats and violence (his home was bombed during the boycott) and his ability to link racial justice with Christian ideals helped the movement gain support among whites outside the South.

In 1957 King and other civil rights leaders founded the Southern Christian Leadership Conference (SCLC), an organization of black churches and ministers dedicated to gaining equal rights for blacks in American society. As the SCLC's most prominent member, King helped shape the group's philosophy of nonviolent protest, which took the form of demonstrations, marches, and boycotts. His frequent speeches on racism and social justice, meanwhile, solidified his status as the civil rights movement's most influential and inspiring spokesman.

Leads marches in Birmingham and Washington, D.C.

During the early 1960s the civil rights movement developed into a powerful force in American society. Civil rights demonstrations such as the May 1963 march in Birmingham, Alabama—in which city authorities brutally attacked peaceful demonstrators (including children) with police dogs, clubs, and high-pressure water hoses—triggered shock and anger in both black and white communities across much of the country. This violence, combined with King's powerful defense of the movement's goals, further increased support for the SCLC and forced the U.S. government to turn its attention to the issue of racial justice.

In August 1963, the civil rights movement held a massive rally in Washington, D.C. During this gathering, which attracted hundreds of thousands of black and white civil rights supporters, King delivered his most famous speech. In this address, commonly known as his "I Have a Dream" speech, King eloquently explained the basic goal that motivated the entire movement: "I have a dream that my four little children will one day live in a nation where they will not be judged by the color of their skin but by the content of their character," he stated.

In 1964 the U.S. government finally began changing some of the laws that had victimized blacks and other minorities for so many years. It passed the Civil Rights Act of 1964, which ended segregation in public places and forbade discrimination in schools and businesses. King received the Nobel Peace Prize in recognition of his key role in guiding this historic legislation into law.

But other racist laws remained in effect, especially in the South, and King and his allies continued their fight. They held numerous rallies and protest marches to publicize their cause and to highlight the problems of poverty and despair that affected many black communities. In 1965 these activities resulted in additional civil rights legislation. The most important of these new laws was the Voting Rights Act of 1965, which barred states from using voter qualification tests that discriminated against blacks.

Martin Luther King and Vietnam

After the passage of the Voting Rights Act, King remained devoted to improving the lives of blacks across the country. He knew that despite the passage of laws that ended discrimination, years of inferior education and limited economic opportunities had plunged many black communities into poverty. With this in mind, he called for the United States to institute new social programs to help black families improve their lives.

President Lyndon B. Johnson (see entry) supported King's calls for economic justice. In fact, Johnson had signed both the Civil Rights Act and the Voting Rights Act into law, and he talked about using new social programs to build a "Great Society" in America. But in 1965 and 1966 King began to see the United States's growing involvement in the Vietnam War as a potential threat to the future of black America and the moral well-being of the country as a whole.

The Vietnam War was a conflict that pitted the U.S.-supported nation of South Vietnam against the Communist nation of North Vietnam and its Viet Cong allies in the South. The Viet Cong were guerrilla fighters who wanted to overthrow the South Vietnamese government and unite the two countries under one Communist government. In the late 1950s and early 1960s the United States sent money, weapons, and advisors to South Vietnam to help it fend off the Viet Cong. In 1965 the

United States began using thousands of American combat troops and extensive air bombing missions to crush the Communists. But deepening U.S. involvement in the war failed to defeat the Viet Cong or the North Vietnamese. Instead, the war settled into a bloody stalemate that claimed the lives of thousands of young American troops and divided communities all across the United States.

President Johnson's decision to begin bombing North Vietnam in 1965 greatly bothered King. As the civil rights leader studied the history of American involvement in the conflict, he determined that U.S. policies toward Vietnam had been "morally and politically wrong" for years. He also concluded that the money spent waging war in Vietnam should instead be used to fund social programs to reduce poverty and discrimination in American society. Finally, he noted that in terms of percentage, black soldiers were dying in much greater numbers than white soldiers in Vietnam.

King Reacts to "The Children of Vietnam"

Many scholars believe that Martin Luther King, Jr.'s opposition to the Vietnam War increased dramatically after he read an article called "The Children of Vietnam" by William Pepper in *Ramparts* magazine in early 1967. King aide Bernard Lee recalled in David Garrow's book *Bearing the Cross* that the text and pictures in the article had a devastating impact on the civil rights leader. "When he came to *Ramparts* magazine he stopped. He froze as he looked at the pictures from Vietnam. He saw a picture of a Vietnamese mother holding her dead baby, a baby killed by our military. Then Martin just pushed the plate of food away from him. I looked up and said, 'Doesn't it taste any good?,' and he answered, 'Nothing will ever taste any good for me until I do everything I can to end that war.'"

Speaks out against the war

In 1965 King made his first public criticisms of the war. He argued that U.S. forces were "accomplishing nothing" in Vietnam, and he called on the Johnson administration to end hostilities and negotiate a peace settlement. But King's remarks, which were made when the American antiwar movement was just beginning to form, were denounced by other civil rights leaders. They warned King that by criticizing American policy in Vietnam, he risked losing Johnson's support for civil rights and antipoverty legislation. The criticism of black civil rights leaders was quickly echoed by national politicians and prominent magazines, who said that King did not know what he was talking about.

Stung by the criticism, King stopped speaking out about Vietnam for several months. But in 1966 he decided that he could no longer remain silent. He accepted the cochairmanship of the antiwar group Clergy and Laity Concerned About Vietnam (CALCAV) and begin delivering sermons critical of the war. At the end of 1966, he declared in testimony before a Senate subcommittee that "poverty . . . and social programs are ignored when the guns of war become a national obsession . . . . The bombs in Vietnam explode at home; they destroy hopes and possibilities for a decent America."

King delivered his most famous antiwar speech on April 4, 1967, at Riverside Church in New York City before an audience of CALCAV religious leaders. In this speech, known variously as the "Riverside Speech," the "Beyond Vietnam" speech, and "A Time to Break Silence," King condemned America's military policies in Vietnam as evil. He also repeated his charge that America's poor were suffering because of the country's decision to pour its resources into bombs, tanks, helicopters, and other weaponry. "Somehow this madness must cease," King declared. "I speak as a child of God and brother to the suffering poor of Vietnam and the poor of America who are paying the double price of smashed hopes at home and death and corruption in Vietnam. I speak as a citizen of the world, for the world as it stands aghast [with shock and horror] at the path we have taken. I speak as an American to the leaders of my own nation. The great initiative in this war is ours. The initiative to stop must be ours."

Leaders of America's antiwar movement praised King's speech and rejoiced that he was lending his moral authority to their cause. In addition, many other civil rights leaders supported King's stand. They agreed that the war drained attention and funding away from America's internal problems, and they characterized his speech as a brave attempt to turn America away from an evil war. "King's actions prove that he had a more compelling and complex view of American patriotism," stated Eric Michael Dyson in *I May Not Get There with You.* "His willingness to criticize his country when it was wrong proved his concern for its moral destiny."

But King's Riverside address attracted fierce condemnation from other quarters. Some black leaders claimed that his remarks showed that civil rights were no longer a priority for him. In addition, his speech angered President Johnson and his administration. And many of the nation's leading magazines attacked him for his antiwar stance. *Time, Newsweek,* and *U.S. News and World Report* all published negative articles on King's antiwar beliefs, and a *Life* magazine editorial charged that by connecting "civil rights with a proposal that amounts to abject [total] surrender in Vietnam . . . . King comes close to betraying the cause for which he has worked so long."

But King refused to back down. Instead, he continued to express his deep opposition to the war, and made a special effort to unite the antiwar movement and the civil rights movement under one banner. Many historians believe that King's stand against Vietnam increased public opposition to the war among both blacks and whites in late 1967 and early 1968.

On April 4, 1968—exactly one year after he gave his Riverside address—King was assassinated by a sniper during a visit to Memphis, Tennessee. News of his death triggered riots in dozens of American cities and caused feelings of shock and outrage throughout the world. In 1969 a white man named James Earl Ray pleaded guilty to murdering King. He was sentenced to ninety-nine years in prison. Since then, many historians have speculated that Ray did not act alone, but no accomplices have ever been found.

King's murder robbed America of one of its greatest voices. But his message of black pride and racial justice lived on and became an essential part of the nation's history. In 1983 the U.S. government formally recognized King's life and contributions to American society by establishing a national holiday in his honor. This holiday is observed on the third Monday in January so that it takes place on or near King's January 15 birthday.

Sources

Albert, Robert J., and Ronald Hoffman, eds. *We Shall Overcome: Martin Luther King Jr. and the Black Freedom Struggle.* New York: Pantheon Books, 1990.

Dyson, Michael Eric. *I May Not Get There with You: The True Martin Luther King Jr.* New York: Free Press, 2000.

Fairclough, Adam. "Martin Luther King, Jr. and the War in Vietnam." *Phylon,* January 1984.

Garrow, David J. *Bearing the Cross: Martin Luther King, Jr. and the Southern Christian Leadership Conference*. New York: Random House, 1986.

King, Martin Luther, Jr. *Autobiography of Martin Luther King, Jr.* Edited by Clayborne Carson. New York: Warner Books, 1998.

King, Martin Luther, Jr. *I Have a Dream: Writings and Speeches That Changed the World*. New York: HarperCollins, 1986.

Oates, Stephen B. *Let the Trumpet Sound: The Life of Martin Luther King, Jr.* New York: Harper and Row, 1982.

Henry A. Kissinger

Born May 27, 1923
Furth, Germany

U.S. national security advisor, 1969–75,
and secretary of state, 1973–77

Henry Kissinger was a major force behind American foreign policy for more than a decade. As U.S. national security advisor during the Vietnam War, he helped President Richard M. Nixon (see entry) develop U.S. strategy and acted as the lead American negotiator at the Paris Peace Talks. After several years of discussions, he and North Vietnamese negotiator Le Duc Tho (see entry) finally reached an agreement to end U.S. involvement in January 1973. Although this agreement ultimately failed to end the war, Kissinger had several other important achievements as U.S. Secretary of State under President Gerald Ford.

A German-born scholar

Heinz Alfred Kissinger, who later changed his first name to Henry, was born May 27, 1923, in Furth, Germany. His parents, Louis and Paula Kissinger, were Jewish. As Adolf Hitler and the Nazi Party rose to power in Germany and began persecuting Jews, the Kissinger family fled the country. They settled in the United States in 1938, and Henry became a naturalized American citizen five years later.

"We cannot by our actions alone ensure the survival of South Vietnam. But we can, alone, by our inaction assure its demise [death]."

Henry A. Kissinger.
Courtesy of the Library of Congress.

Upon arriving in the United States, Kissinger lived in New York City. He worked in a factory by day to help support his family, and he studied accounting at the City College of New York at night. In 1943 he was drafted into the military to serve in World War II (1939–45). He spent most of the next three years in Germany, acting as an interpreter for an American general. After his discharge in 1946 he returned to the United States. Longing to continue his education, he entered Harvard University in 1946. Kissinger stayed at Harvard for his bachelor's and master's degrees, and he completed his education by earning a Ph.D. there in 1954.

After leaving Harvard, Kissinger took a job with the Council on Foreign Relations in New York City. He led a group of scholars who studied the politics of the Cold War—an intense rivalry between the United States and Soviet Union that developed in the late 1940s as both countries competed to spread their political philosophies and influence around the world. In 1957 Kissinger wrote a book called *Nuclear Weapons and Foreign Policy* outlining his opinions on how the United States should relate to the Soviet Union. Although Kissinger opposed communism, he believed that the threat of nuclear weapons made it impossible for either side to "win" the Cold War. Instead, he recommended that the two superpowers agree on a balance of power. Kissinger's book, which won several awards and became a surprise best-seller, brought him to national attention as a leading scholar on international relations.

Advises presidents on policies toward Vietnam

After the publication of his book, Kissinger began teaching classes on government at Harvard. He also served as a consultant and unofficial advisor to Presidents Dwight D. Eisenhower, John F. Kennedy (see entry), and Lyndon B. Johnson (see entry). One of the most pressing issues of foreign relations in the late 1950s and early 1960s was U.S. involvement in Vietnam. Vietnam had won its independence from France in 1954, but the Geneva Peace Accords had divided the nation into two sections—Communist-led North Vietnam, and U.S.-supported South Vietnam. The peace agreement also provided for nationwide free elections to be held in 1956 to reunite the two parts of Vietnam under one government. But U.S. leaders worried that elections would give power to the Communists who had led the war for independence from France. They encouraged the government of South Vietnam to refuse to hold the elections.

A short time later, a new war began between the two parts of Vietnam. The U.S. government sent money, military equipment, and advisors to help South Vietnam defend itself against the Communists. In 1965 President Lyndon Johnson sent U.S. combat troops to fight on the side of South Vietnam. But increasing U.S. involvement failed to defeat the Communists. Instead, the war settled into a bloody stalemate, and the American people became bitterly divided over the government's policies toward Vietnam.

Kissinger visited Vietnam several times beginning in 1965. In 1968 he participated in early negotiations with North Vietnam on behalf of the Johnson administration. Kissinger's initial position in the negotiations was that both American and Communist forces should be withdrawn from South Vietnam. Once this occurred, the two sides could discuss various plans for the country's political future. But his North Vietnamese counterpart, Le Duc Tho, refused to go along with this plan. Instead, he insisted that North Vietnam would continue fighting until the U.S. troops were withdrawn. He also demanded that the South Vietnamese government be replaced by a coalition government that included Communist representatives. With such a wide gap between the two sides, the negotiators made little progress and eventually broke off their talks.

National security advisor under President Nixon

When Richard Nixon became president of the United States in 1969, he promised the American people that he would bring them "peace with honor" in Vietnam. Toward this end, Nixon named Kissinger as his national security advisor. In this position Kissinger advised Nixon on all issues related to national security and foreign affairs. But his main responsibility was representing the United States in peace negotiations with North Vietnam when the talks resumed in Paris, France. Kissinger wanted to bring an end to the war, but he did not want it to seem like the United States had lost. He felt that the way in which the United States withdrew from the conflict would have a lasting effect on its future reputation in world affairs. Kissinger also believed in negotiating from a position of strength. As a result, he encouraged Nixon to use bombing raids and other shows of force to pressure North Vietnam into serious negotiations.

In August 1969 Kissinger and Le Duc Tho began meeting secretly in hopes of negotiating a settlement. Their talks continued off and on for more than two years. As the war dragged on, the American people grew increasingly frustrated, and antiwar demonstrations took place across the country. In the meantime, the Communist countries of China and the Soviet Union began to reduce their support for North Vietnam. These factors made both sides more willing to reach a compromise.

In October 1972 Kissinger and Tho reached a preliminary agreement. In fact, Kissinger announced that "peace is at hand." But the deal fell apart when South Vietnamese President Nguyen Van Thieu (see entry) objected to it. Determined to force the Communists' hand, Nixon then ordered the heaviest bombing raids of the war over North Vietnamese cities. These attacks, which took place in late December, became known as the "Christmas bombings." Kissinger supported the bombings as a way to draw North Vietnam back to the bargaining table.

The Paris Peace Accords

On January 25, 1973, Kissinger and Tho announced that they had reached a final agreement to end U.S. involvement in the Vietnam War. It was signed by the governments of the United States, North Vietnam, and South Vietnam two days later. Under the terms of the agreement, the United States agreed to withdraw its troops from Vietnam within sixty days. Kissinger also agreed to allow some Communist forces to remain in the South. In exchange, North Vietnam agreed to let President Thieu remain in power. But the agreement also established a National Council of Reconciliation—which would include representatives from both North and South Vietnam—to organize elections and form a new government. Finally, the peace agreement provided for the return of all American soldiers held by North Vietnam as prisoners of war.

When the Paris Peace Accords were signed, both sides claimed that they had achieved their goals. But some observers pointed out that very little had changed between this agreement and the agreements that had been considered years earlier. In addition, some people criticized the agreement because it left the political future of South Vietnam uncertain. After all, that had been the main issue the two sides had been fighting to decide.

As many people expected, the peace in Vietnam did not last long. The last American troops withdrew from the country in early 1973. Almost immediately, the South Vietnamese forces under President Thieu began clashing with the Communist forces that remained in the countryside. Each side blamed the other for breaking the treaty. In June 1973 Kissinger and Tho met again and issued a joint statement urging both sides to comply with the terms of the peace agreement. But the fighting continued.

In September 1973 Nixon named Kissinger to the position of secretary of state. On October 16, 1973, Kissinger and Tho received the Nobel Peace Prize for their efforts in ending the Vietnam War. The decision to give the award to the two negotiators created a great deal of controversy, especially since the agreement had not actually led to peace in Vietnam. In fact, some observers sarcastically called it the "Nobel War Prize." In recognition of the crisis that still gripped his country, Tho refused to accept his part of the honor.

Other achievements in foreign relations

In 1974 President Nixon resigned from office in disgrace over his involvement in the Watergate scandal. Vice President Gerald Ford took over the White House, and Kissinger remained secretary of state under Ford. In the meantime, the Communist forces continued to gain ground in the ongoing war in Vietnam. Kissinger tried to convince Ford and the U.S. Congress to send American troops back to Vietnam to enforce the peace agreements. "Despite the agony of this nation's experience in Indochina and the substantial reappraisal which has taken place concerning our proper role there, few would deny that we are still involved or that what we do—or fail to do—will still weigh heavily on the outcome," he told a Senate committee. "We cannot by our actions alone ensure the survival of South Vietnam. But we can, alone, by our inaction assure its demise [death]."

But U.S. lawmakers recognized how unpopular the war had become among the American people, and they refused to take action in support of South Vietnam. In 1975 North Vietnamese forces captured the South Vietnamese capital of Saigon to win the Vietnam War and reunite the country under a Communist government. Kissinger bitterly blamed Congress for the defeat.

Although the peace agreement he negotiated failed to end the Vietnam War, Kissinger registered several other successes as Secretary of State. He helped the United States and the Soviet Union reach an agreement, called the Strategic Arms Limitation Treaty (SALT), that placed limits on the number of nuclear weapons each side possessed. He also arranged for Nixon to make a historic visit to China in 1972, which reopened American diplomatic and trade relations with the Communist nation. In 1973 Kissinger worked to achieve peace in the Middle East during a war between Israel and the Arab nations.

Kissinger left office in 1977, when Democrat Jimmy Carter became president. He then opened his own consulting firm, Kissinger Associates, and began advising clients about the political climate for doing business in other countries. He also became a professor at Georgetown University in Washington, D.C., provided commentary for television news programs, published several books, and attracted high fees as a paid lecturer. He made a brief return to politics in the 1980s, when he advised President Ronald Reagan on U.S. policy in the Middle East.

In 1997 Kissinger came under heavy criticism for using his diplomatic ties with China to arrange deals for his business clients. His critics claimed that he stood to benefit personally from these deals, which grew out of the special access he had received as a public figure. Since leaving the government, Kissinger has lived in Kent, Connecticut, with his second wife, Nancy Maginnes. He has two grown children from an earlier marriage to Ann Fleisher.

Sources

Encyclopedia of World Biography. Farmington Hills, MI: Gale, 1999.

Goodman, Allan E. *The Lost Peace: America's Search for a Negotiated Settlement of the Vietnam War.* 1978.

Hersh, Seymour. *The Price of Power: Kissinger in the Nixon White House.* Simon and Schuster, 1984.

Kissinger, Henry. *White House Years.* Boston: Little, Brown, 1979.

Kissinger, Henry. *Years of Upheaval.* Boston: Little, Brown, 1982.

Kissinger, Henry. *Years of Renewal.* Boston: Little, Brown, 1999.

Porter, Gareth. *A Peace Denied: The United States, Vietnam, and the Paris Agreement.* Bloomington: Indiana University Press, 1975.

Ron Kovic

Born July 4, 1946
Ladysmith, Wisconsin

American Vietnam War veteran
and antiwar activist

> "All I could feel was cheated. All I could feel was the worthlessness of dying right here in this place at this moment for nothing."

Ron Kovic.
Reproduced by permission of Corbis Corporation.

R on Kovic volunteered to serve with the U.S. Marines in Vietnam because he loved his country and wanted to be a hero. But his wartime service—which ended when he received a severe wound that left him paralyzed from the chest down—taught him the cruel reality of war. After returning to the United States and facing life in a wheelchair, he joined the antiwar movement. Kovic wrote about his journey from patriotic soldier to disabled veteran to antiwar activist in a critically acclaimed 1976 autobiography, *Born on the Fourth of July.* In 1989, Kovic's book was made into a popular movie of the same name.

Eager to serve his country

Ron Kovic was born July 4, 1946, in Ladysmith, Wisconsin. He was the second of six children in a patriotic, working-class, Catholic family. When Kovic was a boy, his family moved to Massapequa, Long Island, New York. He loved spending time outdoors, playing baseball or staging mock battles in the woods with his friends. In high school Kovic joined the wrestling team and became a pole-vaulter on the track team. He was also invited to try out for the New York Yankees. "I was a natural athlete," he recalled in *Born on the Fourth of July*, "and there wasn't much of anything I wasn't able to do with my body back then."

Throughout his childhood, Kovic viewed war as an exciting way for young American men to prove their courage. His father had served proudly in World War II (1939–1945). Kovic had attended holiday parades and cheered for the passing veterans. He had also grown up watching patriotic movies starring John Wayne, which had made war seem glamorous to him. As a result, he often dreamed of escaping from the routine of small-town life by serving his country and becoming a war hero.

When a group of recruiters from the U.S. Marine Corps gave a presentation at his high school, Kovic was deeply impressed. In 1964 he enlisted in the Marines to serve in the Vietnam War. "I stayed up most of the night before I left, watching the late movie," he recalled in his memoir. "Then 'The Star-Spangled Banner' played. I remember standing up and feeling very patriotic, chills running up and down my spine. I put my hand over my heart and stood rigid at attention until the screen went black."

Experiences tragedy in combat

The Vietnam War pitted the Communist nation of North Vietnam against the U.S.-supported nation of South Vietnam. North Vietnam wanted to overthrow the South Vietnamese government and reunite the two countries under one Communist government. But U.S. government officials felt that a Communist government in Vietnam would increase the power of the Soviet Union and threaten the security of the United States. In the late 1950s and early 1960s the U.S. government sent money, weapons, and military advisors to help South Vietnam defend itself. In 1965 President Lyndon Johnson (see entry) sent American combat troops to join the fight on the side of South Vietnam.

Kovic went to Vietnam with one of these early shipments of American troops. Within a short time, he began to realize that war was very different than he thought it would be. In his book Kovic recalled two experiences that fundamentally changed the way he viewed the war and his service in it. First, he accidentally shot and killed one of his own men in the confusion of a battle. When he tried to admit his tragic mistake to a superior officer, the officer refused to believe him and promoted him to lead a combat patrol.

The second incident occurred a few weeks later, when Kovic's patrol tracked a group of enemy soldiers to a Vietnamese village. They thought they saw rifles pointing through the window of a small hut. Kovic's men began shooting without a formal order to fire and then continued firing until they had destroyed the hut. Afterward, Kovic went inside to count how many enemy soldiers had been killed. But instead of enemy soldiers, he found that the hut had contained Vietnamese women, children, and old men. "The floor of the small hut was covered with them, screaming and thrashing their arms back and forth, lying in pools of blood, crying wildly," he recalled.

After these two incidents, Kovic was desperate to escape his feelings of guilt and horror. He began volunteering for dangerous duty and taking foolish chances in hopes of being wounded and sent home. During one battle against enemy forces, he remembered thinking: "Here was my chance to win a medal, here was my chance to fight against the real enemy, to make up for everything that had happened."

On January 20, 1968, Kovic was wounded in battle. First, a bullet hit his foot and blew off most of his heel. Still, he continued firing until his rifle locked. Then another bullet went through his shoulder and lung and shattered his spinal cord. As he lay on the battlefield, waiting to be evacuated to a hospital, he recalled, "All I could feel was cheated. All I could feel was the worthlessness of dying right here in this place at this moment for nothing."

Returns from Vietnam in a wheelchair

The second bullet left Kovic paralyzed from the mid-chest down. He returned to the United States as a paraplegic in a wheelchair. He spent the next several months recovering in a New York hospital run by the Veterans Administration (a U.S. government agency responsible for providing medical care and other benefits to former soldiers). Unfortunately, Kovic and the other patients received very poor care in the VA hospital. The facility was dirty, understaffed, and lacking in basic medical supplies and equipment. It was also infested with rats. While there, Kovic grew angry and disgusted at the way the U.S. government was treating its veterans.

"I realized in Vietnam that the real experience of war was nothing like the comic books or movies I had watched as a kid," Kovic told Robert Seidenberg in an interview for *American Film*. "I realized when the war was over and I had come home in a wheelchair that . . . the whole . . . thing was a sham. My best intentions, my innocence, my youth, my beautiful young spirit had been desecrated [violated] by men who never went where I went, men who would never have to go through what I was about to endure."

Upon returning home from the hospital, Kovic received a Purple Heart and a Bronze Star in recognition of his service. He expected his family and his community to greet him as a hero. But as the Vietnam War dragged on, the American people had become bitterly divided over U.S. involvement. Antiwar demonstrations were taking place across the country. Some people viewed Vietnam veterans as symbols of an increasingly unpopular war. Kovic found that most people seemed to treat him with disinterest or even hostility. When he rode in a Fourth of July parade in Massapequa, people just stared at him instead of cheering.

"It was the end of whatever belief I'd still had in what I'd done in Vietnam," he recalled in his book. "Now I wanted to know what I had lost my legs for, why I and the others had gone at all. But it was still very hard for me to think of speaking out against the war, to think of joining those [antiwar protestors] I'd once called traitors." As time passed, Kovic grew increasingly angry, depressed, and bitter about his military service and the treatment he received when he returned home. He spent the summer of 1969 in Mexico with a group of other disabled veterans, drinking, doing drugs, and visiting prostitutes in order to ease his physical and emotional pain.

Begins speaking out against the war

In 1970 events at home convinced Kovic to begin speaking out against the war. That May, four unarmed student protestors were shot and killed by Ohio National Guard troops on the campus of Kent State University. A few days later, Kovic attended a peace rally in Washington, D.C. He found that he identified with members of the antiwar movement. "There was a togetherness, just as there had been in Vietnam, but it was a togetherness of a different kind of people and for a much different reason," he noted in *Born on the Fourth of July.* "In the war we were killing and maiming people. In Washington on that Saturday afternoon in May we were trying to heal them and set them free."

In 1971 Kovic joined an antiwar group called Vietnam Veterans Against the War (VVAW). He began speaking out about a variety of issues, including U.S. involvement in Vietnam and the poor treatment of veterans in VA hospitals. In 1972 he joined several other VVAW members in a protest at the Republican National Convention in Miami, Florida. As the Republican political party officially nominated Richard Nixon (see entry) to run for a second term as president, Kovic and his friends disrupted Nixon's acceptance speech by repeatedly shouting "Stop the bombing, stop the war." When a reporter interviewed Kovic live on television, he used the opportunity to present his views about the war. "What's happening in Vietnam is a crime against humanity," he stated. "If you can't believe the veteran who fought in the war and was wounded in the war, who can you believe?"

Tells his story in a book and a movie

In 1976 Kovic published his autobiography, *Born on the Fourth of July,* in which he discussed his childhood, his decision to join the Marines, his experiences in Vietnam, his struggles to recover from his war wounds, and his transformation into an antiwar activist. Kovic's memoir received a great deal of critical praise upon its publication. In the *New York Times Book Review,* C. D. B. Bryan called it "the most personal and honest testament published thus far by any young man who fought in the Vietnam War." Kovic noted that writing the book also helped him come to terms with his military service. "My book is a miracle," he told Philip A. McCombs of the *Washington Post.* "It was written because I decided not to hate anymore."

Following the success of his book, Kovic was invited to speak at the 1976 Democratic National Convention in New

York City. He gave a moving speech before the Democratic party formally nominated Jimmy Carter as their presidential candidate. It was a completely different experience than his uninvited appearance at the Republican convention four years earlier. In fact, in the interview with McCombs, Kovic called it "the biggest moment in my life, the vindication [reward for being proven right] of all the years that the government had tried to shut me up, to spit in my face. I was addressing the whole U.S.A."

In the late 1970s and early 1980s Kovic continued writing and published a novel, *Around the World in Eighty Days*. He also acted as a consultant for the film *Coming Home*, which starred Jon Voight as a disabled Vietnam veteran struggling to cope with his feelings about the war. In 1987 Kovic received word that *Born on the Fourth of July* was going to be turned into a movie. It would be directed by Oliver Stone (see entry), a Vietnam veteran who had recently won an Academy Award for his Vietnam War movie *Platoon*.

Tom Cruise portrays Vietnam veteran Ron Kovic in the movie "Born on the Fourth of July." *Reproduced by permission of The Kobal Collection.*

Kovic spent the next two years working on the film version of his life story. He helped Stone write the screenplay, and he helped actor Tom Cruise prepare to play the leading role. Cruise spent several weeks in a wheelchair and visited VA hospitals in order to get a feel for Kovic's life. "Tom Cruise was agonizing over this part, and he didn't know if he could go on, either," Kovic recalled in *American Film*. "All of a sudden, I realized that Cruise understood, that I had a brother, I had a friend." When the filming was completed, Kovic presented Cruise with the Bronze Star he had earned in Vietnam.

The movie *Born on the Fourth of July* became a big success upon its release in 1989. It was popular at the box office, and it also received strong critical reviews. In fact, it won four Golden Globes and two Academy Awards. Kovic hoped that seeing the film would teach young people about the reality of war. "My sacrifice, my paralysis, the difficulties, the frustrations, the impossibilities of each and every day would now be for something very valuable, something that would help protect the young people of this country from having to go through what I went through," he told Seidenberg.

Since completing work on the film, Kovic has lived in Redondo Beach, California. He spends his time gardening, painting, and playing the piano. "I never thought I would say this, but I believe that my wound has become a blessing in disguise," he told Jon Kalish in *New York Newsday*. "It's enabled me to reach millions of people with a message of peace and a message of hope."

Sources

Current Biography, August 1990.

Hellman, John. *American Myth and the Legacy of Vietnam.* New York: Columbia University Press, 1986.

Kovic, Ron. *Born on the Fourth of July.* New York: McGraw Hill, 1976.

MacPherson, Myra. *Long Time Passing: Vietnam and the Haunted Generation.* Garden City, NY: Doubleday, 1984.

Moss, Nathaniel. *Ron Kovic: Antiwar Activist.* New York: Chelsea House, 1994.

Where to Learn More

Against the Vietnam War: Writings by Activists. New York: Syracuse University Press, 1999.

Agnew, Spiro. *Go Quietly . . . or Else.* New York: William Morrow, 1980.

Ambrose, Stephen E. *Nixon.* 3 vols. New York: Simon and Schuster, 1987, 1989, 1991.

American Writers of the Vietnam War, Vol. 9 of *Dictionary of Literary Biography Documentary Series.* Detroit: Gale Research, 1991.

Anderson, David L., ed. *Shadow on the White House: Presidents and the Vietnam War, 1945-1975.* Lawrence, KS: University Press of Kansas, 1993.

Andrews, Owen, et al. *Vietnam: Images from Combat Photographers.* Washington: Starwood, 1991.

Anson, Robert S. *McGovern: A Biography.* New York: Holt, Rinehart and Winston, 1972.

Baez, Joan. *And a Voice to Sing With.* New York: Summit Books, 1978.

Beidler, Philip D. *Re-Writing America: Vietnam Authors in Their Generation.* Athens: University of Georgia Press, 1991.

Berman, Larry. *Lyndon Johnson's War.* New York: W.W. Norton, 1989.

Berman, Larry. *Planning a Tragedy: The Americanization of the War in Vietnam.* New York: W.W. Norton, 1982.

Bernstein, Irving. *Guns or Butter: The Presidency of Lyndon Johnson.* New York: Oxford University Press, 1996.

Berrigan, Daniel. *Night Flight to Hanoi.* New York: Macmillan, 1968.

Berrigan, Daniel. *To Dwell in Peace: An Autobiography.* New York: Harper, 1987.

Bird, Kai. *The Color of Truth: McGeorge Bundy and William Bundy, Brothers in Arms: A Biography.* New York: Simon and Schuster, 1998.

Blair, Anne E. *Lodge in Vietnam: A Patriot Abroad.* New Haven, CT: Yale University Press, 1995.

Boetcher, Thomas D. *Vietnam: The Valor and the Sorrow.* Boston: Little, Brown, 1985.

Calley, William L., as told to John Sack. *Lieutenant Calley: His Own Story.* New York: Viking Press, 1971.

Chandler, David P. *Brother Number One: A Political Biography of Pol Pot.* Boulder, CO: Westview Press, 1992.

Chong, Denise. *The Girl in the Picture: The Story of Kim Phuc, The Photograph, and the Vietnam War.* New York: Viking, 2000.

Cohen, Warren I. *Dean Rusk.* Totowa, NJ: Cooper Square, 1980.

Conkin, Paul K. *Big Daddy from the Pedernales: Lyndon Baines Johnson.* Boston: Twayne Publishers, 1986.

Currey, Cecil B. *Edward Lansdale: The Unquiet American.* Boston: Houghton Mifflin, 1988.

Dear, John, ed. *Apostle of Peace: Essays in Honor of Daniel Berrigan.* Maryknoll, New York: Orbis, 1996.

DeBenedetti, Charles, and Charles Chatfield. *An American Ordeal: The Antiwar Movement of the Vietnam Era.* New York: Syracuse University Press, 1990.

Dellinger, David. *From Yale to Jail: The Life Story of a Moral Dissenter.* New York: Pantheon, 1993.

Denton, Jeremiah A., Jr., with Edwin H. Broadt. *When Hell Was in Session.* Clover, South Carolina: Commission Press, 1976.

Duiker, William J. *Ho Chi Minh.* New York: Hyperion, 2000.

Dyson, Michael Eric. *I May Not Get There with You: The True Martin Luther King Jr.* New York: Free Press, 2000.

Eisen, Arlene. *Women and Revolution in Vietnam.* London: Zed Books, 1984.

Elliff, John T. *Crime, Dissent, and the Attorney General: The Justice Department in the 1960s.* 1971.

Ellsberg, Daniel. *Papers on the War.* New York: Simon and Schuster, 1972.

Elwood-Akers, Virginia. *Women Correspondents in the Vietnam War, 1961–1975.* Metuchen, NJ: Scarecrow Press, 1988.

Encyclopedia of World Biography. Detroit: Gale Research, 1999.

Engelmann, Larry. *Tears Before the Rain: An Oral History of the Fall of South Vietnam.* New York: Oxford University Press, 1990.

Fall, Bernard B. *Hell in a Very Small Place: The Siege of Dien Bien Phu.* Philadelphia: Lippincott, 1967.

Fall, Bernard B. *Last Reflections on a War.* New York: Doubleday, 1968.

Fall, Bernard B. *Viet-Nam Witness, 1953–1966.* New York: Praeger, 1967.

Farber, David, ed. *The Sixties: From Memory to History.* Chapel Hill, NC: University of North Carolina Press, 1994.

Farber, David. *Chicago '68.* Chicago: University of Chicago Press, 1988.

Fenn, Charles. *Ho Chi Minh: A Biographical Introduction.* New York: Scribner's, 1973.

Figley, Charles R., and Seymour Leventman, eds. *Strangers at Home: Vietnam Veterans Since the War.* New York: Praeger, 1980.

FitzGerald, Frances. *Fire in the Lake: The Vietnamese and the Americans in Vietnam.* Boston: Little, Brown, 1987.

Freedland, Michael. *Jane Fonda: A Biography.* London: Weidenfeld and Nicolson, 1988.

Fulbright, J. William. *The Arrogance of Power.* New York: Random House, 1967.

Furguson, Ernest B. *Westmoreland: The Inevitable General.* Boston: Little, Brown, 1968.

Garfinkle, Adam. *Telltale Hearts: The Origins and Impact of the Vietnam Antiwar Movement.* New York: St. Martin's Press, 1995.

Garrow, David J. *Bearing the Cross: Martin Luther King, Jr. and the Southern Christian Leadership Conference.* New York: Random House, 1986.

Giap, Vo Nguyen. *The People's War for the Defense of the Homeland in the New Era.* Hanoi: Foreign Languages Publishing House, 1981.

Giap, Vo Nguyen. *Unforgettable Days.* Hanoi: Foreign Languages Publishing House, 1974.

Gitlin, Todd. *The Sixties: Years of Hope, Days of Rage.* New York: Bantam Books, 1987.

Goldberg, Robert Alan. *Barry Goldwater.* New Haven, CT: Yale University Press, 1995.

Goldwater, Barry, with Jack Casserly. *Goldwater.* New York: Doubleday, 1988.

Halberstam, David. *Ho.* New York: Random House, 1971.

Halberstam, David. *The Best and the Brightest.* New York: Random House, 1972.

Halberstam, David. *The Making of a Quagmire: America and Vietnam During the Kennedy Era.* Rev. ed. New York: Knopf, 1988.

Halberstam, David. *The Unfinished Odyssey of Robert Kennedy.* New York: Random House, 1969.

Hall, Mitchell K. *Because of Their Faith: CALCAV and Religious Opposition to the Vietnam War.* New York: Columbia University Press, 1990.

Hammer, Ellen J. *A Death in November: America in Vietnam, 1963.* New York: Dutton, 1987.

Harrison, James Pincklney. *The Endless War: Vietnam's Struggle for Independence.* New York: McGraw-Hill, 1982.

Hayden, Tom. *Reunion: A Memoir.* New York: Random House, 1988.

Hayslip, Le Ly, with James Hayslip. *Child of War, Woman of Peace.* New York: Anchor Books, 1993.

Hayslip, Le Ly, with Jay Wurts. *When Heaven and Earth Changed Places: A Vietnamese Woman's Journey from War to Peace.* New York: Doubleday, 1989.

Heath, Jim F. *Decade of Disillusionment: The Kennedy–Johnson Years.* Bloomington: Indiana University Press, 1975.

Heller, Jeffrey. *Joan Baez: Singer with a Cause.* Chicago: Children's Press, 1991.

Hellman, John. *American Myth and the Legacy of Vietnam.* New York: Columbia University Press, 1986.

Hendrickson, Paul. *The Living and the Dead: Robert McNamara and Five Lives of a Lost War.* New York: Knopf, 1996.

Herr, Michael. *Dispatches.* New York: Knopf, 1977.

Herring, George C. *LBJ and Vietnam: A Different Kind of War.* Austin: University of Texas Press, 1994.

Herring, George. *The Secret Diplomacy of the Vietnam War: The Negotiating Volumes of the Pentagon Papers.* Austin: University of Texas Press, 1983.

Hersh, Seymour M. *My Lai 4: A Report on the Massacre and Its Aftermath.* New York: Random House, 1970.

Hersh, Seymour M. *The Price of Power: Kissinger in the Nixon White House.* New York: Summit Books, 1983.

Hilty, James W. *Robert Kennedy, Brother Protector.* Philadelphia: Temple University Press, 1997.

Ho Chi Minh. *Against U.S. Aggression, for National Salvation.* Hanoi, Vietnam: Foreign Languages Publishing House, 1967.

Hoffman, Abbie. *The Best of Abbie Hoffman.* New York: Four Walls, Eight Windows, 1990.

Howes, Craig. *Voices of the Vietnam POWs: Witnesses to Their Fight.* 1993.

Hubbell, John, with Andrew Jones and Kenneth Y. Tomlinson. *P.O.W.: A Definitive History of the American Prisoner-of-War Experience in Vietnam, 1964–1973.* New York: Reader's Digest Press, 1976.

Isaacs, Arnold R. *Vietnam Shadows: The War, Its Ghosts, and Its Legacy.* Baltimore: Johns Hopkins University Press, 1997.

Isaacs, Arnold R. *Without Honor: Defeat in Vietnam and Cambodia.* Baltimore: Johns Hopkins University Press, 1983.

Johnson, Lady Bird. *A White House Diary.* New York: Holt, Rinehart and Winston, 1970.

Johnson, Lyndon B. *The Vantage Point: Perspectives of the Presidency, 1963–1969.* New York: Holt, Rinehart and Winston, 1971.

Kamm, Henry. *Cambodia: Report from a Stricken Land.* New York: Arcade Publishing, 1998.

Kaplan, Steven. *Understanding Tim O'Brien.* Columbia, SC: University of South Carolina Press, 1994.

Karnow, Stanley. *Vietnam: A History.* New York: Viking, 1983.

Katakis, Michael. *The Vietnam Veterans Memorial.* New York: Crown, 1988.

Kaye, Tony. *Lyndon B. Johnson.* New York: Chelsea House, 1987.

Kearns, Doris. *Lyndon Johnson and the American Dream.* New York: Signet Books, 1976.

Kennedy, Robert F. *To Seek a Newer World.* Garden City, NY: Doubleday, 1967.

Kimball, Jeffrey. *Nixon's Vietnam War.* Lawrence: University Press of Kansas, 1998.

King, Martin Luther, Jr. *Autobiography of Martin Luther King, Jr.* Edited by Clayborne Carson. New York: Warner Books, 1998.

King, Martin Luther, Jr. *I Have a Dream: Writings and Speeches That Changed the World.* New York: HarperCollins, 1986.

Kinnard, Douglas. *The Certain Trumpet: Maxwell Taylor and the American Experience in Vietnam.* 1991.

Kirk, Donald. *Wider War: The Struggle for Cambodia, Thailand, and Laos.* New York: Praeger, 1971.

Kissinger, Henry. *White House Years*. Boston: Little, Brown, 1979.

Kovic, Ron. *Born on the Fourth of July*. New York: McGraw Hill, 1976.

Lansdale, Edward G. *In the Midst of Wars: An American's Mission to Southeast Asia*. New York: Harper and Row, 1972.

Le Duan. *The October Revolution and the Vietnamese Revolution*. Hanoi: Foreign Languages Publishing House, 1978.

Lodge, Henry Cabot. *The Storm Has Many Eyes: A Personal Narrative*. New York: Norton, 1973.

Lukas, Anthony J. *Nightmare: The Underside of the Nixon Years*. New York: Viking Press, 1976.

Macdonald, Peter. *Giap: The Victor in Vietnam*. New York: W.W. Norton, 1993.

Maclear, Michael. *The Ten Thousand Day War: Vietnam, 1945–1975*. New York: St. Martin's Press, 1979.

MacPherson, Myra. *Long Time Passing: Vietnam and the Haunted Generation*. Garden City, NY: Doubleday, 1984.

Mailer, Norman. *Armies of the Night*. New York: New American Library, 1968.

Malone, Mary. *Maya Lin: Architect and Artist*. Springfield, NJ: Enslow, 1995.

Manchester, William. *Portrait of a President: JFK in Profile*. Boston: Little, Brown, 1967.

Marshall, Kathryn. *In the Combat Zone: An Oral History of American Women in Vietnam*. Boston: Little, Brown, 1987.

McCain, John, with Mark Salter. *Faith of My Fathers: A Family Memoir*. New York: Random House, 1999.

McGovern, George. *Grassroots: The Autobiography of George McGovern*. New York: Random House, 1977.

McGovern, George. *Vietnam, Four American Perspectives: Lectures*. West Lafayette, IN: Purdue University Press, 1990.

McNamara, Robert S., and others. *Argument Without End: In Search of Answers to the Vietnam Tragedy*. Public Affairs, 1999.

McNamara, Robert S., with Brian VanDeMark. *In Retrospect: The Tragedy and Lessons of Vietnam*. New York: Times Books, 1995.

Moss, Nathaniel. *Ron Kovic: Antiwar Activist*. New York: Chelsea House, 1994.

Myers, Thomas. *Walking Point: American Narratives of Vietnam*. Oxford University Press, 1988.

Newman, John M. *JFK and Vietnam: Deception, Intrigue, and the Struggle for Power*. New York: Warner Books, 1992

Nguyen Cao Ky. *Twenty Years and Twenty Days*. New York: Stein and Day, 1976.

Nguyen Thi Dinh. *No Other Road to Take: Memoir of Mrs. Nguyen Thi Dinh*. Translated by Mai V. Elliott. New York: Cornell University Southeast Asian Studies Program, 1976.

Nixon, Richard M. *No More Vietnams*. New York: Arbor House, 1985.

Nixon, Richard M. *The Memoirs of Richard Nixon*. New York: Grosset and Dunlap, 1978.

Norman, Elizabeth M. *Women at War: The Story of Fifty Military Nurses Who Served in Vietnam*. Philadelphia: University of Pennsylvania Press, 1990.

Oates, Stephen B. *Let the Trumpet Sound: The Life of Martin Luther King, Jr.* New York: Harper and Row, 1982.

Osborne, Milton E. *Sihanouk: Prince of Light, Prince of Darkness*. Honolulu: University of Hawaii Press, 1994.

O'Brien, Tim. *If I Die in a Combat Zone, Box Me Up and Ship Me Home*. New York: Delacorte, 1973.

O'Brien, Tim. *The Things They Carried*. Boston: Seymour Lawrence/Houghton Mifflin, 1990.

O'Grady, Jim, and Murray Polner. *Disarmed and Dangerous: The Radical Lives and Times of Daniel and Philip Berrigan*. New York: Basic Books, 1997.

Page, Tim. *Derailed in Uncle Ho's Victory Garden: Return to Vietnam and Cambodia*. New York: Touchstone, 1995.

Page, Tim. *Page after Page: Memoirs of a War-Torn Photographer*. New York: Atheneum, 1989.

Pham Van Dong. *Selected Writings*. Hanoi: Foreign Language Publishing House, 1977.

Ponchaud, Francois. *Cambodia: Year Zero*. New York: Holt, Rinehart, and Winston, 1977.

Porter, Gareth. *A Peace Denied: The United States, Vietnam, and the Paris Agreement*. Bloomington: Indiana University Press, 1975.

Prochnau, William W. *Once Upon a Distant War: David Halberstam, Neil Sheehan, Peter Arnett—Young War Correspondents and Their Early Vietnam Battles*. New York: Times Books, 1995.

Rokyo, Mike. *Boss: Richard J. Daley of Chicago*. New York: New American Library, 1970.

Rusk, Dean, as told to Richard Rusk. *As I Saw It*. New York: Norton, 1990.

Sainteny, Jean. *Ho Chi Minh and His Vietnam: A Personal Memoir*. Chicago: Cowles, 1972.

Schanberg, Sydney H. *The Death and Life of Dith Pran*. New York: Viking Penguin, 1980.

Schlesinger, Arthur, Jr. *A Thousand Days: John F. Kennedy in the White House*. Boston: Houghton Mifflin, 1965.

Schlesinger, Arthur, Jr. *Robert Kennedy and His Times*. Boston: Houghton Mifflin, 1978.

Schrag, Peter. *Test of Loyalty: Daniel Ellsberg and the Rituals of Secret Government*. New York: Simon and Schuster, 1974.

Schroeder, Eric James. *Vietnam, We've All Been There: Interviews with American Writers*. Westport, CT: Praeger, 1992.

Schulzinger, Robert D. *A Time for War: The United States and Vietnam, 1941–1975*. New York: Oxford University Press, 1997.

Scruggs, Jan C., and Joel L. Swerdlow. *To Heal a Nation: The Vietnam Veterans Memorial*. New York: Harper and Row, 1985.

Scruggs, Jan C., ed. *Why Vietnam Still Matters: The War and the Wall*. Vietnam Veterans Memorial Fund, 1996.

Shapley, Deborah. *Promise and Power: The Life and Times of Robert McNamara*. Boston: Little, Brown, 1993.

Sheehan, Neil. *A Bright Shining Lie: John Paul Vann and America in Vietnam*. New York: Random House, 1988.

Sihanouk, Norodom, with Wilfred Burchett. *My War with the CIA: The Memoirs of Prince Norodom Sihanouk*. New York: Pantheon, 1973.

Small, Melvin. *Johnson, Nixon, and the Doves*. New Brunswick, NJ: Rutgers University Press, 1988.

Snepp, Frank. *Decent Interval: An Insider's Account of Saigon's Indecent End*. New York: Random House, 1977.

Sorenson, Theodore. *The Kennedy Legacy*. New York: Macmillan, 1969.

Steel, Ronald. *In Love with Night: The American Romance with Robert Kennedy*. New York: Simon and Shuster, 2000.

Stieglitz, Perry. *In a Little Kingdom: The Tragedy of Laos, 1960–1980*. Armonk, NY: M.E. Sharpe, 1990.

Taylor, John M. *General Maxwell Taylor: The Sword and the Pen*. New York: Doubleday, 1989.

Timberg, Robert. *John McCain: An American Odyssey*. New York: Simon and Schuster, 1999.

Vanden Heuvel, William J. *On His Own: Robert F. Kennedy, 1964–1968*. Garden City, NY: Doubleday, 1970.

Van Devanter, Lynda, and Joan Furey, eds. *Visions of War, Dreams of Peace: Writings of Women in the Vietnam War*. New York: Warner Books, 1991.

Van Devanter, Lynda, with Christopher Morgan. *Home before Morning: The Story of an Army Nurse in Vietnam.* New York: Beaufort Books, 1983.

The Vietnam Hearings. Introduction by J. William Fulbright. New York: Random House, 1966.

Wells, Tom. *The War Within: America's Battle Over Vietnam.* Berkeley: University of California Press, 1994.

Werner, Jayne, and Luu Doan Huynh, eds. *The Vietnam War: Vietnamese and American Perspectives.* Armonk, NY: M.E. Sharpe, 1993.

Westmoreland, William C. *A Soldier Reports.* New York: Doubleday, 1976.

White, Theodore H. *The Making of the President, 1972.* New York: Atheneum, 1973.

Wicker, Tom. *One of Us: Richard Nixon and the American Dream.* New York: Random House, 1991.

Willenson, Kim. *The Bad War: An Oral History of the Vietnam War.* New York: New American Library, 1987.

Woods, Randall Bennett. *Fulbright: A Biography.* New York: Cambridge University Press, 1995.

Wyatt, Clarence. *Paper Soldiers: The American Press and the Vietnam War.* New York: W.W. Norton, 1993.

Zafiri, Samule. *Westmoreland: A Biography.* New York: Morrow, 1994.

Zaroulis, Nancy, and Gerald Sullivan. *Who Spoke Up? American Protest Against the War in Vietnam, 1963–1975.* Garden City, NY: Doubleday, 1984.

Index

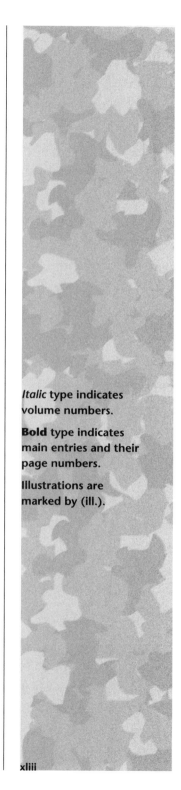

Italic type indicates volume numbers.

Bold type indicates main entries and their page numbers.

Illustrations are marked by (ill.).